A Handbook of Ethical Theory

George Stuart Fullerton

A Handbook of Ethical Theory

Contact:
BibliotechPress@gmail.com

The present edition is a reproduction of 1922 publication of this work. Minor typographical errors may have been corrected without note, however, for an authentic reading experience the spelling, punctuation, and capitalization have been retained from the original text.

ISBN: 978-1-61895-175-5

CONTENTS

PART V
THE SOCIAL WILL

PART VI
THE REAL SOCIAL WILL

PART VII
THE SCHOOLS OF THE MORALISTS

PART VIII
THE ETHICS OF THE SOCIAL WILL

PREFACE

We are all amply provided, with moral maxims, which we hold with more or less confidence, but an insight into their significance is not attained without reflection and some serious effort. Yet, surely, in a field in which there are so many differences of opinion, clearness of insight and breadth of view are eminently desirable.

It is with a view to helping students of ethics in our universities and outside of them to a clearer comprehension of the significance of morals and the end of ethical endeavor, that this book has been written.

I have, in the Notes appended to it, taken the liberty of making a few suggestions to teachers, some of whom have fewer years of teaching behind them than I have. I make no apology for writing in a clear and untechnical style, nor for reducing to a minimum references to literatures in other tongues than our own. These things are in accord with the aim of the volume.

I take this opportunity of thanking Professor Margaret F. Washburn, of Vassar College, and Professor F. J. E. Woodbridge, of Columbia University, for kind assistance, which I have found helpful.

G. S. F. New York, 1921

PART I

THE ACCEPTED CONTENT OF MORALS

CHAPTER I

IS THERE AN ACCEPTED CONTENT?

1. THE POINT IN DISPUTE.—Is there an accepted content of morals? Can we use the expression without going on to ask: Accepted where, when, and by whom?

To be sure, certain eminent moralists have inclined to maintain that men are in substantial agreement in regard to their moral judgments. Joseph Butler, writing in the first half of the eighteenth century, came to the conclusion that, however men may dispute about particulars, there is an universally acknowledged standard of virtue, professed in public in all ages and all countries, made a show of by all men, enforced by the primary and fundamental laws of all civil constitutions: namely, justice, veracity, and regard to common good. [1] Sir Leslie Stephen, writing in the latter half of the nineteenth, tells us that "in one sense moralists are almost unanimous; in another they are hopelessly discordant. They are unanimous in pronouncing certain classes of conduct to be right and the opposite wrong.

---

[1] *Dissertation on the Nature of Virtue.*

No moralist denies that cruelty, falsity and intemperance are vicious, or that mercy, truth and temperance are virtuous." [2]

In other words, these writers would teach us that men are, on the whole, agreed in approving, explicitly or implicitly, some standard of conduct sufficiently definite to serve as a code of morals. But that there is such a substantial agreement among men has not impressed all observers to the same degree. Locke, who wrote before Butler, based his arguments against the existence of innate moral maxims upon the wide divergencies found among various classes of men touching what is right and what is wrong. [3] The historian, the anthropologist and the sociologist reinforce his reasonings with a wealth of illustration not open to the men of an earlier time. They present us with codes, not a code; with multitudinous standards, not a single standard; with what has been accepted here or there, at this time or at that; and we may well ask ourselves where, amid this profusion, we are to find the one and acceptable code.

2. WHAT CONSTITUTES SUBSTANTIAL AGREEMENT?—To be sure, we may be very generous in our interpretation of what constitutes substantial agreement; we may deny significance to all sorts of discrepancies by relegating them to the unimpressive class of "disputes about particulars." Such an impressionistic indifference to detail may leave us with something on our hands as little serviceable as a composite photograph made from individual objects which have little in common, a blur lacking all definite outline and not recognizable as any object at all. No man can guide his conduct by the common core of many or of all moral codes. Taken in its bald abstraction, it is not a code or anything like a code. Who can walk, without walking in some particular way, in some direction, at some time? Who can mind his manners without being mannerly in accordance with the usages of some race or people?

Those who content themselves with enunciating very general moral principles may, it is true, be of no little service to their fellow-men; but that is only because their fellow-men are able to supply the details that convert the blur into a picture. Some twenty-four hundred years ago Heraclitus told his contemporaries "to act according to nature with understanding"; we are often told today that the rule of our lives should be "to do good." Had the ancient Greek not possessed his own notions of what might properly be meant by nature and by understanding, did we not ourselves have some rather definite conception of what actions may properly fall under the caption of doing good, such admonitions could not lead to the stirring of a finger. Who would appeal to his physician for advice as to diet,

---

[2] *The Science of Ethics*, chapter i, Sec. 1.
[3] *Essay Concerning Human Understanding*, Book I, chapter iii.

if he expected from him no more than the counsel to eat, at the proper hours, enough, but not too much, of suitable food?

If, then, we confine our admonitions to the group of abstractions which constitute the universally acknowledged standard of virtue when all the individual differences which characterize different codes have been ignored, we preach what, taken alone, no man can live by, and no community of men has ever attempted to live by. If we leave it to our hearers to drape our naked abstractions with concrete details, each will set to work in a different way. The method of the composite photograph seems unprofitable in attempting to solve the problem of morals.

3. DOGMATIC ASSUMPTION.—There is, however, a second way by which the variations which characterize different codes may come to be relegated to a position of relative insignificance. We may assume that our own code is the ultimate standard by which all others are to be judged, and we may set down deviations from it to the account of the ignorance or the perversity of our fellowmen. So regarded, they are aberrations from the normal, and only true code of conduct; interesting, perhaps, but little enlightening, for they can have little bearing upon our conception of what we ought to do.

A presumption against this arbitrary assumption that we have the one and only desirable code is suggested the unthinking acceptance of the traditional by those who are lacking in enlightenment and in the capacity reflection. Is it not significant that a contact with new ways of thinking has a tendency, at least, to make men broaden their horizon and to revise some of their views?

In other fields, we hope to attain to a capacity for self-criticism. We expect to learn from other men. Why should we, in the sphere of morals, lay claim to the possession of the truth, the whole truth, and nothing but the truth? Why should we refuse to learn from anyone? Such a position seems unreasoning. It puts moral judgments beyond the pale of argument and intelligent discussion. It is an assumption of infallibility little in harmony with the spirit of science. The fact that a given standard of conduct is in harmony with our traditions, habits of thought, and emotional responses, does not prove to other men that it is, not one of a number of accepted codes, but in a quite peculiar sense acceptable, a thing to put in a class by itself—the class into which each mother puts her own child, as over against other children.

Moreover, such an unreasoned assumption of superiority must make one little sympathetic in one's attitude toward the moral life of other peoples. Into the significance of their social organization, of their customs, their laws, one can gain no insight. Their hopes, their fears, their strivings, their successes and their failures, their approval and disapproval of their fellows, their peace of conscience and their remorse, must leave us cold and aloof.

It is not profitable for us to assume at the outset that the differences exhibited in the moral judgments of individuals or of peoples are of minor significance. They are facts to be dealt with in the light of some theory. An ethical theory which ignores them must rest upon a narrow and insecure foundation. It is exposed to assault from many quarters. It may, in default of better means of defence, be compelled to take refuge behind the blind wall of dogmatic assertion. On the other hand, a theory which gives them frank recognition, and strives to exhibit their real significance in the life of the individual and of the race, may be able to show lying among them the golden cord of reason which saves them from the charge of being incoherent facts. It may even lead us back to a conservatism no longer unreasoning, but rationally defensible and conscious of its proper limits. The blindly conservative man seems to be faced with the alternative of stagnation or revolution. The rationally conservative may regard the development of the moral life as a Pilgrim's Progress, not without its untoward accidents, but, in spite of them, a gradual advance toward a desirable goal.

CHAPTER II

THE CODES OF COMMUNITIES

4. THE CODES OF COMMUNITIES: JUSTICE.—In view of the existing tendency in the average man, and even in some philosophers, to pass lightly over the diversities exhibited by different codes, it is well to cast a brief preliminary glance at the content of morals as accepted, both by communities of men, and by their more reflective spokesmen, the moralists. Let us first take a look at the codes of communities.

We have seen that Butler viewed justice, veracity and regard to common good as virtues accepted among men everywhere. But we may also see, if we look into his pages, that he neglected to point out that there may be the widest divergencies in men's notions of what constitutes justice, veracity and common good. And men differ widely on the score of the degree of emphasis to be laid upon their observance.

Take justice. Where men possess a code, written or unwritten, that may properly be called moral, we expect of them the judgment that guilt should be punished. But what shall be accounted guilt? What shall be the measure of retribution? Who shall be fixed upon as guilty?

As to what constitutes guilt. We have only to remind ourselves that the Dyak head-hunter is not condemned by his fellows, but is admired; [4] that the fattening and eating of a slave may, in a given primitive community, be accounted no crime; [5] that infanticide has been most widely approved, and that not merely in primitive communities, for Greece and Rome, when they were far from primitive, practiced certain forms of it with a view to the good of the state; [6] that the holding of a fellow-creature in bondage, and exploiting him for one's own advantage, even under the lash, was, until recently, not a crime in the eye of the law even in the most civilized states. On the other hand, it may be a crime to eat a female opossum. [7] The impressive imperative: Thou shalt not! appears to bear unmistakable reference to time and circumstance.

And what is the natural and proper measure of punishment? The ancient and primitive rule of an eye for an eye and a tooth for a tooth suggests the figure of the scales, the impartially meting out to each man of his due. It is obviously a rule that cannot be applied in all cases. One cannot take the tooth of a toothless man, or compel a thievish beggar to restore fruit which he has eaten. We should be horrified were any serious attempt made to make the rule the basis of legislation in any civilized state today, but men have not always been so fastidious. Approximations to it have been incorporated into the laws of various peoples.

But all have modified it to some degree, and the modifications have taken many forms—the punishment of someone not the criminal, compensation in money or in goods, incarceration, and what not. Nor have the modifications been made solely on account of the difficulty of applying the rule baldly stated. Other influences have been at work.

—————————————————

[4] WESTERMARCK, *The Origin and Development of the Moral Ideas*, London, 1906, I, chapter xiv.
[5] WESTERMARCK, *op. cit.* II, chapter xlvi.
[6] *Ibid.*, I, chapter xvii.
[7] *Ibid.*, I, chapter iv, p. 124.

Thus, in the famous Babylonian code, the man who struck out the eye of a patrician lost his own eye in return, and his tooth answered for the tooth of an equal—but the rule was not made general. [8] In state after state it has been found just to treat differently the patrician, the plebeian, the slave, the man, the woman, the priest. In the very state to which Butler belonged, benefit of clergy could be claimed, up to relatively recent times, by those who could read. The educated criminal escaped hanging for offences for which his illiterate neighbor had to swing. [9]

Nor is there any clear concensus of opinion touching the question of who shall be selected as the bearer of punishment. If a man has injured another unintentionally, shall he be held to make amends? It has seemed just to men that he should. [10] That one man should be made responsible for the misdeeds of another, under the principle of collective responsibility, has commended itself as just to a multitude of minds. Not merely the sins of the fathers, but those of the most distant relations, those of neighbors, of fellow-tribesmen, of fellow-citizens, have been visited upon those whose sole guilt lay in such a connection with the directly guilty parties. This is not a sporadic phenomenon. Among the ancient Hebrews, in Babylonia, in Greece, in the later legislation of Rome, in medieval and even in modern Europe, the principle of collective responsibility has been accepted and has seemed acceptable. Asia, Africa and Oceania have cast votes for it. So have the Americas. [11]

5. THE CODES OF COMMUNITES: VERACITY.—As to veracity: It has undoubtedly been valued to some degree, and with certain limitations, by tribes and nations the most diverse in their degrees of culture. Did men never speak the truth they might well never speak at all. But to maintain that absolute veracity has at all times been greatly valued would be an exaggeration. The lie of courtesy, the clever lie, the lie to the stranger, have been and still are, in many communities both uncivilized and more advanced, not merely condoned, but approved. With the defence which has been made of the doctrines of mental reservation and pious fraud students of church history are familiar. In diplomacy and in war today highly civilized nations find deceptions of many sorts profitable to them, nor are such generally condemned. [12]

---

[8] 5 HOBHOUSE, *Morals in Evolution,* I, chapter iii, Sec 3; New York, 1906.
[9] *Ibid.,* Sec. 11.
[10] WESTERMARCK, chapter ix.
[11] WESTERMARCK, I, chapter ii; DEWEY AND TUFTS, *Ethics,* New York, 1919, Part I, chapter ii.]
[12] WESTERMARCK, II, chapters xxx and xxxi

What modern government does not employ secret service agents, and value them in proportion to the degree of skill with which they manage to deceive their fellows, while limiting the exercise of professional good faith to their intercourse with their paymaster? The secret service agent of transparent frankness, who could not bear to deceive his neighbor, would not hold his post for a day. He would be a subject for Homeric laughter.

Moreover, if the question may be raised: what constitutes justice? may one not equally well ask: what constitutes veracity or its opposite? Where does the silence of indifference shade into purposed concealment, and the latter into what is unequivocally deception? At what point does deception blossom out into the unmistakable lie? One may take advantage of an accidental misunderstanding of what one has said; one may use ambiguous language; one may point instead of speaking. Between going about with a head of glass, with all one's thoughts displayed as in a show-case to every comer, and the settled purpose to deceive by the direct verbal falsification, there is a long series of intermediate positions. The commercial maxim that one is not bound to teach the man with whom one is dealing how to conduct his business, and the lawyer's dictum that the advocate is under no obligation to put himself in the position of the judge, obviously, will bear much stretching.

6. THE CODES OF COMMUNITIES: THE COMMON GOOD.—Nor are the facts which confront us less perplexing when we turn to that "regard to the common good" which Butler finds to be acknowledged and enforced by the primary and fundamental laws of all civil constitutions. Whether we look at the past or view the present, whether we study primitive communities or confine ourselves to civilized nations, we see that common good is not, apparently, conceived as the good of all men, however much the words "justice" and "humanity" may be upon men's lips.

Has any modern state as yet succeeded in incorporating in its civil constitution such provisions as will ensure to all classes of its subjects any considerable share in the common good? Slaves and animals, said Aristotle, have no share in happiness, nor do they live after their own choice. [13] The pervading unrest of the modern economic community is due to the widespread conviction that the existing organization of society does not sufficiently make for the happiness of all. Some states with a high degree of culture have not even made a pretence of having any such aim. They have deliberately legislated for the few. [14] Even where the avowed

---

[13] *Politics*, iii, 9.

[14] The "citizens" of the ancient Greek state were a privileged class who legislated in their own interest. Let the reader look into Plato's *Laws* and

7

aim is the common good of all, states have assumed that some must be sacrificed for others. Certain individuals are selected to die in the trenches in the face of the enemy, that others may be guaranteed liberty and the pursuit of happiness. Grotius, the famous jurist of the seventeenth century, has been criticized for holding that a beleaguered town might justly deliver up to the enemy a small number of its citizens in order to purchase immunity for the rest. How far do the cases differ in principle? "Among persons variously endowed," wrote Hegel, "inequality must occur, and equality would be wrong." [15] Commonwealths of many degrees of development have recognized inequalities of many sorts, and have treated their subjects accordingly.

"For diet," said Bentham with repellent frankness, "nothing but self-regarding affection will serve." Benevolence he considered a valuable addition "for a dessert." He had in mind the individual, and he did injustice to individuals in certain of their relations. But how do things look when we turn our attention to the relations between states? Does any state actually make it a practice to treat its neighbor as itself? Would its citizens approve of its doing so?

The Roman was compelled to formulate a *jus gentium*, a law of nations, to deal with those who held, to him, a place beyond the pale of law as he knew it. [16] Many centuries have elapsed since pagan philosophers taught the brotherhood of man, and since Christian divines began to preach it with passionate fervor. Yet civilized nations today are still seeking to find a *modus vivendi*, which may put an end to strife and enable them to live together. The *jus gentium*, or its modern equivalent, is, alas! still in its rudiments.

To obviate misunderstanding at this point, it is well to state that, in adducing all the above facts, I do not mean to argue that it is abnormal and an undesirable thing that the scales of justice should, at times, be weighted in divers ways. I am not maintaining that the distribution of common good should proceed upon the principle of strict impartiality. What is possible

---

Aristotle's *Politics* and see how inconceivable the cultivated Greek found what is now the ideal of a modern democracy. "Citizens" should own landed property, and work it by slaves, barbarians and servants. They should not be "ignoble" mechanics or petty traders. Compare the spirit of Froissart's *Chronicles*, in the Middle Ages. See what Bryce (*South America*, New York, 1918, chapters xi and xv) says about the position of the Negro in our Southern states, and of the Indians in South American republics.

[15] Hegel, *The Philosophy of Right*, translated by Dyde, London, 1896, p. 56.
[16] See SIR HENRY MAINE, *Ancient Law*, chapter iii.

and is desirable in this field is not something to be decided off-hand. But the facts suffice to illustrate the truth that the discrepancies to be found in the codes of different communities can scarcely be dismissed as unimportant details. They are something far too significant for that.

CHAPTER III

THE CODES OF THE MORALISTS

7. THE MORALISTS.—If, from the codes, or the more or less vague bodies of opinion, which have characterized different communities, we turn to the moralists, we find similar food for thought.

But who are the moralists? Can we put into one class those who preach a short-sighted selfishness or a calculating egoism and those who urge upon us the law of love? Those who recommend a contempt of mankind, and those who inculcate a reverence for humanity? Those who incline to leave us to our own devices, telling us to listen to conscience, and those who draw up for us elaborate sets of rules to guide conduct? The histories of ethics are rather tolerant in herding together sheep and goats. And not without reason. Those whom they include have been in a sense the spokesmen of their fellows. Their words have found an echo in the souls of many. They are concerned with a rule of life, and their rule of life, such as it is, rests upon some principle which has impressed men as being not wholly unreasonable.

In taking a glance at what they have to offer us, I shall not go far afield, and shall exercise a brevity compatible with the purpose of mere illustration. To the moralists of ancient Greece, and, to a lesser degree, to those of the Roman Empire, to the Christian teachers who succeeded to their heritage in the centuries which followed, and to the more or less independent thinkers who made their appearance after the Reformation, we can trace our ethical pedigree. For our purpose we need seek no wider field. Here we may find sufficiently notable contrasts of opinion to disturb the dogmatic slumber of even an inert mind. The most cursory glance makes us inclined to accept with some reserve Stephen's claim that "the difference between different systems is chiefly in the details and special application of generally admitted principles."

8. EPICUREAN AND STOIC.—Thus, Aristippus of Cyrene advised men to grasp the pleasure of the moment rather than to await the more uncertain pleasure of the future; but he also counselled, for prudential reasons, the avoidance of a conflict with the laws. Such advice takes cognizance of the self-love of the individual, and is not self-love reasonable? Nevertheless, such advice might be given by a discouraged criminal of a reflective turn of mind, on his release from prison, to a comrade not yet chastened by incarceration. Epicurus praises temperance and fortitude, but only as measures of prudence. He praises justice, but only in so far as it enables us to escape harm, and frees us from that dread of discovery that haunts the steps of the evil-doer. His more specific maxims, do not fall in love with a woman, become the father of a family, or, generally, go into politics, smack strongly of the rule of life recommended to Feuillet's hero, Monsieur de Camors, by his worldly-wise and cynical father.

Contrast with these men the Stoics, whose rule of life was to follow Nature, and to eschew the pursuit of pleasure. Man's nature, said Epictetus, is social; wrongdoing is antisocial; affection is natural. [17] Said Marcus Aurelius, it is characteristic of the rational soul for a man to love his neighbor. The cautious bachelor imbued with Epicurean principles would find strange and disconcerting the Stoic position touching citizenship: "My nature is rational and social; and my city and country, so far as I am Antoninus, is Rome, but so far as I am a man, it is the world. The things then which are useful to these cities are alone useful to me." [18]

9. PLATO; ARISTOTLE; THE CHURCH.—No more famous classification of the virtues—those qualities of character which it is desirable for a man to have, and which determine his doing what it is desirable that he should do—has ever been drawn up than that offered us by Plato: Wisdom, Courage, Temperance and Justice. [19] It is interesting to lay beside it the longer list drawn up by Aristotle, and to compare both with that which commended itself to the mind of the mediaeval churchman.

---

[17] *Discourses*, Book I, chapter xxiii—a clever answer to Epicurus.

[18] *Thoughts*, Book VI, 44; translated by GEORGE LONG.

[19] For PLATO's account of the virtues see the *Republic*, Book IV, and the *Laws*, Book I.

With Aristotle, the virtues are made to include: [20] Wisdom
High-mindedness
Justice
Ambition
Courage
Gentleness
Temperance
Friendliness
Liberality
Truthfulness
Magnificence
Decorous Wit

and it is suggested that, although scarcely a virtue, a sense of shame is becoming in youth.

We find the Christian teachers especially recommending: [21]

Obedience
Patience
Benevolence
Purity
Humility
Alienation from the "World"
Alienation from the "Flesh"

and their lists of the "deadly sins" they select from the following:

Pride
Arrogance
Anger
Gluttony
Unchastity
Envy
Vain-Glory
Gloominess
Languid Indifference.

---

[20] *Ethics*; I refer the reader to the admirable exposition and criticism by SIDGWICK, *History of Ethics*, London, 1896, chapter ii, Sec 10-12; compare ZELLER, *Aristotle and the Earlier Peripatetics*, English translation London, 1897, Volume II, chapter xii.
[21] See SIDGWICK'S sympathetic account of the Churchman's view of the virtues, *loc. cit.*, chapter iii.

Could there be a more striking contrast than that between the mediaeval code and those of the great Greek thinkers? Plato recommended as virtues certain general characteristics of character much admired by the Greek of his day. Aristotle accepted them and added to them. He has painted much more in detail the gifts and graces of a well-born and well-situated Greek gentleman as he conceived him. The personage would cut a sorry figure in the role of a mediaeval saint; the mediaeval saint would wear a tarnished halo if endowed with the Aristotelian virtues.

The one ideal, the Greek, breathes an air of self-assertion; the other one of self-abnegation. Benevolence, Purity, Humility and Unworldliness are not to be found in the former; Justice, Courage and Veracity appear to be missing in the latter. Wisdom, insight, has given place to the Obedience appropriate to a man clearly conscious of a Law, not man-made, to which man feels himself to be subject.

Indeed, the discrepancy between the ideals is such that Aristotle's virtuously high-minded man would have been conceived by the mediaeval churchman to be living in deadly sin, as the very embodiment of pride and arrogance. We find him portrayed as neither seeking nor avoiding danger, for there are few things about which he cares; as ashamed to accept favors, since that implies inferiority; as sluggish and indifferent except when stimulated by some great honor to be gained or some great work to be performed; as frank, for this is characteristic of the man who despises others; as admiring little, for nothing is great to him. His pride prevents him from harboring resentment, from seeking praise, and from praising others. This Nietzschean hero would attract attention upon any stage: "The step of the high-minded man is slow, his voice deep, and his language stately, for he who feels anxiety about few things is not apt to be in a hurry; and he who thinks highly of nothing is not vehement." [22]

To be sure, virtues not on a given list may be found in, or read into, some of the writings of the man who presents it. It would be absurd to maintain that the mediaeval churchman had no regard for justice, courage and veracity, as he would define them, or that Plato and Aristotle were wholly deaf to the claims of benevolence. Nevertheless, the variations in the emphasis laid on this virtue or on that, or in the conception of what constitutes this virtue or that, may yield ideals of character and of conduct which bear but a slight family resemblance. Imagine St. Francis of Assisi lowering his voice, slowing his step, and cultivating "high- mindedness," or striving to make himself a pattern of decorous wit.

---

[22] *Ethics*, Book IV, chapter in, 19, translation by R. W. BROWNE, London, 1865.

10. LATER LISTS OF THE VIRTUES.—The codes proposed by the moralists of a later time are numerous and widely scattering. It is impossible to do justice to them in any brief compass. A very few instances, selected from among those most familiar to English readers, must suffice to indicate the diversity of their nature.

Hobbes, [23] deeply concerned to discover some *modus vivendi* which should put a check upon strife between man and his fellow-man, and save us from a life "solitary, poor, nasty, brutish and short," recommends among other virtues:

Justice
Equity
Requital of benefits
Sociability
A moderate degree of forgiveness
The avoidance of pride and arrogance.

Locke, [24] who believes that moral principles must be intuitively evident to one who contemplates the nature of God and the relations of men to Him and to each other, thinks it worth while to set down such random maxims as:

No government allows absolute liberty.
Where there is no property there is no injustice.
All men are originally equal.
Men ought not to harm one another.
Parents have a right to control their children.

Hume, [25] whose two classes of virtues comprise the qualities immediately agreeable or useful to ourselves and those immediately agreeable or useful to others, offers us an extended list. He puts into the first class:

Discretion
Caution
Enterprise
Industry
Frugality
Economy
Good Sense, etc.

---

[23] *Leviathan*, chapter xv.
[24] *Essay*, Book IV, chapter iii, Sec. 18; *Of Civil Government*, Book II, chapter ii.
[25] An Enquiry Concerning the Principles of Morals, Sec 6, Part I.

Temperance
Sobriety
Patience
Perseverance
Considerateness
Secrecy
Order, etc.

In the second class he includes:

Benevolence
Justice
Veracity
Fidelity
Politeness
Wit
Modesty
Cleanliness.

Manifestly, the lists may be indefinitely prolonged. Why not add to the first class the pachydermatous indifference to rebuffs which is of such service to the social climber, and, to the second, taste in dress and the habit of not repeating stories?

Thomas Reid lays stress upon the deliverances of the individual conscience, when consulted in a quiet hour. Nevertheless he proposes five fundamental maxims: [26]

We ought to exercise a rational self-love, and prefer a greater to a
  lesser good.
We should follow nature, as revealed in the constitution of man.
We should exercise benevolence.
Right and wrong are the same for all in the same circumstances.
We should venerate and obey God.

With such writers we may contrast the Utilitarians and the adherents of the doctrine of Self-realization, [27] who lay little stress upon lists of virtues or duties, but aim, respectively, at the greatest happiness of the greatest number, and at the harmonious development of the faculties of man, regarding as virtues such qualities of character as make for the attainment, in the long run, of the one or the other of these ends.

---

[26] *On the Active Powers of Man*, Essay V, chapter i.
[27] These will be discussed below, chapters xxv and xxvi.

11. THE STRETCHING OF MORAL CONCEPTS.—The instances given suffice to show that the moralists speak with a variety of tongues. The code of one age is apt to seem strange and foreign to the men of another. Even where there is apparent agreement, a closer scrutiny often reveals that it has been attained by a process of stretching conceptions. Take for example the so-called "cardinal" virtues [28] dwelt upon by Plato. The Stoics, who made use of his list, changed its spirit. Cicero stretches justice so as to make it cover a watery benevolence. St. Augustine finds the cardinal virtues to be different aspects of Love to God. The great scholastic philosopher of the thirteenth century, St. Thomas, places in the first rank the Christian graces of Faith, Hope and Charity, but still finds it convenient to use the Platonic scheme in ordering a list of the self- regarding virtues taken from Aristotle. Thus may the pillars of a pagan temple be utilized as structural units in, or embellishments of, a Christian church.

Our own age reveals the same tendency. Thomas Hill Green, the Oxford professor, follows Plato. But with him we find wisdom stretched to cover artistic creation; we see that courage and temperance have taken on new faces; and justice appears to be able to gather under its wings both benevolence and veracity. [29] A still wider divergence from the original understanding of the cardinal virtues is that of Dewey, who conceives of them as "traits essential to all morality." He treats, under temperance, of purity and reverence; he makes courage synonymous with persistent vigor; he extends justice so as to include love and sympathy; he transforms wisdom into conscientiousness. [30]

This variation in the content of moral concepts may be illustrated from any quarter in the field of ethics. Cicero's circumspect "benevolence" advances the doctrine that "whatever one can give without suffering loss should be given even to an entire stranger." Among such obligations he reckons: to prohibit no one from drinking at a stream of running water; to permit anyone who wishes to light fire from fire; to give faithful advice to one who is in doubt; which things, as he naively remarks, "are useful to the receiver and do no harm to the giver." [31]

Compare with this the admonition to love one's neighbor as oneself; Sidgwick's "self-evident" proposition that "I ought not to prefer my own

---

[28] From *cardo*, a hinge. These virtues were supposed to be fundamental. The name given to them was first used by AMBROSE in the fourth century A.D. See SIDGWICK, *History of Ethics*, chap, ii, p. 44.
[29] *Prolegomena to Ethics*, Book III, chapter iii, and Book IV, chapter v.
[30] DEWEY AND TUFTS, *Ethics*, pp. 404-423.
[31] De Officiis, Book I, chapter xvi.

lesser good to the greater good of another;" [32] Bentham's utilitarian formula, "everybody to count for one, and nobody for more than one." The admonition, "be benevolent," may mean many things.

12. THE REFLECTIVE MIND AND THE MORAL CODES.—Even the cursory glance we have given above to the moral codes of different communities and those proposed by individual moralists must suffice to bring any thoughtful man to the consciousness that they differ widely among themselves, and that the differences can scarcely be dismissed as insignificant. A little reflection will suffice to convince him, furthermore, that to treat all other codes as if they were mere pathological variations from his own is indefensibly dogmatic.

On the other hand, the differences between codes should not be unduly emphasized. The core of identity is there, and, although in its bald abstractness it is not enough to live by, it is vastly significant, nevertheless. If there were not some congruity in the materials, they would never be brought together as the subject of one science. Unless "good," "right," "obligation," "approval," etc., or the rudimentary conceptions which foreshadow them in the mind of the most primitive human beings, had a core of identity which could be traced in societies the most diverse, there would be no significance in speaking of the enlightened morality of one people and the degraded and undeveloped morality of another. There could be no history of the development of the moral ideas. Collections of disparate and disconnected facts do not constitute a science, nor are they the proper subject of a history.

As a matter of fact, we all do speak of degraded moral conceptions, of a perverted conscience, of a lofty morality, of a fine sense of duty; we do not hesitate to compare, i. e., to treat as similar and yet dissimilar, the customs, laws and ethical maxims of different ages and of different races. This means that we have in our minds some standard, perhaps consciously formulated, perhaps dimly apprehended, according to which we rate them. The unreflective man is in danger of taking as this standard his own actual code, such as it is; of accepting, together with such elements of reason as it may contain, the whole mass of his inherited or acquired prejudices; the more reflective man will strive to be more rationally critical.

---

[32] The Methods of Ethics, Book III, chapter xiii, Sec 3.

PART II

ETHICS AS SCIENCE

CHAPTER IV

THE AWAKENING TO REFLECTION

13. THE DOGMATISM OF THE NATURAL MAN.—In morals and in politics it seems natural for man to be dogmatic, to take a position without hesitation, to defend it vehemently, to maintain that others are in the wrong.

This is not surprising. We are born into a moral environment as into an all-embracing atmosphere. From the cradle to the grave, we walk with our heads in a cloud of exhortations and prohibitions. From our earliest years we have been urged to make decisions and to act, and we have been furnished with general maxims to guide our action. When, therefore, we approach the solution of a moral problem, we do not, as a rule, acutely feel our fitness to solve it, even though we may be judged quite unfit by others.

This unruffled confidence in one's possession of an adequate supply of indubitable moral truth may be found in men who differ widely in their degree of intelligence and in the extent of their information. Some individuals seem born to it. We may come upon it in the ethical philosopher; we may meet it in the man of science, who knows that it has taken him a quarter of a century to fit himself to be an authority in matters chemical or physical, but who wanders in his hours of leisure into the field of ethics and has no hesitation in proposing radical reforms. But it is more natural to look for the unwavering confidence which knows no questionings among persons of restricted outlook, who have been brought into contact with but one set of opinions. It is characteristic of the child, of the uncultivated classes in all communities, of whole communities primitive in their culture and relatively unenlightened.

14. THE AWAKENING.—Manifestly, even the beginnings of ethical science are an impossibility where such a spirit prevails. Where there are no doubts, no questionings, there can be no attempt at rational construction.

Fortunately for the cause of human enlightenment there are forces at work which tend to arouse men from this state of lethargy. Horizons are broadened, new ideas make their appearance, there is a conflict of authorities, the birth of a doubt, and, finally, a more or less articulate appeal to Reason.

Even a child is capable of seeing that paternal and maternal injunctions and reactions are not wholly alike, and it sets them off against each other. Nor have all the children in the home precisely the same nature. One is temperamentally frank and open, but unsympathetic; another is affectionate, and prone to lying as the sparks fly upward. The virtues and vices are not spontaneously arranged in the same order of importance by children, and differences of opinion may arise. Nor does it take the child long to discover that the law of its own home is not identical with that of the house next door. At school the experience is repeated on a larger scale; many homes are represented, and, besides that, two codes of law claim allegiance, the code of the schoolboy and that of the master. They may be by no means in accord.

And when, in college, the student for the first time seriously addresses himself to the task of the study of ethics as science, he comes to it by no means wholly unprepared. He has had rather a broad experience of the contrasts which obtain between different codes. He is familiar with the code of the home, of the school, of the social class, of the religious community, of the civil community. There sit on the same benches with him the sensitively conscientious student who doubts whether it is a permissible deception of one's neighbor to apply a patch to an old garment so skillfully that it will escape detection; the sporting character who takes it to be the mutual understanding among men that truth shall not be demanded of those who deal in horses and dogs; the youth from Texas who claims that the French philosopher, Janet, cannot be an authority on morals, since he asserts that he who cheats at cards must feel a burning shame. With the ethics of the ancient Hebrews, of the Greeks, of the Romans, our young moralist has had the opportunity to acquire some familiarity, and he can compare them, if he will, with the Christian ethics of his own day. He knows something of history and biography; he has read books of travel, and has some acquaintance with the manners and customs of other peoples. Were he given to reflection, it ought not to surprise him to find a Portuguese sea-cook maintaining that it is wrong to steal, except

18

from the rich; or to learn that a Wahabee saint rated the smoking of tobacco as the worst possible sin next to idolatry, while maintaining that murder, robbery, and such like, were peccadilloes which a merciful God might properly overlook.

Material for reflection he has in abundance—and he often remains relatively dogmatic and unplagued by doubt. But only relatively so; and only so long as the claims of conflicting authorities are not forced upon his attention, rendered importunate in the light of discussion, made so familiar as to seem real and substantial. It is the tendency of the widening of the horizon to arouse men to reflection, to stimulate to criticism. From such criticism the science of ethics has its birth.

What is true of the individual is true of men in the mass. The blind life of social classes long laid in chains by custom and tradition may come to be illuminated by new ideas, and passive acquiescence may give way to active participation in social endeavor. Nor can primitive peoples remain wholly primitive except in isolation. With the increased intercourse between races and peoples, men are brought to a clear consciousness that the accepted in morals is manifold and diverse; the next step is to question whether it is, in any given instance, of unquestionable authority; thus do men become ripe for the search for the *acceptable*.

CHAPTER V

ETHICAL METHOD

15. INDUCTIVE AND DEDUCTIVE METHOD.—Professor Henry Sidgwick has defined a method of ethics as "any rational procedure by which we determine what is right for individual human beings to do, or to seek to realize by voluntary action." [33]

---

[33] *The Methods of Ethics*, Book I, chapter i, Sec I.

He points out that many methods are natural and are habitually used, but claims that only one can be rational. By which he means that the several methods of determining right conduct urged by the different schools of the moralists must be reconciled, or all but one must be rejected. [34]

In this chapter I shall not discuss in detail the schools of the moralists and the specific methods which characterize them. I am here concerned only with the general distinction between the scientific methods of deduction and induction, and its bearing upon ethical investigations.

How do we discover that, in an isosceles triangle, the sides which subtend the equal angles are equal? We do not go about collecting the opinions of individuals upon the subject, nor do we consult the records of other peoples, past or present. We do not measure a great number of triangles and arrive at our conclusion after a calculation of the probable error of our measurements. The appeal to authorities does not interest us; that measurements are always more or less inaccurate, and that all actual triangles are more or less irregular, we freely admit, but we do not regard such facts as significant. We use a single triangle as an illustration, and from what is given in, or along with, that individual instance, we deduce certain consequences in which we have the highest confidence. Here we follow the method of deduction. We accept a "given," with its validity we do not concern ourselves; our aim is the discovery of what may be gotten out of it.

In the inductive sciences the individual instance has an importance of quite a different sort. It is not a mere illustration, unequivocally embodying a general truth to which we may appeal directly, treating the instance as a mere vehicle, in itself of little significance. Individual instances are observed and compared; uniformities are searched for; it is sought to establish general truths, not directly evident, but whose authority rests upon the particular facts that have been observed and classified.

It is a commonplace of logic that both induction and deduction may be employed in many fields of science. We may attain by inductive inquiry to more or less general truths, which we no longer care to call in question, and which we accept as a "given," to be exploited and carried out in its consequences. Indeed, we need not betake ourselves to science to have an illustration of this method of procedure. In everyday life men have maxims by which they judge of the probable actions of their fellow-men and in the light of which they direct their dealings with them. Such maxims as that men may be counted upon to consult their own interests have certainly not been adopted independently of an experience of what, on particular

---

[34] *Ibid.*, chapter i, Sec 3.

occasions, men have shown themselves to be. But, once adopted, they may be treated as, for practical purposes, unquestionable; men are concerned to apply them, not to substantiate them. In so far, men reason from them deductively and pass from the general rule to the particular instance.

16. THE AUTHORITY OF THE "GIVEN."—Obviously the "given," in the sense indicated, may possess, in certain cases, a very high degree of authority, and, in others, a very low degree.

In the case of the mathematical truth referred to above, men do not, in fact, find it necessary to call in question the "given," though they may be divided in their notions touching the general nature of mathematical evidence and whence it draws its apparently indisputable authority. In certain of the inductive sciences, as in mechanics, physics and chemistry, generalizations have been attained in which even the critical repose much confidence. In other fields men are constantly making general statements which are promptly contradicted by their fellows, and are drawing from them inferences the justice of which is in many quarters disallowed. There are axioms and axioms, maxims and maxims. The confidence felt by a given individual in a particular "given" does not guarantee its acceptance by all men of equal intelligence. Where, however, the evidence upon which a disputed "given" is based is forthcoming, there is, at least, ground for rational discussion.

Not a few famous writers have treated moral truths as analogous to mathematical. [35] To take here a single instance. Sidgwick, in his truly admirable work on "The Methods of Ethics," maintains [36] that "the propositions, 'I ought not to prefer a present lesser good to a future greater good,' and 'I ought not to prefer my own lesser good to the greater good of another,' do present themselves as self-evident; as much (*e.g.*) as the mathematical axiom that 'if equals be added to equals the wholes are equals.'"

But it is one thing to claim that we are in possession of a "given" with ultimate and indisputable authority; it is another to convince men that we really do possess it. Locke's efforts at deduction fall lamentably short of the model set by Euclid. "Professor Sidgwick's well-known moral axiom, 'I ought not to prefer my own lesser good to the greater good of another,' would," writes Westermarck, [37] "if explained to a Fuegian or a Hottentot, be regarded by him, not as self-evident, but as simply absurd; nor can it claim general acceptance even among ourselves. Who is that 'Another' to

---

[35] See the chapter on "Intuitionism," Sec 90, note.
[36] Book III, chapter xiii, Sec 3.
[37] *Op. cit.*, Volume I, chapter i, p. 12.

whose greater good I ought not to prefer my own lesser good? A fellow-countryman, a savage, a criminal, a bird, a fish—all without distinction?" To Bentham's "everybody to count for one and nobody for more than one" may be opposed Hartley's preference of benevolent and religious persons to the rest of mankind. [38]

The fact that men eminent for their intellectual ability and for the breadth of their information are, in morals, inclined to accept, as ultimate, principles not identical, and thus to found different schools, would seem to indicate that, to one who aims at treating ethics as a science, principles, as well as the deductions from them, should be objects of closest scrutiny. They should not be taken for granted. The history of ethical theory appears to make it clear that the "given" of the moralist is not of the same nature as that of the geometer.

The ethical philosopher cannot, hence, confine himself to developing deductively the implications of some principle or principles assumed without critical examination. He must establish the validity even of his principles. This we should bear in mind when we approach the study of the different ethical schools.

CHAPTER VI

THE MATERIALS OF ETHICS

17. HOW THE MORALIST SHOULD PROCEED.—The above reflections on method suggest the materials of which the moralist should avail himself in rearing the edifice of his science.

(1) Evidently he should reflect upon the moral judgments which he finds in himself, the moral being with whom he is best acquainted. He should

---

[38] *Observations on Man*, Part II, chapter iii, 6.]

endeavor to render consistent and luminous moral judgments which, as he finds, have too often been inconsistent and more or less blind.

(2) He should take cognizance of his own setting—of the social conscience embodied in the community in which he lives.

(3) And since, as we have seen, the significance, either of the individual conscience, or of the social conscience revealed in custom, law and public opinion, can hardly become apparent to one who does not bring within his horizon many consciences individual and social, he should enlarge his view so as to include such. The moralists, in our day, show an increasing tendency to pay serious attention to this mass of materials. They do not confine their attention to the moral standard which this man or that has accepted as authoritative for him, nor to that accepted as authoritative in a given community. They study *man*— man in all stages of his development and in material and social settings the most diverse.

(4) Nor should the student of ethics overlook the work which has been done by those moralists who have gone before him. He who has studied descriptive anatomy is aware of the immense service which has been done him by the unwearied observations of his predecessors; observations which have been put on record, and which draw his attention to numberless details of structure that would, without such aid, certainly escape his attention. Ethics is an ancient discipline. It has fixed the attention of acute minds for many centuries. He who approaches the subject naively, without an acquaintance with the many ethical theories which have been advanced and the acute criticisms to which they have been subjected, will almost certainly say what someone has said before, and said, perhaps, much better. The valor of ignorance will involve him in ignominious defeat.

(5) It is evident that the moralist must make use of materials offered him by workers in many other fields of science. The biologist may have valuable suggestions to make touching the impulses and instincts of man. The psychologist treats of the same, and exhibits the work of the intellect in ordering and organizing the impulses. He studies the phenomena of desire, will, habit, the formation of character. The anthropologist and the sociologist are concerned with the codes of communities and with the laws of social development. The fields of economics, politics and comparative jurisprudence obviously march with that cultivated by the student of ethics.

18. THE PHILOSOPHER AS MORALIST.—In all these sciences at once it is not possible for the moralist to be an adept. The mass of the material they furnish is so vast that the ethical writer who starts out to master it in

all its details may well dread that he may be overcome by senility before he is ready to undertake the formulation of an ethical theory.

It does not follow, however, that he should leave to those who occupy themselves professionally with any of these fields the task of framing a theory of morals. He must have sufficient information to be able to select with intelligence what has some important bearing upon the problem of conduct, but there are many details into which he need not go. It is well to note the following points:

(1) A multitude of details may be illustrative of a comparatively small number of general principles. It is with these general principles that the moralist is concerned. The anthropologist may regard it as his duty to spend much labor in the attempt to discover why this or that act, this or that article of food, happens in a given community to be taboo to certain persons. The student of ethics is not bound to take up the detailed investigation of such matters. Human nature, in its general constitution, is much the same in different races and peoples. The influence of environment is everywhere apparent. There are significant uniformities to be discovered even by one who has a limited amount of detailed information. "Those who come after us will see nothing new," said Antoninus, "nor have those before us seen anything more, but in a manner he who is forty years old; if he has any understanding at all, has seen by virtue of the uniformity which prevails all things which have been and all that will be." 39 Which is, to be sure, an overstatement of the case, but one containing a germ of truth.

(2) We find, by looking into their books, that men most intimately acquainted with the facts of the moral life as revealed in different races and peoples may differ widely in the ethical doctrine which they are inclined to base upon them. Not all men, even when endowed with no little learning, are gifted with the clearness of vision which can detect the significance of given facts; nor are all equally capable of weaving relevant facts into a consistent and reasonable theory. The keenness and the constructive genius of the individual count for much. And breadth of view counts for much also. We have seen that ethics touches many fields of investigation, and the philosopher is supposed, at least, to let his vision range over a broad realm, and to grasp the relations of the different sciences to each other. He is, moreover, supposed to be trained in reflective analysis, and of this ethical theory appears to stand in no little need.

(3) Finally, the mere fact that ethics has for so many centuries been regarded as one of the disciplines falling within the domain of the

---

39 *Thoughts*, XI, 1. London, 1891, translated by GEORGE LONG.

philosopher is not without its significance. One may deplore the tendency to base ethics upon this or that metaphysical doctrine, and desire to see it made an independent science; and yet one may be compelled to admit that it is not easy to comprehend and to estimate the value of many of the ethical theories which have been evolved in the past, without having rather an intimate acquaintance with the history of philosophy. The ethical teachings of Plato, of Aristotle, of St. Thomas, of Kant, of Hegel, of Green, lose much of their meaning when taken out of their setting. The history of ethical theory is blind when divorced from the history of philosophy, and with the history of ethical theory the moralist should be acquainted.

The philosopher has no prescriptive right to preempt the field of ethics. Many men may cultivate it with profit. Nevertheless, he, too, should cultivate it, not independently and with a disregard of what has been done by others, but in a spirit of hearty cooperation, thankfully accepting such help as is offered him by his neighbors.

CHAPTER VII

THE AIM OF ETHICS AS SCIENCE

19. THE APPEAL TO REASON.—The proper aim of the scientific study of ethics appears to be suggested with sufficient clearness by what has been said in the chapters on the accepted content of morals.

Where individuals take up unreflectively the maxims which are to control their conduct, human life can scarcely be said to be under the guidance of reason. Where, moreover, the codes of individuals clash with each other or with the social conscience of their community, and where the codes of different communities are disconcertingly diverse, planful concerted action with a view to the control of conduct appears to be impracticable. Historical accident, blind impulse and caprice, cannot serve as guides for a rational creature seeking to live, along with others, a rational life.

"The aim of ethics," says Sidgwick, [40] "is to render scientific—i.e., true, and as far as possible systematic—the apparent cognitions that most men have of the rightness or reasonableness of conduct, whether the conduct be considered as right in itself, or as the means to some end conceived as ultimately reasonable." The use here of the word "cognitions" calls our attention to the fact that, when men say, "this is right, that is wrong," they mean no more than, "this I like, that I do not like"; and the use of the word "apparent" indicates that the judgments expressed may be approved by the man who makes them, and yet be erroneous. The appeal is to an objective standard; there is a demand for proof.

That most men recognize, in some cases dimly, in some cases clearly and explicitly, that the appeal to such a standard is justifiable, can scarcely be denied. Between "I choose" and "I ought to choose," between "the community demands," and "the community ought to demand," men generally recognize a distinction when they have attained to a capacity for reflection.

It has, however, been denied that the appeal is justifiable, and denied by no mean authority. "The presumed objectivity of moral judgments," writes Westermarck, [41] "being a chimera, there can be no moral truth in the sense in which this term is generally understood. The ultimate reason for this is, that the moral concepts are based upon emotions, and that the contents of an emotion fall entirely outside the category of truth. But it may be true or not that we have a certain emotion, it may be true or not that a given mode of conduct has a tendency to evoke in us moral indignation or moral approval. Hence a moral judgment is true or false according as its subject has or has not that tendency which the predicate attributes to it. If I say that it is wrong to resist evil, and yet resistance to evil has no tendency whatever to call forth in me an emotion of moral disapproval, then my judgment is false." The conclusion drawn from this is that there are no general moral truths, and that "the object of scientific ethics cannot be to fix rules for human conduct"; it can only be "to study the moral consciousness as a fact."

20. THE APPEAL TO REASON JUSTIFIED.—The words of so high an authority should not be passed over lightly. One is impelled to seek for their proper appreciation and their reconciliation with the judgment of other moralists. Such can be found, I think, by turning to two truths dwelt upon in what has preceded: the truth that the moralist should not assume that he is possessed of a "given" analogous to that of the geometer—a standard in no need of criticism; and the equally important truth that the moralist cannot hope to frame a code which will simply replace the codes

---

[40] *The Methods of Ethics*, Book I, chapter vi, Sec 1.
[41] *The Origin and Development of the Moral Ideas*, chapter i, p. 17.

of individual communities and will prescribe the details of human conduct while ignoring such codes altogether.

But it does not seem to follow that, because the moralist may not set up an arbitrary code of this sort, he is also forbidden to criticize and compare moral judgments, to arrange existing codes in a certain order as lower and higher, to frame some notion of what constitutes progress. He may hold before himself, in outline, at least, an ideal of conduct, and not one taken up arbitrarily but based upon the phenomena of the moral consciousness as he has observed them. And in the light of this ideal he may judge of conduct; his appeal is to an objective standard.

Thus, he who says that it is false that it is right to reduce to slavery prisoners taken in war may, if he be sufficiently unreflective, have no better reason for his judgment than a feeling of repugnance to such conduct. But, if he has risen to the point of taking broad views of men and their moral codes, he may very well assert the falsity of the statement even when he feels no personal repugnance to the holding of certain persons as slaves. His appeal is, in fact, to such a standard as is above indicated, and his condemnation of certain forms of conduct is based upon their incompatibility with it.

Hence, a man may significantly assert that certain conduct is objectively desirable, although it may not be desired by himself or by his community. He may judge a thing to be wrong without *feeling* it to be wrong. Whether anything would actually be judged to be wrong, if no one ever had any emotions, is a different question. With it we may class the question whether anything would be judged to be wrong if no one were possessed of even a spark of reason. There is small choice between having nothing to see and not being able to see anything. [42]

---

[42] That, in the citation above given, WESTERMARCK'S attention was concentrated upon the extreme position taken by some moralists touching the function of the reason in moral judgments seems to me evident. He is far too able an observer to overlook the significance of the diversity of moral codes and the meaning of progress. He writes: "Though rooted in the emotional side of our nature, our moral opinions are in a large measure amenable to reason. Now in every society the traditional notions as to what is good or bad, obligatory or indifferent, are commonly accepted by the majority of people without further reflection. By tracing them to their source it will be found that not a few of these notions have their origin in sentimental likings and antipathies, to which a scrutinizing and enlightened judge can attach little importance; whilst, on the other hand, he must account blamable many an act and omission which public opinion,

An appeal, thus, from the actual to the ideal appears to be possible. And, since the natural man, unenlightened and unreflective, is not more inclined to show himself to be a reasonable being in the sphere of morals than elsewhere, it seems that there is no little need of ethical science. Its aim is to bring about the needed enlightenment. Its value can only be logically denied by those who maintain seriously that it is easy to know what it is right to do. Do men really hold this, if they are thoughtful?

out of thoughtlessness, treats with indifference." Vol. I, pp. 2-3. See also his appeals to reason where it is a question of the attitude of the community toward legal responsibility on the part of the young, toward drunkenness, and toward the heedless production of offspring doomed to misery and disease, pp. 269 and 310.

PART III

MAN AND HIS ENVIRONMENT

CHAPTER VIII

MAN'S NATURE

21. THE BACKGROUND OF ACTIONS.—In estimating human actions we take into consideration both the doer and the circumstances under which the deed was done. Actions may be desirable or undesirable, good or bad, according to their setting. How shall we judge of the blow that takes away human life? It may be the involuntary reaction of a man startled by a shock; it may be a motion of justifiable self-defence; it may be one struck at the command of a superior and in the defence of one's country; it may be the horrid outcome of cruel rapacity or base malevolence.

Nor are the emotions, torn out of their context, more significant than actions without a background. They are mental phenomena to be observed and described by the psychologist; to the moralist they are, taken alone, as unmeaning as the letters of the alphabet, but, like them, capable in combination of carrying many meanings. Anger, fear, wonder, and all the rest are, as natural emotions, neither good nor bad; they are colors, which may enter into a picture and in it acquire various values.

In morals, when men have attained to the stage of enlightenment at which moral estimation is a possible process, they always consider emotions, intentions, and actions in the light of their background. We do not demand a moral life of the brutes; we do not look for it in the intellectually defective and the emotionally insane; nor do we expect a savage caught in the bush to harbor the same emotions, or to have the same ethical outlook, as the missionary with whom we may confront him. The concepts of moral responsibility, of desert, of guilt, are emptied of all significance, when we lose sight of the nature, inborn or acquired, of the creature haled before the bar of our judgment, and of the environment, which on the one hand, impels him to action, and, on the other, furnishes the stage upon which the drama of his life must be played out to the end.

Hence, he who would not act as the creature of blind impulse or as the unthinking slave of tradition, but would exercise a conscious and intelligent control over his conduct, seems compelled to look at his life and its setting in a broad way, to scrutinize with care both the nature of man and the environment without which that nature could find no expression. When he does this, he only does more intelligently what men generally do instinctively and somewhat at haphazard. He seeks a rational estimate of the significance of conduct, and a standard by which it may be measured.

22. MAN'S NATURE.—Moralists ancient and modern have had a good deal to say about the nature of man. To some of them it has seemed rather a simple thing to describe it. Its constitution, as they have conceived it, has furnished them with certain principles which should guide human action. Aristotle, who assumed that every man seeks his own good, conceived of his good or "well-being" as largely identical with "well- doing." This "well-doing" meant to him "fulfilling the proper functions of man," or in other words acting as the nature of man prescribes. [43] To the Stoic man's duty was action in accordance with his nature. [44] Butler, [45] many centuries later, found in man's nature a certain "constitution," with conscience naturally supreme and the passions in a position of subordination. This "constitution" plainly indicated to him the conduct appropriate to a human being.

Such appeals to man's nature we are apt to listen to with a good deal of sympathy. Manifestly, man differs from the brutes, and they differ, in their kind, from each other. To each kind, a life of a certain sort seems appropriate. The rational being is expected to act rationally, to some degree, at least. In our dealings with creatures on a lower plane, we pitch our expectations much lower.

And the behavior we expect from each is that appropriate to its kind. The bee and the ant follow unswervingly their own law, and live their own complicated community life. However the behavior of the brute may vary in the presence of varying conditions, the degree of the variation seems to be determined by rather narrow limits. These we recognize as the limits of

---

[43] *Politics*, i, 2. See, further, on *Man's Nature*, chapter xxvi.
[44] MARCUS AURELIUS, *Thoughts*, v, 1.
[45] *Sermons on Human Nature*, ii

the nature of the creature. It dictates to itself, unconsciously, its own law of action, and it follows that law simply and without revolt.

When we turn to man, "the crown and glory of the universe," as Darwin calls him, we find him, too, endowed with a certain nature in an analogous sense of the word. He has capacities for which we look in vain elsewhere. The type of conduct we expect of him has its root in these capacities. Human nature can definitely be expected to express itself in a human life,—one lower or higher, but, in every case, distinguishable from the life of the brute. It means something to speak of the physical and mental constitution of man, that mysterious reservoir from which his emotions and actions are supposed to flow. We feel that we have a right to use the expression, even while admitting that the brain of man is, as far as psychology is concerned, almost unexplored territory, and that the relation of mind to brain is, and is long likely to remain, a subject of dispute with philosophers and psychologists.

23. HOW DISCOVER MAN'S NATURE?—Nevertheless, in speaking of the nature of any living creature, we are forced to remind ourselves that the original endowment of the creature studied can never be isolated and subjected to inspection independently of the setting in which the subject of our study is found. Who, by an examination of the brain of a bee or of an ant, could foresee the intricate organized industry of the hive or the anthill? The seven ages of man are not stored ready-made in the little body of the infant. At any rate, they are beyond the reach of the most penetrating vision. In the case of the simple mechanisms which can be constructed by man a forecast of future function is possible on the basis of a general knowledge of mechanics. But there is no living being of whose internal constitution we have a similar knowledge. From the behavior of the creature we gather a knowledge of its nature; we do not start with its nature as directly revealed and infer its behavior. That there are differences in the internal constitution of beings which react to the same environment in different ways, we have every reason to believe. What those differences are in detail we cannot know. And our knowledge of the capacities inherent in this or that constitution will be limited by what we can observe of its reaction to environment.

Sometimes the reaction to environment is relatively simple and uniform. In this case we feel that we can attain without great difficulty to what may be regarded as a satisfactory knowledge of the nature of the creature studied. The conception of that nature appears to be rather definite and unequivocal. When it is once attained, we speak with some assurance of the way in which the creature will act in this situation or in that. If, however, the capacities are vastly more ample, and the environment to which this creature is adjusted is greatly extended, the difficulty of describing in any unequivocal way the nature of the creature becomes indefinitely greater.

Is it possible to contemplate man without being struck with the breadth and depth of the gulf which separates the primitive human being from the finished product of civilization? What a difference in range of emotion, in reach of intellect, in stored information, in freedom of action, between man at his lowest and man at his highest! Can we describe in the same terms what is natural to man everywhere and always?

For the filthy and ignorant savage, absorbed in satisfying his immediate bodily needs, standing in the simplest of social relations, taking literally no thought for the morrow, profoundly ignorant of the world in which he finds himself, possessing over nature no control worthy of the name, the sport and slave of his environment, it is natural to act in one way. For enlightened humanity, acquainted with the past and forecasting the future, developed in intellect and refined in feeling, rich in the possession of arts and sciences, intelligently controlling and directing the forces of nature, socially organized in highly complicated ways, it is natural to act in another way. And to each of the intermediate stages in the evolution of civilization some type of conduct appears to be appropriate and natural.

Whither, then, shall we turn for our conception of man's nature? Shall we merely draw up a list of the instincts and impulses which may be observable in all men? Shall we say no more than that man is gifted with an intelligence superior to that of the brutes? To do this is, to be sure, to give some vague indication of man's original endowment. But it can give us little indication of what it is possible for man, with such an endowment, and in such an environment as makes his setting, to become. And what man becomes, that he is.

If man's nature can be revealed only through the development of his capacities, it is futile to seek it in a return to undeveloped man. The nature of the chicken is not best revealed in the egg. And, as man can develop only in interaction with his environment, we must, to understand him, study his environment also.

CHAPTER IX

MAN'S MATERIAL ENVIRONMENT

24. THE STRUGGLE WITH NATURE.—It is not possible to disentangle from each other and to consider quite separately the diverse elements which enter into the environment of man and which influence his development. His environment is two-fold, material and social; but his material setting may affect his social relations, and it is social man, not the individual as such, that achieves a conquest over nature. However, it is possible, and it is convenient, to direct attention successively upon the one and the other aspect of his environment.

At every stage of his development, man must have food, shelter, some means of defense. If they are not easily obtainable, he must strain every nerve to attain them. Are his powers feeble and his intelligence undeveloped, it may tax all his efforts to keep himself alive and to continue the race in any fashion. The rules which determine his conduct seem rather the dictates of a stern necessity than the products of anything resembling free choice.

He who is lashed by hunger and haunted by fear, who cannot provide for the remote future, but must accept good or ill fortune as the accident of the day precipitates his lot upon him, lives and must live a life at but one remove from that of the brute. In such a life the instincts of man attain to a certain expression, but intelligence plays a feeble part. The man remains a slave, under dictation, and moved by the dread of immediate disaster. For an interest in what is remote in time and place, for the extension of knowledge for its own sake, for the development of activities which have no direct bearing upon the problem of keeping him alive and fed, there can be little place. One must be assured that one can live, and live in reasonable security and physical well-being, before the problem of enriching and embellishing life can fairly present itself as an important problem. One must be set free before one can deliberately set out to shape one's life after an ideal.

Not that a severe struggle with physical nature is necessarily and of itself a curse. It may call out man's powers, stimulate to action, and result in growth and development. Where a prodigal nature amply provides for man's bodily necessities without much effort on his part, the result may be, in the absence of other stimulating influences giving rise to new wants, a paralyzing slothfulness, an animal passivity and content. This may be observed in whole peoples highly favored by soil and climate, and protected by their situation from external dangers. It may be observed in certain favored classes even in communities which, by long and strenuous effort, have conquered nature and raised themselves high in the scale of civilization. The idle sons of the rich, relieved from the spur of necessity, may undergo the degeneration appropriate to parasitic life. In the midst of a strenuous activity adapted to call out the best intellectual and moral powers of man, they may remain unaffected by it, incapable of effort, unintelligent, slothful, the weak and passive recipients of what is brought to them by the labor of others.

But the struggle with physical nature, sometimes a spur to progress and issuing in triumph, may also issue in defeat. Nature may be too strong for man, or, at least, for man at an early stage of his development. She may thwart his efforts and dwarf his life. It was through no accident that the Athenian state rose and flourished upon the shores of the Aegean; no such efflorescence of civilization could be looked for among the Esquimaux of the frozen North.

25. THE CONQUESTS OF THE MIND.—Physical environment counts for much, but the physical environment of man is the same as that of the creatures below him who seem incapable of progress. It is as an intelligent being that he succeeds in bringing about ever new and more complicated adjustments to his environment.

From the point of view of his animal life in many respects inferior to other creatures—less strong, less swift, less adequately provided with natural means of defense, less protected by nature against cold, heat and the inclemencies of the weather, endowed with instincts less unerring, less prolific, through a long period of infancy helpless and dependent— man nevertheless survives and prospers.

He has conquered the strong, overtaken the swift, called upon his ingenuity to furnish him with means of defence. He has defied cold and heat, and we find him, with appliances of his own devising, successfully combating the rigors of Arctic frosts and the torrid sun of the tropics. Intelligence has supplemented instinct and has guaranteed the survival of the individual and of the race.

It has even protected man against himself, against the very dangers arising out of his immunity from other dangers. A gregarious creature, increasing and multiplying, he would be threatened with starvation did not his intelligent control over nature furnish him with a food-supply which makes it possible for vast numbers of human beings to live and thrive on a territory of limited extent. Moreover, he has compassed those complicated forms of social organization which reveal themselves in cities and states, solving problems of production, transportation and distribution before which undeveloped man would stand helpless.

And from the problem of living at all he has passed to that of living well. He has created new wants and has satisfied them. He has built up for himself a rich and diversified life, many of the activities of which appear to have the remotest of bearings upon the mere struggle for existence, but the exercise of which gives him satisfaction. Thus, the primitive instinct of curiosity, once relatively aimless and insignificant, has developed into the passion for systematic knowledge and the persistent search for truth; the rudimentary aesthetic feeling which is revealed in primitive man, and traces of which are recognizable in creatures far lower in the scale, has blossomed out in those elaborate creations, which, at an enormous expense of labor and ingenuity, have come to enrich the domains of literature, music, painting, sculpture, architecture. Civilized man is to a great extent occupied with the production of what he does not need, if need be measured by what his wants are at a lower stage of his development. But these same things he needs imperatively, if we measure his need by his desires when they have been multiplied and their scope indefinitely widened.

26. THE CONQUEST OF NATURE AND THE WELL-BEING OF MAN.—It is evident that the successful exploitation of the resources of material nature is of enormous significance to the life of man. It may bring emancipation; it offers opportunity. One is tempted to affirm, without stopping to reflect, that the development of the arts and sciences, the increase of wealth and of knowledge, must in the nature of things increase human happiness.

One is tempted, further, to maintain that an advance in civilization must imply an advance in moralization. Man has a moral nature which exhibits itself to some degree at every stage of his development. What more natural to conclude than that, with the progressive unfolding of his intelligence, with increase in knowledge, with some relaxation of the struggle for existence which pits man against his fellow-man, and subordinates all other considerations to the inexorable law of self- preservation, his moral nature would have the opportunity to show itself in a fuller measure?

When we compare man at his very lowest with man at his highest such judgments appear to be justified. But man is to be found at all sorts of intermediate stages.

His knowledge may be limited, the development of the arts not far advanced, his control over nature far from complete, and yet he may live in comparative security and with such wants as he has reasonably well satisfied. His competition with his fellows may not be bitter and absorbing. The simple life is not necessarily an unhappy life, if the simplicity which characterizes it be not too extreme. In judging broadly of the significance for human life of the control over nature which is implied in the advance of civilization, one must take into consideration several points of capital importance:

(1) The multiplication of man's wants results, not in happiness, but in unhappiness, unless the satisfaction of those wants can be adequately provided for.

(2) The effort to satisfy the new wants which have been called into being may be accompanied by an enormous expenditure of effort. Where the effort is excessive man becomes again the slave of his environment. His task is set for him, and he fulfills it under the lash of an imperious necessity. The higher standard may become as inexorable a task-master as was the lower.

(3) It does not follow that, because a given community is set free from the bondage of the daily anxiety touching the problem of living at all, and may address itself deliberately to the problem of living well, it will necessarily take up into its ideal of what constitutes living well all those goods upon which developed man is apt to set a value. A civilization may be a grossly material one, even when endowed with no little wealth. With wealth comes the opportunity for the development of the arts which embellish life, but that opportunity may not be embraced. Man may be materially rich and spiritually poor; he may allow some of his faculties to lie dormant, and may lose the enjoyments which would have been his had they been developed. The Athenian citizen two millenniums ago had no such mastery over the forces of nature as we possess today. Nevertheless, he was enabled to live a many-sided life beside which the life of the modern man may appear poor and bare. It is by no means self- evident that the good of man consists in the multitude of the material things which he can compel to his service.

(4) Moreover, it does not follow that, because the sum of man's activities, his behavior, broadly taken, is vastly altered, by an increase in his control over his material environment, the result is an advance in moralization. An advance in civilization—in knowledge, in the control over nature's resources, in the evolution of the industrial and even of the fine arts—does not necessarily imply a corresponding ethical advance on the part of a given community. New conditions, brought about by an increase of knowledge, of wealth, of power, may result in ethical degeneration.

What constitutes the moral in human behavior, what marks out right or wrong conduct from conduct ethically indifferent, we have not yet considered. But no man is wholly without information in the field of morals, and we may here fall back upon such conceptions as men generally possess before they have evolved a science of morals. In the light of such conceptions a simple and comparatively undeveloped culture may compare very favorably with one much higher in the scale of civilization.

In the simplest groups of human beings, justice, veracity and a regard to common good may be conspicuous; the claim of each man upon his fellow-man may be generally acknowledged. In communities more advanced, the growth of class distinctions and the inequalities due to the amassing of wealth on the part of individuals may go far to nullify the advantage to the individual of any advance made by the community as a whole. The social bonds which have obtained between members of the same group may be relaxed; the devotion to the common good may be replaced by the selfish calculation of profit to the individual; the exploitation of man by his fellow-man may be accepted as natural and normal. It is not without its significance that the most highly civilized of states have, under the pressure of economic advance, come to adopt the institution of slavery in its most degraded forms; that the problem of property and poverty may present itself as most pressing and most difficult of solution where national wealth has grown to enormous proportions. The body politic may be most prosperous from a material point of view, and at the same time, considered from the point of view of the moralist, thoroughly rotten in its constitution.

It is well to remember that, even in the most advanced of modern civilizations, whatever the degree of enlightenment and the power enjoyed by the community as a whole, it is quite possible for the individual to be condemned to a life little different in essentials from that of the lowest savage. He whose feverish existence is devoted to the nerve- racking occupation of gambling in stocks, who goes to his bed at night scheming how he may with impunity exploit his fellow-man, and who rises in the morning with a strained consciousness of possible fluctuations in the market which may overwhelm him in irretrievable disaster, lives in perils which easily bear comparison with those which threaten the precarious existence of primitive man. To masses of men in civilized communities the problem of the food supply is all-absorbing, and may exclude all other and broader interests. The factory-worker, with a mind stupefied by the mechanical repetition of some few simple physical movements of no possible interest to him except as resulting in the wage that keeps him alive, has no share in such light as may be scattered about him.

The control of the forces of nature brings about great changes in human societies, but it may leave the individual, whether rich or poor, a prey to dangers and anxieties, engaged in an unequal combat with his environment, absorbed in the satisfaction of material needs, undeveloped, unreflective and most restricted in his outlook. Of emancipation there can here be no question.

And a civilization in which the control of the forces of nature has been carried to the highest pitch of development may furnish a background to the darkest of passions. It may serve as a stage upon which callous indifference, greed, rapacity, gross sensuality, play their parts naked and unashamed. That some men sunk in ignorance and subject to such passions live in huts and have their noses pierced, and others have taken up from their environment the habit of dining in evening dress, is to the moralist a relatively insignificant detail. He looks at the man, and he finds him in each case essentially the same—a primitive and undeveloped creature who has not come into his rightful heritage.

CHAPTER X

MAN'S SOCIAL ENVIRONMENT

27. MAN IS ASSIGNED HIS PLACE.—The old fable of a social contract, by virtue of which man becomes a member of a society, agreeing to renounce certain rights he might exercise if wholly independent, and to receive in exchange legal rights which guarantee to the individual the protection of life and property and the manifold advantages to be derived from cooperative effort, points a moral, like other fables.

The contract in question never had an existence, but neither did the conversation between the grasshopper and the ant. In each case, a truth is illustrated by a play of the imagination. Contracts there have been in plenty, between individuals, between families, between social classes, between nations; but they have all been contracts between men already in a social state of some sort, capable of choice and merely desirous of modifying in some particular some aspect of that social state. The notion of an original contract, lying at the base of all association of man with man, is no more than a fiction which serves to illustrate the truth that the desires and wills of men are a significant factor in determining the particular forms under which that association reveals itself.

No man enters into a contract to be born, or to be born a Kaffir, a Malay, a Hindoo, an Englishman or an American. He enters the world without his own consent, and without his own connivance he is assigned a place in a social state of some sort. The reception which is accorded to him is of the utmost moment to him. He may be rejected utterly by the social forces presiding over his birth. In which case he does not start life independently, but is snuffed out as is a candle-flame by the wind. And if accepted, as he usually is in civilized communities, he takes his place in the definite social order into which he is born, and becomes the subject of education and training as a member of that particular community.

28. VARIETIES OF THE SOCIAL ORDER.—The social order into which he is thus ushered may be most varied in character. He may find himself a member of a small and primitive group of human beings, a family standing in more or less loose relations to a limited number of other families; he may belong to a clan in which family relationship still serves as a real or fictive bond; his clan may have its place in a confederation; or the body politic in which he is a unit may be a nation, or an empire including many nationalities.

His relations to his fellow-man will naturally present themselves to him in a different light according to the different nature of the social environment in which he finds himself. The community of feeling and of interests which defines rights, determines expectations, and prescribes duties, cannot be the same under differing conditions. Social life implies cooperation, but the limits of possible cooperation are very differently estimated by man at different stages of his development. To a few human beings each man is bound closely at every stage of his evolution. The family bond is everywhere recognized. But, beyond that, there are wider and looser relationships recognized in very diverse degrees, as intelligence expands, as economic advance and political enlightenment make possible a community life on a larger scale, as sympathy becomes less narrow and exclusive.

It is not easy for a member of a community at a given stage of its development even to conceive the possibility of such communities as may come into existence under widely different conditions. The simple, communistic savage, limited in his outlook, thinks in terms of small numbers. A handful of individuals enjoy membership in his group; he recognizes certain relations, more or less loose, to other groups, with which his group comes into contact; beyond is the stranger, the natural enemy, upon whom he has no claim and to whom he owes no duty.

At a higher level there comes into being the state, including a greater number of individuals and internally organized as the simpler society is not. But even in a highly civilized state much the same attitude towards different classes of human beings may seem natural and inevitable. To Plato there remained the strongly marked distinctions between the Athenian, the citizen of another Hellenic community, and the barbarian. War, when waged against the last, might justifiably be merciless; not so, when it was war between Greek states. [46] Into such conceptions of rights and duties men are born; they take them up with the very air that they breathe, and they may never feel impelled to subject them to the test of criticism.

It is instructive to remark that neither the speculative genius of a Plato nor the acute intelligence of an Aristotle could rise to the conception of an organized, self-governing community on a great scale. To each it seemed evident that the group proper must remain a comparatively small one. Plato finds it necessary to provide in his "Laws" that the number of households in the State shall be limited to five thousand and forty. Aristotle, less arbitrarily exact, allows a variation within rather broad limits, holding that a political community should not comprise a number of citizens smaller than ten, nor one greater than one hundred thousand. [47] That a highly organized state, a state not composed of a horde of subjects under autocratic control, but one in which the citizens are, in theory, self-governing, should spread over half a continent and include a hundred millions of souls, would have seemed to these men of genius the wildest of dreams. Yet such a dream has been realized.

29. SOCIAL ORGANIZATION.—The social body of which man becomes, by the accident of birth, an involuntary member, may stand at any point in the scale of economic evolution. It may be a primitive group living from hand to mouth by the chase, by fishing or by gathering such food as nature spontaneously produces. It may be a pastoral people, more or less nomadic, occupied with the care of flocks and herds. It may be an agricultural community, rooted to the soil, looking forward from seed-time to harvest, capable of foresight in storing and distributing the fruits of its labors. It may combine some of the above activities; and may, in addition, have arrived at the stage at which the arts and crafts have attained to a considerable development. In its life commerce may have come to play an important role, bringing it into peaceful relations with other communities and broadening the circle of its interests. That human societies at such different stages of their development should differ greatly in their internal organization, in their relations to other communities, and in the demands which they make upon the individuals who compose them,

---

[46] Republic, Book V.
[47] PLATO, *Laws*, v. ARISTOTLE, *Ethics*, ix, 10.

is to be expected. Some manner of life, appropriate to the status of the community, comes to be prescribed. The ideal of conduct, whether unconsciously admitted or consciously embraced and inculcated, is not the same in different societies. The virtues which come to be prized, the defects which are disapproved, vary with their setting.

Moreover, the process of inner development results in differentiation of function. Clearly marked social classes come into existence, standing in more or less sharply defined relations to other social classes, endowed with special rights and called to the performance of peculiar duties.

Man is not merely born into this or that community; he is born into a place in the community. In very primitive societies that place may differ little from other places, save as such are determined by age or sex. But in more highly differentiated societies it may differ enormously, entail the performance of widely different functions, and prescribe distinct varieties of conduct.

"What will be the manner of life," said Plato, [48] "among men who may be supposed to have their food and clothing provided for them in moderation, and who have entrusted the practice of the arts to others, and whose husbandry, committed to slaves paying a part of the produce, brings them a return sufficient for living temperately?"

His ideal leisure class is patterned after what he saw before him in Athens. He conceives those who belong to it to be set free from sordid cares and physical labors, in order that they may devote themselves to the perfecting of their own minds and bodies and to preparation for the serious work of supervising and controlling the state. Their membership in the class defined their duties and prescribed the course of education which should fit them to fulfill them. It is not conceived that the functions natural and proper to one human being are also natural and proper to another in the same community.

The flat monotony which obtains in those simplest human societies, resembling extended families, where there is scarcely a demarcation of classes, a distinction of occupations and a recognition of private property in any developed sense, has given place in such a state to sharp contrasts in the status of man and man. Such contrasts obtain in all modern civilized communities. Man is not merely a subject or citizen; he is a subject or citizen of this class or of that, and the environment which molds him varies accordingly.

---

[48] Laws, vii.

30. SOCIAL ORDER AND HUMAN WILL.—We have seen that the material environment of a man, the extent of his mastery over nature and of his emancipation from the dictation of pressing bodily needs, is a factor of enormous importance in determining what he shall become and what sort of a life he shall lead. That his social setting is equally significant is obvious. What he shall know, what habits he shall form, what emotions he shall experience in this situation and in that, what tasks he shall find set before him, and what ideals he shall strive to attain, are largely determined for him independently of his choice.

To be sure, it remains true that man is man, endowed with certain instincts and impulses and gifted with human intelligence. Nor are all men alike in their impulses or in the degree of their intelligence. Within limits the individual may exercise choice, reacting upon and modifying his environment and himself. But a moment's reflection reveals to us that the new departure is but a step taken from a vantage-ground which has not been won by independent effort. The information in the light of which he chooses, the situation in the face of which he acts, the emotional nature which impels him to effort, the habits of thought and action which have become part of his being—these are largely due to the larger whole of which he finds himself a part. He did not build the stage upon which he is to act. His lines have been learned from others. He may recite them imperfectly; he may modify them in this or in that particular. But the drama from which, and from which alone, he gains his significance, is not his own creation.

The independence of the individual in the face of his material and social environment makes itself more apparent with the progressive development of man. But man attains his development as a member of society, and in the course of a historical evolution. It was pointed out many centuries ago that a hand cut off from the human body cannot properly be called a hand, for it can perform none of the functions of one. And man, torn from his setting, can no longer be considered man as the proper subject of moral science.

It is as a thinking and willing creature in a social setting that man becomes a moral agent. To understand him we must make a study of the individual and of the social will.

PART IV

THE REALM OF ENDS

CHAPTER XI

IMPULSE, DESIRE, AND WILL

31. IMPULSE.—Commands and prohibitions address themselves to man as a voluntary agent. But it seems right to treat as willed by man much more than falls under the head of conscious and deliberate volition. We do not hesitate to make him responsible for vastly more; and yet common sense does not, when enlightened, regard men as responsible for what is recognized as falling wholly beyond the direct and indirect control of their wills.

Motions due to even the blindest of impulses are not to be confounded with those brought about by external compulsion. They may have the appearance of being vaguely purposive, although we would never attribute purpose to the creature making them. The infant that cries and struggles, when tormented by the intrusive pin, the worm writhing in the beak of a bird,—these act blindly, but it does not appear meaningless to say that they act. The impulse is from within.

Some impulses result in actions very nicely adjusted to definite ends. Such are winking, sneezing, swallowing. These reflexes may occur as the mechanical response to a given stimulus. They may occur without our being conscious of them and without our having willed them.

Yet such responses to stimuli are not necessarily unconscious and cut off from voluntary control. He who winks involuntarily when a hand is passed before his eyes may become conscious that he has done so, and may, if he chooses, even acquire some facility in controlling the reflex. One may resist the tendency to swallow when the throat is dry, may hold back a sneeze, or may keep rigid the hand that is pricked by a pin. That is to say, actions in their origin mechanical and independent of choice may be raised out of their low estate, made the objects of attention, and brought within the domain of deliberate choice.

Furthermore, many actions which, at the outset, claimed conscious attention and were deliberately willed may become so habitual that the doer lapses into unconsciousness or semi-unconsciousness of his deed. They take on the nature of acquired reflexes. The habit of acting appears to have been acquired by the mind and then turned over to the body, that the mind may be free to occupy itself with other activities. The man has become less the doer than the spectator of his acts; perhaps he is even less than that, he is the stage upon which the action makes its appearance, while the spectator is his neighbor. The complicated bodily movements called into play when one bites one's nails had to be learned. It requires no little ingenuity to accomplish the act when the nails are short. Yet one may come to the stage of perfection at which one bites one's nails when one is absorbed in thought about other things. And one may learn to slander one's neighbor almost as mechanically and unthinkingly as one swallows when the throat is dry.

When we speak of man's impulses, we are using a vague word. There are impulses which will never be anything more. There are impulses which may become something more. There are impulses which are no longer anything more. Impulses have their psychic aspect. At its lower limit, impulse may appear very mechanical; at its upper, one may hesitate to say that desire and will are wholly absent. It is not wise to regard impulse as lying wholly beyond the sphere of will.

32. DESIRE.—At its lower limit, desire is not distinguished by any sharp line from mere impulse. Is the infant that stretches out its hands toward a bright object conscious of a desire to possess it? Or does the motion made follow the visual sensation as the wail follows the wound made by the pin? At a certain stage of development the phenomena of desire become unmistakable. The idea of something to be attained, the notion of means to the attainment of an end, the consciousness of tension, may stand out clearly. The analysis of the psychologist, which finds in desire a consciousness of the present state of the self, an idea of a future state, and a feeling of tension towards the realization of the latter, may represent faithfully the elements present in desire in the higher stages of its development, but it would be difficult to find those elements clearly marked in desire which has just begun to differentiate itself from impulse. There may be a desire where there can scarcely be said to be a self as an

object of consciousness; one may desire where there is no clear consciousness of a future state as distinct from a present one.

Moreover, the consciousness of desire may be faint and fugitive, as it may be intense and persistent. Desire is the step between the first consciousness of the object and the voluntary release of energy which works toward its attainment. This step may be passed over almost unnoticed. The thought of shifting my position when I feel uncomfortable may be followed by the act with no clear consciousness of a tension and its voluntary release. The mere thought, itself but faintly and momentarily in consciousness, appears to be followed at once by the act, and desire and will to be eliminated. It does not follow that they are actually eliminated; they may be present as fleeting shadows which fail to attract attention.

If, however, the desire fails to find its immediate fruition, if it is frustrated, consciousness of it may become exceedingly intense. There is the constant thought of the object, a vivid feeling of tension, of a striving to attain the object. Desire may become an obsession, a torment filling the horizon, and the volition in which it finds its fruition stands forth as a marked relief. This condition of things may be brought about by the inhibition occasioned by the physical impossibility of attaining the object; but it may also be brought about by the struggle of incompatible desires among themselves. The man is drawn in different directions, he is subject to various tensions, and he becomes acutely conscious that he is impelled to move in several ways and is moving in none.

I have used the word "tension" to describe the psychic fact present in desire. I have done so for want of a better word. Of the physical basis of desire, of what takes place in the brain, we know nothing. With the psychic fact, the feeling of agitation and unrest, we are all familiar. Of the tendency of desire to discharge itself in action we are aware. A desire appears to be an inchoate volition—that which, if ripened successfully and not nipped in the bud, would become a volition. It may be looked upon as the first step toward action—a step which may or may not be followed by others. It does not seem out of place to call it a state of tension, of strain, of inclination. In speaking, thus, we use physical metaphors, but they do not appear out of place.

33. DESIRE OF THE UNATTAINABLE.—But if a desire may be regarded as an unripe act of will, an inchoate volition, how is it that we can desire the unattainable, a sufficiently common experience? I may bitterly regret some act of my own in the past; I may earnestly wish that I had not performed it. But the past is irrevocable. Hence, the desire for the attainment of what is in this case the object, a different past, can hardly be regarded as even a preparatory step toward attainment.

In this case it can not, and were all desires directed upon what is in the nature of the case wholly unattainable by effort, it would occur to no one to speak of desire as a first step toward action. But normally and usually desires are not of this nature. They usually do constitute a link in the chain of occurrences which end in action. Did they not, they would have little significance in the life-history of the creature desiring. With the appearance of free ideas, with an extension of the range of memory and imagination, objects may be held before the mind which are not properly objects to be attained. Yet such objects are of the kind which attract or repel, i.e., of the kind which men endeavor to realize in action. They cannot be realized; we do not will to realize them; but we should will to do so were they realizable. The psychic factor, the strain, the tension, is unmistakably present. Real desire is revealed, and common speech, as well as the language of science, recognizes the fact.

This general attraction or repulsion exercised by objects, in spite of the fact that the objects may not appear to be realizable, is not without significance. The hindrance to realization may be an accidental one; it may not be wholly insuperable. The presence of a persistent desire may result in persistent effort, which may ultimately be crowned by success. Or it may show itself as a permanent readiness for effort. Were every frustrated desire at once dismissed from consciousness, the result would show itself in a passivity detrimental to action in general. Where the object is intrinsically an impossible one, persistent desire is, of course, futile. The dog baying at the cat in the tree is the prey of such a desire, but he does not realize it, or he might discontinue his inefficacious leaps. The man tormented by his unworthy act in the past is quite aware of the futility of his longings. His condition is psychologically explicable, but to a rational being, in so far as rational, it is not normal.

Normally, desire is the intermediate step between the recognition of an object and the will to attain it. The most futile of desires may be harbored. The imaginative mind may range over a limitless field, and give itself up to desires the most extravagant. But indulgence in this habit serves as a check to action serviceable to the individual and to the race. As a matter of fact, desire is usually for what seems conceivably within the limit of possible attainment. The man desires to catch a train, to run that he may attain that end; his mind is little occupied with the desire to fly, nor does his longing center upon the carpet of Solomon. To the desirability of dismissing from the mind futile desires current moral maxims bear witness.

34. WILL.—The natural fruition of a desire is, then, an act of will; the tension is normally followed by that release of energy which makes for the attainment of the object or end of the desire.

The question suggests itself, may there not be present, even in blindly impulsive action, something faintly corresponding to desire and will? That there should be an object in the sense of something aimed at, held in view as an idea to be realized, appears to be out of the question. But may there not be a more or less vague and evanescent sense of tension, and some psychic fact which may be regarded as the shadowy forerunner of the consciousness of the release of tension which, on a higher plane, reveals itself as the consciousness of will? There may be: introspection is not capable of answering the question, and one is forced to fall back upon an argument from analogy. Blindly impulsive action and action in which will indubitably and consciously plays a part are not wholly unlike, but they differ by a very wide interval. The interval is not an empty gap, however, for, as we have seen, all volitions do not stand out upon the background of our consciousness with the same unmistakable distinctness. There are volitions no one would hesitate to call such. And there are phenomena resembling volition which we more and more doubtfully include under that caption as we pass own on the descending scale.

Naturally, in describing desire and volition we do not turn to the twilight region where all outlines are blurred and indistinct. We fix our attention upon those instances in which the phenomena are clearly and strongly marked. They are most clearly marked where desire does not, at once and unimpeded, discharge itself in action, but where action is deferred, and a struggle takes place between desires.

The man is subject to various tensions, he is impelled in divers directions, he hesitates, deliberates, and he finally makes a decision. During this period of deliberation he is apt to be vividly conscious of desire as such—as a tension not yet relieved, as an alternation of tensions as the attention occupies itself, first with one desirable object, then with another. And the decision, which puts an end to the strife, is clearly distinguished from the desires as such.

In the reflective mind, which turns its attention upon itself and its own processes, the distinction between desire and will seems to be a marked one. But it is not merely the developed and reflective mind which is the seat of deliberation. The child deliberates between satisfying its appetite and avoiding possible punishment; it reaches for the forbidden fruit, and withdraws its hand; it wavers, it is moved in one direction as one desire becomes predominant, and its action is checked as the other gains in ascendency. Deliberation this unmistakably is. And deliberation we may observe in creatures below the level of man; in the sparrow, hopping as close as it dares to the hand that sprinkles crumbs before it; in the dog, ready to dart away in pursuance of his private desires, but restrained by the warning voice of his master. This is deliberation. Such deliberation as we find in the developed and enlightened human being it is not. That, however, there is present even in these humble instances, some psychic fact corresponding to what in the higher mind reveals itself as desire and volition, we have no reason to doubt.

35. DESIRE AND WILL NOT IDENTICAL.—I have had occasion to remark that the modern psychologist draws no such sharp line between desire and volition as the psychologist of an earlier time. That some distinction should be drawn seems palpable. It is not without significance that immemorial usage sanctions this distinction. The ancient Stoic's quarrel was with the desires, not with the will. The will was treated as a master endowed with rightful authority; the desires were subjects, often in rebellion, but justly to be held in subjection. And from the days of the Stoic down almost to our own, the will has been treated much as though it were an especial and distinct faculty of man, not uninfluenced by desire, but in no sense to be identified with it,—above it, its law-giver, detached, independent, supreme. This tendency finds its culmination in that impressive modern Stoic, Immanuel Kant, who desires to isolate the will, and to emancipate it altogether from the influence of desire.

Recently the pendulum has swung in the other direction. It has been recognized that will is the natural outcome of desire, and that without desire there would be no will at all. It has even been maintained that will *is* desire, the desire "with which the self identifies itself." [49]

To this last form of expression objection may be made on the score of its vagueness. What does it mean for the self to "identify" itself with a desire? And if such an identification is necessary to will, can there be volition or anything resembling volition where self-consciousness has not yet been developed? It is very imperfectly developed in young children, and in the lower animals still less developed, if at all; and yet we see in them the struggle of desires and the resultant decision emerging in action. If we call a volition in which consciousness of the self has played its part "volition proper," it still remains to inquire how volitions on a lower plane are to be distinguished from mere desires.

What happens in a typical case of deliberation and decision? Two or more objects are before the mind and the attention occupies itself with them successively. Tensions alternate, wax strong and die away, only to recover their strength again. Finally the attention fixes upon one object to the exclusion of others, the strife of desires come to an end, and there is an inception of action in the direction of the realization of that particular desire. The desire itself is not to be confounded with the decision; the tension, with its release. The psychic fact is in the two cases different. The decision brings relief from the strain. It cannot properly be called a desire,

---

[49] See, for example, GREEN, *Prolegomena to Ethics*, Sec 144-149.

not even a triumphant desire, although in it a desire attains a victory and its realization has begun.

Such a victory not all desires, even when most intense and prolonged, are able to attain. We have seen that the desire for the unattainable may amount to an obsession, and yet it will not ripen into an act of volition. The release of the tension in incipient action does not come. The bent bow remains bent. From the sense of strain in such a case one may be freed, as one is freed from the desires which succumb during the process of deliberation, by the occupation of the attention with other things. But the desire has been forgotten, not satisfied. It may at any time recur in all its strength.

We cannot more nearly describe the psychic fact called decision. Just as we cannot more nearly describe the psychic fact to which we have given the name "tension." Although the nervous basis of the phenomena of desire and will are unknown, we can easily conceive that, during desire, and before desire has resulted in the release of energy which is the immediate forerunner of action, the cerebral occurrence should be different from that which is present when that release takes place. Nor should it be surprising that the psychical fact corresponding to each should be different.

The view here set forth does not confuse desire and will, making will indistinguishable from desire, or, at least, from certain desires. On the other hand, it does not separate them, as though they could not be brought within the one series of occurrences which may properly be regarded as a unit. It has the advantage of making comprehensible the mutual relations of impulse, desire, and will. Blind impulse discharges itself in action seemingly without the psychic accompaniments which distinguish desire and will. But all impulse is not blind impulse, and desiring and willing admit of many degrees of development. To deny will to creatures lower than man, as some writers have done, is to misconceive the nature of the process that issues in action. We are tempted to do it only when we compare will in its highest manifestations with those rudimentary foreshadowings of it which stand at the lower end of the scale. But even in man we can discern blind impulse, dimly conscious desires which ripen into as dimly recognized decisions, and, at the very top of the scale, conscious decisions which follow deliberation, and are the resultant of a struggle between many desires.

For ethical science it is of no little importance to apprehend clearly the relation of decision to desire. Moral rules aim to control human conduct, and conduct is the expression of the whole man. If we have no clear conception of the desires which struggle for the mastery within him, and of the relation of his decisions to those desires, in vain will we endeavor to influence him in the direction in which we wish him to move.

36. THE WILL AND DEFERRED ACTION.—It remains to speak briefly of one point touching the nature of will. It has been suggested that the decision is the psychic fact corresponding to the release of nervous energy which relieves the tension of desire. It is the beginning of action, of realization. But what shall we say of resolves which cannot at once be carried out in action? Of decisions the realization of which is deferred? I may long debate the matter and then determine to pay a bill when it comes due next month. The decision is made; but, for a time, at least, nothing happens. How can I here speak of the beginning of action?

The action does not at once begin, yet it is, in a sense, initiated. The struggle of conflicting considerations has ceased; the man is "set" for action in a certain direction. For the time being the matter is settled, and only an external circumstance prevents the resolve from being carried out. The psychic factor is widely different from that of mere desire, and is not recognized to be different from that present in volition which at once issues in action.

CHAPTER XII

THE PERMANENT WILL

37. CONSCIOUSLY CHOSEN ENDS.—Our volitions, deliberate, less deliberate, and those verging upon what scarcely deserves the name of volition, weave themselves into complicated patterns, which find their expression in long series of the most varied activities. The nature of the pattern as a whole may be determined by the deliberate selection of an end, and to that the other choices which enter into the complex may be subordinate.

Thus, a man may decide that he can afford to give himself the pleasure of a long walk through the country before taking the train at the next town. During the course of the ramble he may make a number of more or less conscious decisions not incompatible with the purpose he originally embraced—to take this bit of road or that, to loiter in the shade, to climb a hill that he may enjoy a view, to hasten lest he find himself too late in arriving at his destination. These decisions may require little deliberation; they spring into being at the call of the moment, are not preceded by deliberation, and leave little trace in the memory. They may be made semi-consciously, and while the mind is largely occupied with other things, with thoughts of the past or the future, with other scenes suggested by the landscape, or with the flowers which skirt the road. Nevertheless, we would not hesitate to call them decisions.

May we apply the word in speaking of the single steps made by the traveler as he advances? His feet seem to move of themselves and to make no demands at all upon his attention.

Yet it is not strictly true to say that they move of themselves. They are under control, and the successive steps follow upon each other not without direction. They serve as expressions of the will to take the walk, and they are adjusted to the end consciously held in view. That attention is not fixed upon the individual steps does not remove them from the sphere of the voluntary, in a proper sense of the words. They are expressions of the man's will, even if they be not the result of a conscious series of deliberations and decisions. Whether we shall use the term decision in connection with the single step is rather a question of verbal usage than of the determination of fact. We have seen that decisions shade down gradually, from those quite unmistakable and characteristic, to occurrences far less characteristic and more disputable. The consciousness of deliberation and decision does not disappear abruptly at some point in the series. It fades away, as the light of day gradually passes, through twilight, into the shades of night. And actions not directly recognizable as consciously voluntary may be obviously under voluntary control. They weave themselves, with actions more palpably voluntary and higher in the scale, into those complicated patterns determined by the conscious selection of an end. As long as they serve their purpose, and require no effort, they may remain inconspicuous and unconsidered. But, as soon as a check is met with, attention is directed upon them and they become the subject of conscious voluntary control.

38. ENDS NOT CONSCIOUSLY CHOSEN.—In the above illustration the end which determines the character of a long chain of actions has been deliberately chosen. It is a consciously selected end. When, however, we contemplate critically the lives of our fellow-men, we seem to become aware of the fact that many of them act in unconsciousness of the ultimate end upon which their actions converge. The attention is taken up with minor decisions, and takes no note of the permanent trend of the will.

Thus, the selfish man may be unaware of the significance of the whole series of choices which he makes in a day; the malicious man may not realize that he is animated by the settled purpose to injure his neighbors; one may be law-abiding without ever having resolved to obey the laws through the course of a life. If called upon to account for this or that subordinate decision, each may exhaust his ingenuity in assigning false causes, while ignoring the permanent attitude of the will revealed in the series of decisions as a whole and giving them what consistency they possess.

Hence, the choice of ends, as well as the adoption of means to the attainment of ends, may reveal itself either in conscious deliberate decisions, or in the working of obscure impulses which do not emerge into the light. Even in the latter case, we have not to do with what is wholly beyond the sphere of intelligent voluntary control. The selfish man may be made aware that he is selfish; the malicious man, that he is malicious; and each may deliberately take steps to remedy the defect revealed.

When we understand the word "will" in the broad sense indicated in the preceding pages, we see that a man's habits may justly be regarded as expressions of the man's will. That, through repetition, his actions have become almost automatic does not remove them from the sphere of the volitional. That he does not clearly see, or that he misconceives, the significance of his habits, and may acquiesce in them even though they be injurious to him, does not make them the less willed, so long as he follows them. It is only when he actively endeavors to control or modify a habit that he may be said to will its opposite.

39. THE CHOICE OF IDEALS.—Nor is it too much to bring under the head of willing the attitudes of approval and disapproval taken by man in contemplating certain occurrences, actual or possible, which lie beyond the confines of the field within which he can exercise control. The field of control, direct and indirect, is as we have seen a broad one, but it has its limits, and many of the things he would like to see accomplished or prevented lie without it.

A man's will may be set upon the preservation of his health, he may strive to attain that end, and circumstances may condemn him to a life of invalidism. He would be healthy if he could, but his strivings are overruled. Or he may earnestly pursue the attainment of wealth, and may end in bankruptcy. He has the will to be rich, but that will is frustrated.

It is the same when we consider his attitude toward the decisions and actions of other men. By mere willing he cannot condition another's choice. But by willing he can often influence indirectly the volitions of his fellows. He can enlighten or misinform, persuade or threaten, reward or punish. In many ways he can weight the scale of his neighbor's mind. But such influences are not all-powerful, and only within limits can we bend other wills to follow a course prescribed for them by our own.

Nevertheless, even beyond those limits, the attitude of a man's mind toward the actions of his neighbor may be a volitional one. His will may be for them or against them; he may approve or disapprove, command or prohibit. We know quite well that commands and prohibitions laid upon children and servants will not always be effective, yet we issue general commands and prohibitions, as though assuming unlimited control. It is quite in accordance with usage to speak of a man as willing an end, even where it is clearly recognized that the will to attain does not guarantee attainment. The man does what he can; could he do more he would do so; in his helplessness the attitude of the will persists unchanged.

It is obvious that, in this large sense of the word "will," we may speak of a man as continuing to will or to approve a given end, even when he is not willing or approving anything, in a narrower sense of the words, at this or that moment. We speak of a man as inspired by the permanent will to be rich, although at many times during the day, and certainly during his hours of sleep, no act of volition with such an end in view has an actual existence.

No man always thinks of the permanent ends which he has selected as controls to his actions. They are selected, they pass from his mind, and, when they recur to it again, the selection is reaffirmed. But, whether he is actually thinking about the ends in question or not, the settled trend of his will is expressed in them.

This settled trend of the will, even when scarcely recognized by the man himself, may be vastly more significant than the passing individual decision, although the latter be accompanied by clear consciousness. In certain cases the latter is a true exponent of character, but not infrequently it is not. It may be the result of a whim, of an irrational impulse little congruous with a man's nature. It may be the outcome of some misconception and in contradiction with what the man would will, if enlightened. The individual volition appears only to disappear; it may leave no apparent trace. The permanent will indicates a habit of mind, a way of acting, which may be expected to make its influence felt with the persistency of that which exerts a steady pressure. To refuse it the name of will seems arbitrary and unjustifiable.

In the permanent will is expressed the *character* of the man. This character is reflected in his *ideals*. Sometimes ideals are clearly recognized and deliberately chosen. Sometimes a man is little aware of the nature of the ideals which control his strivings. He may be said to choose, but to choose more or less blindly. But, whether he chooses with clear vision or without it, he may choose well or ill.

53

CHAPTER XIII

THE OBJECT IN DESIRE AND WILL

40. THE OBJECT AS END TO BE REALIZED.—The expression "the object before the mind in desiring and willing" is not free from ambiguity. It may be used in referring to the idea, the psychic fact, which is present when one desires or wills. Or it may be used to indicate the future fact which is the realization of the idea, that which the idea points to as its end.

The idea and the end are, of course, not identical, but they are related. The idea mirrors the end, foreshadows it. In the attempt to explain a voluntary act we may turn either to the one or to the other; we may regard the idea as the efficient cause which has resulted in the act, or we may account for the act by pointing out the end it was purposed to attain. There is no reason why we should not recognize both the efficient cause and the final cause, or end.

The latter has been the subject of more or less mystification. How, it has been asked, can an end, which does not, as yet, exist, be a cause which sets in motion the apparatus that brings about its own existence? [50]

The difficulty is a gratuitous one. It lies in the confusion of the final cause or end, with the efficient cause. When we realize that the expression "final cause" means simply that which is purposed, or accepted as an end, objections to it fall away. That, in desire and will, in all their higher manifestations, at least, there is consciousness of an end, there can be no question.

If we attempt to give more than a vague physical explanation of actions due to blind impulse, we are compelled to refer to the idea, the psychic fact present, as efficient cause. Not so when we are concerned with actions of a higher order. We constantly refer such actions to the ends they have in view. We regard them as satisfactorily explained when we have pointed out the end upon which they are directed.

To the moralist it is of the utmost importance to know what ends men actually choose, and what they may be induced to choose. He is concerned

---

[50] See JANET, *Les Causes Finales*, Paris, 1901, p. 1, ff.

with conduct, which is intelligent and purposive action. Conduct may be studied without entering upon an investigation of the efficient causes, whether physical or mental, which are the antecedents of action of any kind. Such matters one may leave to the physiologist and the psychologist.

Accordingly, when I speak of "the object" in desiring and willing, I shall use the word to indicate the end held in view, that toward which the creature desiring or willing strives.

41. HUMAN NATURE AND THE OBJECTS CHOSEN.—What objects do men actually desire and will to attain? To give a detailed account of them appears to be a hopeless and profitless task.

I take up my pen, I write, I turn to a book; I look at my watch, change my position, stretch, walk up and down, speak to some one who is present, smile or give vent to irritation; I sit down to a meal, eat of this dish rather than of that, go out to visit a place of amusement, respond to the appeal of the beggar in the street—in short, I fill my day with a thousand actions the most diverse, which follow each other without intermission.

Each of these actions may be the object of desire and will. No novel, however realistic, however prolix in its descriptions, can give us more than the barest outlines of the course of life followed by the personages it attempts to portray. A touch here, a touch there, and a character is indicated. No more, for more would be intolerable.

It is significant, however, that the few points touched upon can serve to give an idea of a character. Not-withstanding their diversity, volitions fall into classes; it is quite possible to indicate in a general way the kind of choices a given creature may be impelled to make. They are a revelation of the nature of the creature choosing. That beings differing in their nature should be impelled to different courses of action can surprise no one. Cats have no temptation to wander in herds; the exhibition of pugnacity in a sheep would strike us with wonder.

To every kind of creature its nature: and, although individuals within a kind differ more or less from one another, we look for approximation to a type. So it is with man. The expression "human nature," so much in the mouths of certain moralists ancient and modern, although somewhat vague, is not without its significance. To it we refer in passing a judgment upon individual human beings, and we regard as abnormal those who vary widely from the type.

42. THE INSTINCTS AND IMPULSES OF MAN.—In sketching for us the outlines of this distinctively human nature, the psychologist proceeds to an

enumeration of the fundamental instincts and general innate tendencies of man, and he draws up a list of the emotions which correspond to them. He mentions the instincts of flight, repulsion, curiosity, pugnacity, self-abasement, self-assertion, the parental instinct, the instinct of sex, the instinct for food, that for acquisition, etc. He points out that man is by nature open to sympathy, is suggestible, and has the impulse to play. In such instincts and inborn general tendencies, blending and reinforcing or opposing and inhibiting one another, he sees the forces which give their direction to desire and will; which select, out of all possible objects, those which are to become objects for man.

It is not necessary here to discuss the nature of instinct, to distinguish between an instinct and a more general inborn tendency, or to attempt a complete list of the instincts and inborn tendencies of man. Nor need I ask whether every choice made by a human being can be traced, directly or indirectly, to one or more of the instincts and other tendencies given in the above or in any similar list. In explaining the individual choices which men make, or the desires to which they are subject, there is much scope for the ingenuity of the psychologist.

But of the significance for human life of the impulses mentioned there can be no question. What would the life of a man be if he could feel no fear or repulsion? Could there be a development of knowledge in the absence of curiosity? How long would the race endure if the parental instinct were wholly lacking? What would become of a man who never desired food? Could a human society of any sort exist if there were no sympathy or tender feeling, no impulse to seek the company of other men? It is men, such as they are, endowed with the qualities which distinguish man, who associate themselves into communities, and the customs and laws of such reflect the fundamental impulses in which they had their origin.

43. THE STUDY OF MAN'S INSTINCTS IMPORTANT.—That a careful study of human nature is of the utmost importance to the moralist is palpable. He must not prescribe for man a rule of conduct which it is not in man to follow. He must not set before him, as inducements to actions, objects which it is impossible for him to desire and, hence, to choose.

To be sure, the main traits of human nature were pretty well recognized many centuries before the modern science of psychology had its birth. Had they not been, man could not have had rational dealings with his fellow-man; could not effectively have persuaded and threatened, rewarded and punished, and, in short, set in motion all the machinery which is at the service of one man when he wants to influence the conduct of another. But moralists ancient and modern have made serious blunders through an imperfect understanding of the impulses natural to man; and the modern psychologist, without claiming to be a wholly original or an infallible guide, may be of no little service in helping us to detect them.

Thus, it was possible for as shrewd an observer of man as Aristotle to explain the affection of a man for his child by regarding it as an extension of self-love, the child being, in a sense, a part of the parent. [51] Aristotle's quaint explanation of the fact that maternal affection is apt to be stronger than paternal is an error of a kindred nature. [52] And the ancient egoists, [53] in setting before man their selfish and anti-social ideal of human conduct, made their appeal, not to the whole man, but only to a part of him. The normal man, whether savage or civilized, whether ancient or modern, cannot desire a life filled only with the objects which they set before him. Nor is the modern moralist, or as he prefers to style himself, "immoralist," Nietzsche, [54] guilty of less gross a blunder. He rails at morality as commonly understood, calling it "the morality of the herd," and he recommends isolation, the repression of sympathy, and a contempt for one's fellows. To be sure, the "herd" is a scornful, rhetorical expression,— what Bentham would have called a "question-begging epithet,"—for men do not, properly speaking, live in herds; but they do normally live in human societies of some sort, and they have the instincts and impulses which fit them to do so. The repression of such instincts and impulses does violence to their nature, and he who advocates other than a social morality should advocate it for some creature other than man. Man is a social creature, and, among the objects of his desire and will, he must give a prominent place to some which are distinctively social.

44. THE BEWILDERING MULTIPLICITY OF THE OBJECTS OF DESIRE, AND THE EFFORT TO FIND AN UNDERLYING UNITY.—The mere enumeration of the characteristics which have been adduced as instincts or fundamental innate tendencies of man is enough to reveal the truth that man is not merely the subject of *desire*, but of *desires*; that is to say, his impulses are directed upon objects widely different from each other.

And when we call to mind that the concepts of the instincts and fundamental tendencies of human nature, as thus enumerated, are products of abstraction and generalization—are general notions gathered from the numberless concrete instances of desire and will furnished by our observation—we are forced to realize that the objects which individual men set before themselves in desiring and willing are really endlessly varied.

---

[51] *Ethics*, Book VIII, chapter xii.

[52] *Ibid.*, Book IX, chapter vii.

[53] See the answer to Epicurus in the *Discourses of Epictetus*, translated by LONG, London, 1890, pp. 69-70.

[54] A sketch of Nietzsche's doctrine is given later, see chapter xxix.

All men are not equally moved by fear, anger, repulsion, tender emotion, or sympathy. Nor do all men find the same things the objects of their fear, anger, repulsion, and the rest. The desire for food is an abstraction; in the concrete, this man eagerly accepts an oyster, and that one turns from it in disgust. In order to deal successfully with our fellow-man, we must not merely know man. We must know men.

Furthermore, not only do individuals set their affections upon different objects, but the same person at different stages of his development desires widely different things. What is a temptation to the boy has no attraction for the man. What fills the savage with longings may inspire in the product of a high civilization no other feeling than repulsion.

And what is true of the individual is true of men in the mass. The objects of desire and of endeavor are not the same in communities of all orders. Each kind of man has its own nature, which differs in some respects from that of each other kind, and dictates what shall be, for this or that man, an object of desire and will. No two men desire precisely the same thing in all particulars. Yet each is a man, and is endowed with the usual complement of human instincts.

The process of abstraction and generalization which resulted in the above-mentioned list of the elements which enter into the constitution of human nature is, nevertheless, not without its uses. It serves to order, to some extent, at least, the bewildering variety of the phenomena presented to us when we view the broad field of the desires and volitions of all sorts and conditions of men. Men's choices fall into *kinds*; there is similiarity in difference. We do not approach an unknown man with the feeling that he is a wholly unknown quantity. He is, at least, a man, and we know something of men. We have *some* notion how to go at him.

But the ordering of the motley multiplicity of men's desires by a reference to the fundamental instincts of man stops far short of a complete unification. We are left with a number of distinct and apparently irreducible impulses and tendencies on our hands. If it is useful to go so far, may it not be much more useful to go still farther?

Aristotle divided things eligible into those eligible in themselves and those eligible for the sake of something else. How it would illuminate the field of action, if it were discovered that men ultimately desire but one thing, and choose all other things on account of it! Would the discovery not facilitate immensely our dealings with our fellows, suggesting new possibilities of control? A notorious instance of the attempt to conjure away the bewildering diversity in men's desires and choices lies in the selection of pleasure as the one thing eligible in itself, the unique ultimate object of human action. Of this object we have, so far, taken no account.

CHAPTER XIV

INTENTION AND MOTIVE

45. COMPLEX ENDS.—I may desire to clear my throat and may do so. The action is a trivial one, is over in a moment, and is forgotten. On the other hand, I may desire to spend my summer on the sea-coast, to grow rich in business, to attain to high social position, or to satisfy political ambition.

When the object is of this complicated description, there may easily be elements in it which, considered alone, I should not desire at all.

The summer on the New Jersey coast may make for health. But it may entail mosquitoes, uncomfortable rooms, unaccustomed food, the lack of wonted occupations, and a distasteful association at close quarters with neighbors not of one's choosing. The road to wealth is an arduous one. The envied social station may imply the swallowing of many rebuffs. The way of the politician is hard.

One may desire, *on the whole*, one of these objects, or a thousand like them; but there are, obviously, many things comprised in the whole, or unavoidably bound up with it, that cannot attract, and are not eligible for their own sake.

46. INTENTION.—An object chosen and realized may bring in its train an indefinite series of consequences foreseen or unforeseen.

The striking of a match to light a candle may result in an unforeseen and disastrous conflagration. The overmastering desire to grow rich may have its fruit in an excessive application to business, the neglect of the family and of the duties of citizenship, and in hard and, perhaps, unscrupulous dealings. These things may be foreseen and accepted as natural accompaniments of the end chosen. But there may also be entailed shattered health, overwhelming anxieties, and the distress of seeing one's sons, brought up in luxury and without incentive to effort, victims to the dangers which menace the idle rich.

Whether such consequences might have been foreseen and provided against or not, it is true that they are frequently not foreseen with clearness. They certainly form no part of the intention of the man who bends his energies to the attainment of wealth. He does not deliberately intend to injure his health, to lose the affection of his family, to leave behind him degenerate children. He does intend to get rich, if he can.

How many of the elements contained in the object chosen, or so bound up with it that they must be accepted along with it, may fairly be said to fall within the intention of the chooser? There may easily be dispute touching the latitude with which the word intention may be used. Some things a man sees clearly to be inseparably connected with the object of his choice; some he is less conscious of; some he overlooks altogether. It does not seem unwarranted to maintain that the first of the three classes of things, at least, may be said to be intended. When Dr. Katzenberger, in his desire to get across the road without sinking in the mire, used as a stepping-stone his old servant Flex, who had fallen down, his complete intention was not simply to cross the road unmuddied. It was to cross the road unmuddied by stepping on Flex.

Evidently the intention—the whole object—gives some revelation of the character of a man. Many men may will to avoid the mud; but not all of these can will to avoid it by stepping upon a fellow-man.

47. MOTIVE.—The stepping upon a fellow-man with whom one is on good terms can scarcely be regarded as a thing desirable in itself. If it is desired, it is because of the complex in which it is an element. Some other element or elements may exert the whole attractive force which moves desire and will. In other words, some things are chosen for the sake of others.

When we have discovered that for the sake of which any object is chosen, we have come upon the *Motive*. The intention may be said to embrace the whole object as foreseen. The motive embraces only a part of it, but the vital part, the part without which the object would not be desired and willed.

48. ETHICAL SIGNIFICANCE OF INTENTION AND MOTIVE.—There has been much dispute among moralists as to the ethical significance of intention and motive. Bentham maintains that "from one and the same motive, and from every kind of motive, may proceed actions that are good, others that are bad, and others that are indifferent." He gives the following illustration: [55]

"1. A boy, in order to divert himself, reads an inspiring book; the motive is accounted, perhaps, a good one; at any rate, not a bad one. 2. He sets his

---

[55] *Principles of Morals and Legislation*, chapter x, Sec 3.]

top a-spinning: the motive is deemed at any rate not a bad one. 3. He sets loose a mad ox among a crowd: his motive is now, perhaps, termed an abominable one. Yet in all three cases the motive may be the very same: it may be neither more nor less than curiosity."

In criticizing this citation I must point out that curiosity is not, properly speaking, an object of choice at all. I have used the word "object" to indicate what is chosen, not to indicate the psychic fact present at the time of the choice. And I have said that the motive is the vital part of the object.

Hence curiosity should not be called the motive. No man chooses curiosity as an object, either in the abstract or in the concrete. Curiosity is a fundamental impulse of human nature; we may elect to satisfy the impulse in any given instance; in other words, we may choose the appropriate object.

In the case of the boy letting loose the bull in the crowd, the object is to see what will happen under the given circumstances. This is what appeals to the boy. Something else might have appealed to him in performing the action. He might have had the deliberate wish to injure certain persons present against whom he harbored resentment. Or his sympathies might have been with the bull, which had been the victim of bad treatment, and to which he wished to grant its liberty. Were the crowd in question a band of ruffians intent upon lynching, he might have been moved by the desire to assist, in a somewhat irregular way, in the re-establishment of law and order. But even if his real object is only to see what will happen, there is no reason to put it on a par with the object in view when a boy spins a top. "To see what will happen" is the vaguest of phrases, and covers a multitude of disparate objects. He who does things to see what will happen has, at least, a very general knowledge of the kind of thing likely to happen, if a given experiment is made. A boy does not hold his finger in the candle-flame to see what will happen. He who does things to see what will happen, in really complete ignorance of what is likely to happen, may be set down as too much of a fool to be the subject of moral judgments.

It is obvious that an act may be done with many different objects in view—I mean real objects, motives. I give money to a beggar whose case is one to inspire pity. My motive, my "vital" object, may be to relieve the man. But it may equally well be to get rid of him, to gratify my self-feeling by becoming the dispenser of bounty, or to inspire admiration in the onlooker. The intention, as I have used the word above, is to relieve the beggar, with such consequences of the act as may be foreseen at the time. Within the limits of this intention, the motive may vary widely, and may, in a given instance, be either admirable or contemptible.

It may be claimed, in answer to this, that the real intention is, in every case, what I have called the motive; that, in the first case, it was to relieve suffering; in the second, to get rid of an annoyance; in the third to satisfy vanity; in the fourth, to be admired.

The word "intention," thus used, is equivalent to "motive." Popular usage gives some sanction to this confusion of the words. We say of a man who has done a questionable act: "His intentions were good," or, "His motives were good." Still, popular usage does not always regard the two expressions as equivalent. To revert to the case of the unhappy Flex. It does not seem inappropriate to say that the use of a man as a stepping-stone was a part of his master's intention. It does appear inappropriate to call it the motive or a part of the motive of the whole transaction.

Intention and motive are convenient words to designate the whole object chosen and the part of the object which accounts for the choice of the whole. That it is important to distinguish between the two is palpable.

The intention gives some indication of character. We know something about a man when we know what kinds of objects he will probably set before himself as aims. But we know more when we know why he chooses these objects rather than others; when we can analyze the complex and can discover just what elements in it attract him.

With an increase of our knowledge comes an increased power of control. Until we know a man's motives, we do not really know the man; and until we know the man, our efforts to influence him must be rather blind.

The search for motives appears to carry us in the direction of the systematization and simplification of the embarrassing wealth of objects which are actually the goal of human desires and volitions. Man may desire a boundless variety of objects. His motives in desiring them may, conceivably, be comparatively few.

It should be apparent that both intention and motive have ethical significance. We have our opinion of men capable of harboring certain intentions. But we recognize that some men may harbor them with better motives than others. And we can see that a man's intention may be bad, and yet his motive, considered in itself, be good. How we are to rate the man, morally, becomes rather a nice question.

CHAPTER XV

FEELING AS MOTIVE

49. FEELING. [56] —Two men may recognize with equal clearness the presence of a danger. That recognition may evoke in the one a violent emotion of fear, and in the other little or no emotion. Two men may be treated with indignity. The one fumes with rage; the other remains calm. It is well recognized that men may be susceptible to emotion in general, or to certain specific emotions, in varying degrees. Knowledge is not always accompanied by a marked manifestation of emotion. Thoughts may be clear, but cold. There are, however, natures whose intellectual processes are steeped in emotion. Such men live in an atmosphere of agitation.

Lists of the emotions which correspond to the instincts and fundamental impulses of man have been drawn up. In them we find mentioned fear, disgust, wonder, anger, elation, tender feeling, and so forth; phenomena which, by earlier writers, were classified as "passions," and to which we may conveniently give the name "feeling." We constantly speak of our emotions as our "feelings," and we contrast the man of feeling with the coldly intellectual mind in which emotion is at a minimum.

But it is not alone to such specific emotions as those above-mentioned that we apply the term feeling. Thoughts are agreeable or disagreeable, pleasurable or painful. So are emotions. The agreeableness or disagreeableness, pleasantness or painfulness, which are the accompaniments of thoughts and emotions, have been called by modern psychologists their feeling-tone. It is not out of harmony with common usage to give them the name of feelings. In so doing we contrast them with knowledge and assimilate them to emotion.

Whether every sensation and every thought gives rise to an emotion of some sort is matter for dispute, as is also the question whether every sensation, thought and emotion is tinged with some degree of pleasurable or painful feeling. In the absence of conclusive evidence, it is open to us to assume that some feeling is always present where there is mental activity of any kind. The feeling may be so faint and evanescent as to escape detection, but this does not prove that it is absent.

---

[56] See the notes on this chapter at the end of this volume.

50. FEELING AND ACTION.—Emotions and feelings of pleasure and pain are the normal accompaniments of the exercise of the instincts and impulses of creatures that desire and will. Within limits, we appear to be able to take them as an index of the strength of the desire and the vigor of the effort at attainment.

An act of cruelty is perpetrated. I see it, and it leaves me, perhaps, cold and unmoved. In such case, it is hardly expected of me that I should take energetic measures to have the evil-doer punished. The man whose face flushes, whose brows descend, whose teeth come together, whose fists clench, whose heart beats thickly, at the recognition of an insult, is, as a rule, the man from whom we look for vigorous efforts at retaliation. The apathetic creature who *feels* no resentment is usually expected to swallow the indignity. The child who jumps for joy at the sight of a new doll is supposed to desire it eagerly, and to be ready to make efforts to obtain it.

But it is only within limits that this relation between feeling and action holds. Men of little emotion may be resolute and prompt to action. Their desires, as evinced by their actions, may be persistent and effective. Nor need the individual fix his choice upon the particular object that arouses in him the most feeling. A man may see his fellow- creature destitute, and may shed tears over his pitiable lot. But he will not bequeath his money to him. He will leave it to his son, for whom, perhaps, he has no respect and has come to have little affection. And he may leave it to him with regret, knowing that it will be dissipated in ways which he cannot approve. It has been pointed out with justice that the exercise of many instincts may be accompanied with little feeling; and we are all aware of the fact that, as action becomes habitual, emotion tends to evaporate and the pleasure of effort and attainment is apt to be reduced to a minimum.

51. FEELING AS OBJECT.—It is well to keep in mind the distinction between feeling as a psychic fact present in the mind of the creature desiring and willing, and feeling as the object of desire and will. A man in a rage is the victim of a storm of feeling. The thought of the injury he has received and the desire for retaliation by no means exhaust the contents of his mind. But the passion which shakes him is not his *object*; that object is revengeful action.

Nevertheless, feeling may be made the object of desire and will. One may attend a religious or political meeting with the deliberate view of arousing in one's self certain complex emotions. Poe's gruesome tales are read for the sake of the thrill which is produced by the perusal. Probably the desire for excitement, for the experiencing of certain vivid emotions, has no little to do with the attraction exercised by certain criminal professions. The burglar desires the booty, but he may desire something more.

Emotions have, as we have seen, their "tone" of pleasure or pain. They are agreeable or the reverse, and it is palpable that men do not, as a rule, deliberately make them the object of desire and will in indifference to the fact that they are pleasant or are painful. We do not normally wish to attain to states of mind in which remorse plays a prominent part; we do not aim to revel in shame; we do not seek to be haunted with fear. Pleasurable emotions are desired, where desire is set on emotions at all; and painful emotions are regarded by the mind as unwelcome guests. At any rate, this appears to be the rule, and to characterize the man whom we regard as normal.

This being the case, it seems natural to ask whether, when we embrace the *intention* of producing in ourselves a given emotion, our *motive* may not be narrower in scope, namely, the attainment of pleasure? and, when we wish to rid the mind of any emotion, our *motive* may not be the avoidance of pain?

The adoption of this view would give to the feelings of pleasure and pain a unique importance. They would be accepted as the only ultimate objects of desire and will. By many they have been thus accepted. It has been insisted that objects of every description are chosen only as they arouse some feeling; and that those which promise pleasant feeling are sought and those which entail pain are avoided. The general recognition of the primacy of pleasure and pain over our other feelings, over the specific emotions mentioned above, is indicated by the fact that ethical writers of eminence sometimes make pleasure and pain synonymous with feeling in general, passing over other feelings, as though it were not important for the moralist to take them into consideration. The dispute whether the proper course for human action to take is prescribed by reason or is dictated by feeling often resolves itself into the problem whether we should be guided by reason, or by a consideration of pleasure to be attained or pain to be avoided.

52. FREEDOM AS OBJECT.—The acceptance of pleasure and pain as the ultimate motives of human action seems, at first sight, to be of inestimable assistance to us in threading our way through the labyrinth of diverse choices made by creatures that desire and will.

But only at first sight. Even if it be true that every creature seeks only to attain pleasure and to avoid pain, and uses the means it finds to hand in the attainment of these ends, the endless diversity of the means remains as a thing to reckon with. The knowledge that all men desire pleasure does not help us a whit in dealing with men, unless we know what things will give pleasure to this man or to that. All men may desire pleasure; but it remains true that what gives pleasure to the spendthrift gives pain to the miser; what appeals to the glutton disgusts a man of refined tastes. If all men were alike and precisely alike, and if their natures were very simple and remained unchanged, the problem of the distribution of pleasures would be vastly simplified.

Whether the pursuit of pleasure and the avoidance of pain may be regarded as the only ultimate ends proper to man will be discussed later. [57] Here, it is important to insist that so general a formula gives us little useful information touching the set of the will either of classes of men or of individuals. This we can attain to only as a result of the study of the complex nature of man as revealed in the choices which he actually makes. The ends of man are many and various; some of these ends are accidental, palpably means for the attainment of other ends more fundamental, and for them other means of attaining the same ends may be substituted. But other ends, and they are by no means to be reduced to a single class, appear to belong to the very nature of man. In seeking them he is giving expression to the impulses which make him what he is.

In so far as these impulses find an unimpeded expression the man is free; otherwise he is under restraint. Without rendering here a final decision upon the importance of the role played in human life by pleasure and pain, one feels impelled to ask the question whether the goal of a man's endeavors may not best be described as *freedom*? Not freedom in the abstract, freedom to do anything and everything, but freedom to live the life appropriate to him as man, and as a man of a given type. That this freedom is limited in a variety of ways, by his material environment, by the clashing of impulses within himself, by the conflict of his desires with the will of the social organism in which he finds his place, is sufficiently palpable.

CHAPTER XVI

RATIONALITY AND WILL

53. THE IRRATIONAL WILL.—As dreams do not consist of an insignificant medley of elements drawn from the experiences of waking life, but, in spite of their fantastic character, bear some semblance of

---

[57] See chapter xxv.

ordered reality, so the impulses of even the most unintelligent and inconsequent of human beings are not wholly chaotic, but differ only in the degree of their organization from those of the most rational and far-seeing.

Where there is even a glimmer of intelligence, ends are recognized and means to their attainment are chosen. Ends are compared, and the preference is given to some over others. But, with all this, there may be much incoherence and planlessness. Men can live somehow without looking far into the future, or keeping well in mind the lessons to be learned from the past. They can manage to exist in the face of no little short- sighted impulsiveness and inconsistency. But it is palpable that they cannot, under such circumstances, live as they might live were they more truly rational.

The individual deficient in foresight and control may, it is true, be carried along and defended from disaster by the presence of these qualities in the greater organism of which he is a part. The infant is a parasite upon society; it is provided for independently of its own efforts. The child would soon come to grief were its ends not chosen by others and its conduct kept under control. And a vast number of persons not children are in much the same position. There is foresight and rational purpose somewhere; they profit by it; but of foresight and rational purpose they themselves possess but a modicum.

Where breadth of view is lacking, where the future is unforeseen or ignored and the past is forgotten, where desires arise and impel to action in relative independence of one another, the man seeks today what tomorrow he rejects. We can scarcely say that the man chooses. He is the scene of independent choices, varied and inconsistent. He is the victim of caprice, and appears to us largely the creature of accident, a prey to the impulse which happens to be in his mind at the moment. From such a man we cannot look for an adherence to distant aims, and the marshalling of the proper means to their attainment. He cannot count upon himself, and he cannot be counted upon. That he can play no significant role in such stable organizations as the state and church is obvious. His desires may be many and varied, but they converge upon no one end. We set him down as irrational.

54. ONE VIEW OF REASON.—Concerning the part played by reason or intelligence in the active life of man there has been no little dispute.

It has been maintained, on the one hand, that reason or intelligence serves its whole purpose in holding before the mind all its impulses and desires, revealing their interrelations, and making possible an enlightened and deliberate choice from among them. Where the horizon is thus extended and mental clarity reigns, the attention can roam unimpeded over the whole field, consider the objects of desire in their true relations and compare them with one another. Congruous desires can reinforce each other; conflicting desires can be brought face to face, and the one or the other can deliberately be dismissed; fundamental and dominant desires may assert their supremacy, and give their stamp to far- reaching decisions which exercise a control over minor decisions and favor or repress a multitude of desires and volitions.

The attainment of perfect rationality in this sense is an ideal never completely realized. No man can hold before his mind all his impulses and desires, see them in their true relations to each other, and come to a decision which will do complete justice to all. But the ideal may be approached.

The reason, in this case, resembles the presiding officer of a deliberative assembly, who insists that all the members shall be heard from, all proposals seriously considered, and that the ultimate decision shall justly represent the true will of the deliberative body as a whole. The specious but fallacious argument is, in the debate, revealed in its true nature; the obstinate insistence of the individual is not allowed to prevail; the loud voice is recognized to be a loud voice and nothing more; fugitive gusts of passion exhaust themselves; the permanent and fundamental will of the assembly is revealed in the final vote. It is claimed that, in such a mind, the result is a harmonization and unification of the multiplicity of the desires and purposes which, in a mind less rational, jostle one another without control, and refuse to fall into an ordered system. That the decisions of a rational mind reveal both a unity and a harmony not evinced by a mind short-sighted and impulsive cannot be denied. But it is well to understand clearly what is meant by such unity and harmony.

55. DOMINANT AND SUBORDINATE DESIRES.—Wherever a group of desires fall into a system and work together toward a common end, we have unity. Such a system may be short-lived, comparatively poor in content, and of no great significance for a man's life as a whole. It may come into competition with another similar system, and be displaced by it. An interest that has dominated our minds for a time, and controlled our desires and volitions, may readily give place to different choices. I may successively bend all my energies upon the winning of a game, the doing of a successful stroke of business, the defeat of a social rival, the success of a philanthropic undertaking. There is no normal human being who does not exhibit such limited volitional units. The most idle and purposeless of vagrants, the most scatter-brained school-boy, the most volatile coquette, may, for a time, be dominated by some desire which calls into its service other desires and thus realizes some chosen end.

Such volitional units do not, however, go far toward unifying the efforts of a life. It is only when some dominant and deep-seated desire, oft recurring, not easily displaced by others, sweeps into its train the other desires of a man, establishing a sovereignty and exacting subservience, that such an effect is accomplished. Then the lesser units fall into a significant relation to each other as constituent elements in the greater unit. The life, as such, may be said to have a purpose; it strives toward a single goal.

Whatever bears upon the attainment of such a dominant purpose may, however trivial in itself, acquire a vital importance and be eagerly desired. To a man of mature mind there can be little interest in hitting a small ball with a stick, abstractly considered. Nor is the dropping of a bit of paper into a box with a slit in it an action in itself calculated to stir profound emotion. But if the hitting of the ball in the right way marks the critical point in winning an eagerly contested game of golf, the interest in it may be absorbing. And if the bit of paper is an offer of marriage committed to the post, the hand may tremble and the heart leap in the breast. A dominant desire may create or reinforce other desires to a degree to which it is not easy to set limits.

56. THE HARMONIZATION OF DESIRES.—And it may actively repress other desires or cause them to dwindle and disappear. A man possessed by a devouring ambition may resolutely scorn delights to which he would otherwise be keenly susceptible, or he may simply ignore them without effort. The attention, fixed upon some chosen end, and busied with the means to its attainment, may leave them unheeded. Finding no place in the volitional pattern that occupies the mind, they are cast aside and soon forgotten.

In so far, hence, as the desires of a man tend to fall thus into groups converging upon a single end, we find not merely unity but harmony. The volitional pattern is of a given kind, and the colors which enter into it are selected.

When, however, we speak of the desires of a rational mind as harmonized, we do not mean that incompatible desires are reconciled. One cannot laugh and drink at the same time, nor can the desire for luxurious ease be made to fall upon the neck of the desire for attainment through strenuous effort. The final harmony attained resembles in some respects the peace enforced by the violent character depicted by Mark Twain, who would have peace at any price, and was willing to sacrifice to it the life and limb of the opposing party. The cessation of strife does not imply the satisfaction of all parties to a contest; nor does the fact that a life is controlled by a ruling motive, which reinforces or calls into being certain desires and robs others of their insistence, imply that by any device all the desires which man has, still less all that he, as a human being, might have, can find their satisfaction. Harmony is obtained at the price of the suppression of many desires; but, where a mind is strongly dominated by a comprehensive volitional unit, the price may be paid without much regret.

57. VARIETIES OF DOMINANT ENDS.—Obviously, the comprehensive and harmonious volitional complexes which may come to characterize different minds may be of very different complexion. Peace of mind, the bubble reputation, the amassing of a fortune, a happy domestic life, humanitarian effort, the perfecting of one's character—each may become the controlling end which furthers or inhibits individual desires and emotions. Or the ends may be such as to appear to most men far more insignificant. To the collection of first editions or the heaping together of bric-a-brac a man may sacrifice his financial security and the welfare of his family. Naturally, the moralist cannot put all such ends upon the same level; but, from the point of view of the psychologist, the processes which take place in the minds thus unified and harmonized are essentially the same.

58. AN OBJECTION ANSWERED.—To the position that it is reason or intelligence that brings about this unity and harmony an objection may be brought. It may be claimed that breadth of information and clarity of vision are quite compatible with highly inconsistent action revealing the temporary dominance of a succession of incongruous desires.

Video meliora proboque, deteriora sequor, confessed the Latin poet. Have we not seen men of the highest intelligence, gifted with foresight, quite capable of grasping the relation of means to ends, nevertheless subject to the baleful influence of momentary desires which drive them hither and thither like a rudderless bark at the mercy of the wind and tide? How does it happen that their intelligence does not help them?

To this we may answer that it is not the same thing to possess intelligence and to use it. One may be supplied with information and quite capable of taking long views and embracing inclusive ends—and the attention may be so preoccupied with the desire of the moment, that the voices of others are stifled. In so far as this is the case, the man can not, at the time, be said to be reasonable or intelligent. He has information, and acts as if he were ignorant; his choices do not issue as a resultant of his desires as a whole; there is no resultant; the single desires make their influence felt separately.

To be sure, an insistent and oft-recurring desire may introduce a good deal of unity and harmony into life, even where long views are not taken and there is little intelligence. The stupid egoist may become rather a consistent egoist, and increasingly so as he grows older. His desires and volitions may converge upon an end of which he is very imperfectly conscious; incompatible desires may come to be repressed. But this does not refute the position that, when reason or intelligence is supreme, the

70

attention is directed upon a wide range of desires, they are weighed in the light of each other, and the ultimate decision is no longer blind, but fairly expresses the permanent push of the man's nature. Even where a desire or group of desires, unilluminated by intelligence, seems so insistent as to take on something of this character, complete unity and harmony of action may be lacking, due to the short-sightedness of the methods employed to attain to the chosen goal. Blind desires may easily defeat their own ends; wealth does not necessarily accumulate in proportion to a man's miserliness; the ardent but unenlightened philanthropist may do his fellow-man more harm than good. Long views are of no little service in weeding out inconsistent actions and introducing order and unity into life.

59. THIS VIEW OF REASON MISCONCEIVED.—In the above view of the function of reason or intelligence it has not been represented as issuing commands to perform certain actions rather than others, nor as furnishing motives not in some way related to the impulses and desires of man. It has been treated, literally, as the presiding officer of a public assembly, who insists that every voice shall be heard; that all proposals shall be weighed and compared with one another; that the consequences of all shall be clearly foreseen. Its function is enlightenment; the driving force which impels to action of any sort has been found in the impulses and the desires.

It is possible to set this view forth in terms which make it highly unpalatable.

Thus Hume, who has a weakness for shocking the susceptibilities of the conservative and the sober-minded, startles us with the remark that "Reason is, and ought only to be, the slave of the passions." [58] This doctrine, taken as the average reader is almost inevitably impelled to take it, seems worthy of instant reprobation. It appears to degrade the rational in man and to exalt the blind and irrational.

But it is not fair to the doctrine to set it forth in such terms. There is no small difference between random and fugitive desires and those more fundamental desires that express truly the nature of a man. Desires organized and harmonized gain great strength, and are enabled to overcome and expel from the mind erratic impulses, the obedience to which may easily be followed by regret. Action taken without a clear foresight of consequences, with an imperfect conception of the relation of means to ends, is blind and irrational action. Reason, as bringing enlightenment, as making possible deliberation, as turning the incoherent clamors of a mob of inconsistent desires into the authoritative voice of an orderly deliberative assembly, is not a faculty to be lightly regarded.

---

[58] A Treatise of Human Nature, iv, Sec 3.

Nor should it be forgotten that, neither to the plain man, nor to the moralist, do desires all stand upon the same level. He who bends his intellectual energies to the satisfaction of his greed, his avarice, his longing for revenge, may fairly be said to be prostituting his mind to the service of passion. But is it a proper use of language to describe as the slave of his passions the man whose thought is set upon the enlightenment of mankind, the alleviation of suffering, the service of a state, the attainment of a noble character? Were Socrates, St. Francis, Abraham Lincoln, Wilberforce, Thomas Hill Green, the slaves of their passions? Yet these men were moved by certain dominant desires, and their unswerving pursuit of their goal was made possible only by the reason that harmonized their lives and substituted deliberate purpose for random impulse.

The doctrine, then, that the reason is to be likened rather to the presiding officer of a deliberative assembly, concerned only to give every voice a fair hearing, than to a legislator issuing commands independently, may be so stated as not to shock the sober-minded.

And the doctrine recommends itself in showing that reason and inclination or desire are not enemies. The possession of reason must lead to the suppression of some desires—those incompatible with a comprehensive purpose deliberately embraced; but the desires and the reason or intelligence work together to a common end. On this view, it is not the rational man who is divided against himself; it is the short-sighted, the impulsive, the inconsistent, the irrational man. He is the prey of warring desires whose strife leads to no permanent peace under the guidance of reason.

60. ANOTHER VIEW OF REASON.—To certain minds this view of reason as the arbiter and reconciler of man's impulses and desires does not appeal.

Thus, Kant, whose doctrine will be more fully considered later, [59] holds that man's reason promulgates a law which takes no account of the impulses and desires of man. Thus, also, Henry Sidgwick, who differs from Kant in making the attainment of happiness the goal of human endeavor, and who, consequently, is not tempted to disregard the desires of man, yet refers to the reason independently certain maxims, which he regards as self-evident, touching our own good and the good of our neighbor. [60]

There are certain considerations which appear to favor the view that the reason is a faculty which may be regarded as an independent law-giver. A

---

[59] Chapter xxix.
[60] *The Methods of Ethics*, chapter iii.

72

man may be possessed of great intelligence; he may be well-informed, acute in his reasonings, and consistent in his strivings to attain some comprehensive end, which, on the whole, appears congruous to his nature, such as it is. Yet we may regard him as highly unreasonable. Judged by some higher standard which we look upon as approved by reason, he is found to fall short. Is reason, then, synonymous with intelligence? Or is it something more—the source of an ultimate standard of action, intuitively known, and by which all man's actions must be judged? Upon this question light will be thrown in the pages following.

PART V

THE SOCIAL WILL

CHAPTER XVII

CHARACTERISTICS OF THE SOCIAL WILL

61. WHAT IS THE SOCIAL WILL?—The social will is not a mysterious entity, separate and distinct from all individual wills. It is their resultant. The resultant of two or more physical forces is a force; it has a character and may be described. The resultant of individual wills in interaction is a will with a given character which it is of no small importance for the moralist to comprehend. This will presents aspects closely analogous to those presented by the will of the individual.

Thus, to begin with, a community of men may be said to will a vast number of things which have never been made by the members of the community the object of conscious reflection. It may unthinkingly move along the groove made for it by tradition. It may be intellectually upon so low a plane that even the possibility of acting in other ways does not occur to it. Nevertheless, ways of action thus unthinkingly pursued cannot properly be said to be beyond the voluntary control of the community. A new situation may draw attention to the fact that they are unsatisfactory, lead to critical examination, to inhibition, to deliberate change. Between the passive acceptance of actions prescribed by tradition and deliberate conscious choice in the presence of recognized alternatives there is no clear line of demarcation.

Under the pressure of circumstances or with the gradual increase of information and intelligence the traditional may undergo slight modifications which scarcely rank as conscious departures from what has been passively accepted. The algebraic sum of such departures may, with the lapse of time, come to be by no means insignificant, yet no individual may have exercised in any considerable degree conscious reflection or shown in any large measure freedom of choice.

On the other hand, the social will may, at times, reveal itself in deliberate decisions, preceded by much conscious deliberation, and initiating wide departures from established usage. The presence of new enemies or a diminution of the food-supply may awake a primitive community from its lethargy, leading it to modify its habits and adjust itself to new conditions. A barbarous horde may set out upon a career of conquest, and may introduce revolutionary changes into its manner of life. A civilized nation may come to the conclusion that, in the course of human events, it has become necessary for it to dissolve the bands which have held it to another nation; it may frame for itself an independent constitution, embodying new ideals and prescribing a new form of corporate life.

But, as in the case of the individual, so in that of the community, the tendency to fall again into a rut is always apparent. Laws, once enacted, lend a passive resistance to change, even when they no longer serve well the ends they were intended to serve. The independence of thought and action revealed in the adoption of new constitutions are not conspicuous in their maintenance. Man collective, as well as man individual, falls into habits, and he commits to his unthinking self what was wrought out by himself as thinking and consciously choosing. Passive acceptance of the traditional again wins the day and becomes a ruling factor in action. [61]

This tendency to mechanization should not surprise us, for we meet with the phenomenon everywhere. The man who says, "Good-by" today does not mean "God be with thee," and the "Gruss Dich Gott" of the Bavarian peasant is very properly translated by the American child as "Hallo." The traditional tends to lose or to alter its meaning, but it continues to serve a purpose. A community without traditions, without settled ways of acting, followed, for the most part, without much reflection, would be in the position of a man without habits either good or bad. Human life as we know it could not go on upon such a basis. The rule has, at times, its inconveniences; but it leads somewhere, at least; whereas he who plunges

---

[61] "It is indisputable that much the greatest part of mankind has never shown a particle of desire that its civil institutions should be improved since the moment when external completeness was first given to them by their embodiment in some permanent record." MAINE, *Ancient Law*, chapter ii.

into the unexplored forest may find every step a problem, and may come even to doubt whether any step is a step in advance.

62. SOCIAL WILL AND SOCIAL HABITS.—Within the province of the social will fall what may not inaptly be called the habits of a community— ways of acting acquired largely without premeditation and followed to a great extent through mere inertia. The province of the social will is a broad one. Deliberate choices; those half-conscious choices analogous to the unheeded expressions of preference which fill the days of the individual; impulses and tendencies which scarcely emerge into the light—all are expressions of the social will.

In the next chapter I shall distinguish between customs proper and social habits in a broader sense. But, in discussing the general problem of the relation of habit to will, it is not necessary to mark the distinction.

Some habits rest upon us lightly; some are inveterate. Of some we are well aware; others have to be pointed out to us before we recognize that we have them. Some we approve, some we disapprove, to some we are indulgent or indifferent. All these peculiarities are found in the relation of the social will to social habits. It may recognize them, approve of them, encourage them. It may pay them little attention. It may disapprove them and strive to repress them. Will has brought them into being; it is will that maintains them; it is will that must modify or suppress them.

As a matter of fact, all communities do tend to change their habits, some more slowly, some more rapidly. And for its habits we hold a community responsible. Common sense refers them to its will, and exercises approval or disapproval. This it would not do were the practices upon which judgment is passed recognized as beyond the control of will altogether.

63. SOCIAL WILL AND SOCIAL ORGANIZATION.—Under the general heading of the habits of a society it is not out of place to discuss its social and political organization.

The fact that there never was an original social contract, made with each other by men solitary and unrelated, with the deliberate intent of putting an end to the war of all against all, does not signify that the social state in which men find themselves is a something with which the human will has had, and has, nothing to do.

Social and political organization are the result of a secular process, but behind that process, as moving and directing forces, stand the will and the intelligence of man. The social and political organization of a community is not the creation of any single generation of men. Each generation is born

76

into a given social setting, as the individual is born into the setting furnished by the community. This social setting, the heritage of the community from the past, may be compared to a great estate brought together by the efforts of a man's ancestors, and transmitted to him to hold intact, to add to, to squander, as he may be inclined. It is a product attained by man's nature in its struggle with environment, and that product may be modified by the same forces that made it what it is.

Into this heritage the generation of men who compose a community at any given time may enter with little thought of its significance, with no information, or with false information, touching the manner of its coming into being, and with small inclination to do anything save to leave unchanged the institutions of which it finds itself possessed. Nevertheless, the forms under which societies are organized are subject to the social will, and, if disapproved, are modified or abolished. Some change is taking place even where there is apparent immobility, as becomes evident when the history of institutions is followed through long periods of time. The utmost that can be said is that, where intelligence is little developed and energy at a low ebb, the social will may bear the stamp of passive acceptance of the inherited, rather than exhibit a tendency to innovation. *Will* it remains, but we may hesitate to describe it as a *free will*.

It is at times forced upon our attention with unmistakable emphasis that the forms of social and political organization are under voluntary control. Momentous changes may be made deliberately, and with full consciousness of their significance. Among the more progressive nations in our day the duty of introducing innovations appears to be generally recognized: constitutions are amended; the status of social classes is made the object of legislation; even the domain of the family is invaded, as in legislation touching marriage and divorce. Men appear to feel themselves free to will deliberately the end that shall be served by the mechanism of the state, and to adapt that mechanism to the attainment of the end chosen.

64. THE SOCIAL WILL AND IDEAL ENDS.—The social will, like the wall of the individual, may manifest itself in decisions which it is obviously impossible to carry out to a completely successful issue. A community has a power of control over its members, but that control has its limits. Even a man's actions cannot be completely controlled by the community of which he is a part. There are always individuals who violate rules, and to whom, as it would seem, no motive can be presented which is adequate to keep them in the rut prescribed by society.

Still less can the social will exercise full control over men's thoughts and feelings. Influenced to some degree they may be. A man may be kept in ignorance, or furnished with information calculated to determine his thought in a given direction. His emotions may be played upon; he may be exhorted, rewarded, punished. But thoughts and feelings are not open to direct inspection; they may be concealed or simulated. Much more readily than actions can they withdraw themselves from control.

Nevertheless, the social will may, and does, ignore all such limitations to its powers. Laws are not passed to regulate the changes of the weather, which palpably fall outside the province of the law; but they are passed to regulate the actions of men, which normally fall within it; that is, which can, to a very significant degree, be influenced by the attitude of the social will. For the same reason laws may even take cognizance of men's thoughts. Of the accidental limitations of its power of control within the general sphere in which it has a meaning to speak of control, the social will is not compelled to take cognizance. It may set itself to encourage or repress certain types of character and conduct, and take measures to attain the end it has selected. That the measures taken should sometimes prove inadequate does not alter the fact of the choice of an end, nor does it obscure the revelation of the trend of the social will.

Thus, a community may be said to will that its members shall not be guilty of violence; it may will to live at peace with other communities; it may will to conquer and subjugate. Whether, in each case, the will shall be completely realized or not, may not be determined by the mere fact of its willing. Nevertheless, the permanent volitional attitude may be unmistakably present, and may reveal itself in strivings toward the chosen goal. To describe this attitude as no more than wishing is manifestly to do it an injustice.

65. THE PERMANENT SOCIAL WILL.—The social will may be regarded as something permanent. Its existence is not confined to those moments in which collective decisions are being made. The will to be one which constitutes a group of human beings a nation is not at all times actively exercised, but the settled disposition to action looking toward that end may be always present and ready to be called into action. An autocracy remains such when its irresponsible head is making no decisions; and a democracy is not such only while elections are being held or the legislature is sitting. The organization of a society, the whole body of the usages which it accepts and approves, are revelations of the social will. That will does, it is true, give expression to itself in a series of actual decisions more or less conscious and deliberate, but it is far more than any such series of decisions. It is a disposition, rooted in the past and reaching into the future. It is a guarantee of decisions to come, of whose nature we may make some forecast.

The permanent social will constitutes the *character* of a community. Our study of the will of the individual prepares us for the recognition of the fact that communities may be but dimly aware of their own character, and may be quite unable to give an unbiased account of the ideals which animate them.

CHAPTER XVIII

EXPRESSIONS OF THE SOCIAL WILL

66. CUSTOM.—We have seen above that even the forms of political and social organization may justly be regarded as an expression of the social will. Such forms are the result of past choices, and their acceptance in the present is evidence of present choice.

Between the organization of a society and its customs proper we may distinguish by comparing the former to structure and the latter to function in the case of any organism. But we must bear in mind that, here, structure has been built up by, and is in process of modification by, the same forces that exhibit themselves in function. It would not be wholly out of place to describe a people as having the custom of being ruled by hereditary chiefs, of choosing their monarchs, or of governing themselves through elected representatives. Forms of organization are handed down to successive generations by the same social tradition that transmits customs of every description.

Customs are public habits which are, on the whole, approved by a community. They are ways of acting which are regarded as normal and proper. Where the authority of custom is evoked, pressure is brought to bear upon the individual to adjust himself to the will of the community.

A community, like an individual, may have habits which it does not approve. Such may be tolerated, although disapproved; or active efforts may be made to set them aside. Some habits may be regarded with comparative indifference, although professedly held in condemnation. The individual, in following such habits, may claim that they are not unequivocally condemned by the community, and he is not conscious of the weight of displeasure which visits the violation of the will of the community when unequivocally expressed.

In simple and primitive societies custom prescribes to the individual his course of life in the minutest detail. It possesses the authority of the dictator. In societies upon a higher level it may leave to him some discretion in deciding upon the details of his daily life, while still exercising a paramount control over the general trend of his actions.

Thus the will of the community, expressed in custom, determines what the members of the community *ought* to do, and it takes measures to enforce obedience to its decisions. Is it surprising that the names which have been given to the science which treats of man's rights and duties, *morals, ethics* (*mores, ethica, Sitten*), should reflect this truth? It would be an inadequate statement to maintain that the science of morals is no more than a systematic exposition of the customary in human societies. It is not an inadequate statement to assert that, in many societies, custom has, in fact, furnished the ultimate and complete standard of obligation, and that in all societies it is of enormous significance in moulding men's notions of right and wrong.

67. THE GROUND FOR THE AUTHORITY OF CUSTOM.—Habits are as essential to a society as they are to an individual human being. Without them, society could not live. In any social state—and no man can live except in a social state—there must be cooperation. How can there be cooperation if there are no social habits upon which men may count in their dealings with one another?

Try to conceive all the tacit mutual conventions, the unconscious adaptations to custom, which guide our daily lives, suspended for twenty-four hours. When should one rise in the morning? How should one dress? What and how should one eat? Of business there could be no question, nor could there be cooperation in pleasures. Public order there could not be, for there would be no public worthy of the name. Protection of life and limb would be the creature of accident. Between civility and insult there would be no recognizable distinction. In short, men could not behave either well or ill, for there would be no rule to follow or to violate, nothing to expect, and, hence, no ground for disappointment.

In such a chaotic condition no society of men has ever lived. No actual state of anarchy has ever been complete, nor could it be, and endure. A "reign of terror" is a reign of law in comparison with such a dissolution of all the bonds which knit man to man. When we pass from one community to another, we find one set of public habits exchanged for another. Some sets impress us as better, some as worse. But there is no set which is not better than none. It makes it possible for men to live, if not to live well.

Customs are, then, a necessity. It is equally necessary that they should, in general, have binding force for the individual. But there are customs good and bad. The individual may fall into habits which he, upon reflection, concludes to be injurious to him, and which others see clearly to be injurious. A community sufficiently enlightened to criticize itself at all, may come to disapprove some of its customs and may endeavor to abolish them.

This means that a new act of the social will may set itself in opposition to the social will already crystallized into custom. In a given instance, and where there are differences of opinion, it may be a nice question whether the new or the old should be regarded as the authoritative expression of the social will.

68. THE ORIGIN AND THE PERSISTENCE OF CUSTOMS.—From the fact that customs are, in general, to be regarded as expressions of the social will, it might be assumed that their purposive character and social utility should be a sufficient explanation of their coming into being. But the matter is not so simple. A man may fall into habits which are no indication of what he regards as useful to him. Such habits have not been formed independently of his will, and yet they may appear to be purposeless, or even detrimental. Who wishes to have the inveterate habit of cracking the joints of his fingers or of biting his finger-nails? What purpose do such habits serve?

Although the social utility of customs, taken generally, is easily apparent, yet there are many customs which seem inexplicable upon such a principle. Why, for example, should the king of a primitive community be prohibited from sleeping lying down? or why should it be forbidden that he gaze upon the sea? [62] The origin of such customs is hidden in obscurity. That their adoption was not without its reason, we may assume. That the reason was a reasonable one cannot be maintained. It seems probable, however, that it at some time seemed reasonable to some one. The persistence of habit, social as well as individual, would account for the perpetuation of the custom long after the occasion which gave rise to it had been forgotten.

69. LAW.—Between custom and law, taken generally, it is by no means easy to draw a sharp distinction, although, in some instances, the distinction, may be clearly marked. In primitive communities, laws reduced to writing, and administered by persons deliberately chosen for

---

[62] *Encyclopedia Britannica*, Eleventh edition, article "Taboo."

that end, may be wholly lacking; and yet who would say that such communities do not live under the reign of law in a broad sense of the term? A course of life is prescribed to the individual; failure to come up to the standard meets with punishment.

Nevertheless, as social life rises in the scale and as communities become developed, custom and law become differentiated. The latter stands out upon the background of the former as something more sharply defined. Penalties and the method of their infliction are more exactly fixed. Not all violations of what is customary are taken up into the legal code as punishable offences, although they meet with that indefinite measure of punishment entailed by social disapproval.

Those public habits which it seems to a community it is of especial importance to preserve and enforce come to be embodied in laws. The selection is a matter of more or less deliberate choice, and is an expression of will. The choice is not, normally, an arbitrary one. The laws of a people are, unless accident has intervened, the outcome and expression of its corporate life. For their ultimate authority they rest upon the acquiescence of the social will. Laws contrary to deep-seated and widely accepted custom are not apt to be regarded as of binding force. They are felt to be tyrannous, and are obeyed, if at all, unwillingly, and because of pressure from without.

In a later chapter [63] I shall dwell upon the fact that the accidental may play a very significant role in law. In given instances the laws of a community may be, not the outcome of its will in any sense, but something imposed upon it. Such laws cannot but be felt to be oppressive and a restriction of freedom.

Laws, like customs, may cease to have a significance, and they may be modified or allowed to fall into desuetude. There is, however, much conservatism, as all who are familiar with legal usage know. And laws may fail of their purpose. They may aim to diminish crime, and their undiscriminating severity may foster crime. So may the individual select an end, fall into error in his choice of means, and, as a result of experience, resolve to substitute for such means others which are better adapted to carry out his purpose.

70. PUBLIC OPINION.—Public opinion is manifestly a force broader and more vague than established custom, and still broader than law. Public opinion may approve or condemn what no law touches, and it makes its influence felt beyond the sphere of what is customary.

---

[63] Chapter XX.

Where customs and laws come to be imperfect expressions of the social will, they may stand condemned by public opinion. In such a case their authority is undermined and violations of them are condoned. Where public opinion is strongly against a law; the law becomes ineffective. The conservatism of law is such that a law may be allowed to stand unchanged, and yet may fail to be carried into effect. Juries may refuse to convict, or the unpalatable infliction of punishment may be avoided by granting to the judge a wide discretion in pronouncing sentence.

The gradual development of a strong public sentiment may lead to the passage of new laws, not based upon previously established customs, but deliberately framed with a view to the public weal. Old customs may be modified and new customs may be introduced. That the recommendations of public opinion extend beyond the sphere of the customary is manifest. It is not the custom of most men to leave any large part of their estate to public charity. Except in the case of the very rich, the failure to do so is not, as a rule, expressly condemned. Yet such bequests are approved, the testators are praised, and the attitude of public opinion has no small influence upon the conduct of individuals. Again, extreme self- sacrifice is not customary; it is exceptional; and yet shining examples of unselfishness excite a warm sympathy. The expression of this sympathy is not without its influence.

Public opinion is more palpably an expression of the actual social will than are custom and law. We have seen that the last two may represent, in given instances, rather the inherited will of the past than the living will of the present. But when we call public opinion an expression of the social will we cannot mean that it necessarily reflects the sentiment of all the members of a given community.

In primitive communities custom may be a public habit which embraces all, or nearly all, individuals. Public opinion may scarcely have a separate existence. In communities more developed, some individuals may disapprove and refuse to follow many customs which are characteristic of the society to which they belong. Laws are not approved by all, and, in progressive states, there is usually some agitation which has as its object the repeal of old laws or the passage of new ones. In communities where there is independence of thought, public opinion is usually divided.

Furthermore, the communities to which civilized men belong are not homogeneous aggregations of units. There is the public opinion which obtains within single groups within the state. The adherents of a religious sect may have notions peculiar to themselves of the conduct proper to the individual, and such notions may extend far beyond what is actually prescribed by the tenets of the sect. The several trades and professions, the social classes, neighborhoods, even lesser voluntary associations of men, such as clubs, may be pervaded by a public sentiment which varies with each group. When we speak of public opinion generally we have in mind something broader, a resultant. But the public sentiment of the lesser groups cannot be ignored. The individual feels himself especially influenced by the opinions of those most nearly associated with him.

Under the head of public opinion it is convenient to speak of the opinions of moral teachers who have influenced the race. Such a thinker may enunciate truths far in advance of the opinions of his fellows. His teachings are not, hence, fairly representative of the social will as it reveals itself in his time. But the sentiments of the more enlightened never are completely in accord with those of the mass of their fellows. They are not mere aberrations from the social will; they are its forerunners. The moralist and the religious teacher initiate new choices, which may become the choices of large bodies of men. From them proceed influences which have their issue in new expressions of the social will, characterizing whole societies, and giving birth to new customs, new laws, and a new form of public opinion. One can scarcely imagine what China would be without her Confucius; or the Arabic world, with Mahomet abstracted.

CHAPTER XIX

THE SHARERS IN THE SOCIAL WILL

71. THE COMMUNITY.—It is difficult to state with absolute exactness what constitutes a community.

We may define it as a group of human beings associated in a common life, depending upon and cooperating with each other. This definition will apply, to be sure, to lesser groups within a tribe or state; and even to a collection of tribes or states in so far as such enter into alliances and cooperate to their mutual advantage. As, however, the bond of union is, in the former case, subordinate to the higher authority of a larger group (for the family is subject to the tribe or state); and as, in the latter case, the bond of union is a relatively loose one, and evidently subordinate to that which binds the citizens of individual states, the community proper may be regarded as that group which is characterized by a relatively great degree of inner coherence and by relative external independence.

The type of such communities is, among the more primitive peoples, the tribe, and among the more developed, the state. The authority of such groups over their own members is, theoretically, paramount, although it may be suspended or abolished by the exertion of force from without.

Such a community may be said to be inspired by a social will expressed in its customs, its laws and the public opinion prevalent in it. Its members may be said to be sharers in the social will of the community. Their participation in it is marked by their being endowed with rights and charged with duties.

It has not been characteristic of communities generally that all who find their place in them should be like sharers in the social will. The distinction has been made between the citizen, who enjoys the fullest rights and may, perhaps, directly take part in the government of the state, and those who, while *in* the state, are not *of* it, as they do not enjoy citizenship. Where slavery, in any of its forms, has prevailed, the distinction between those who are significant factors in determining the social will, and those who have not this prerogative, has been very marked. Social classes have often enjoyed, even before the law, privileges of great moment. Women have, as a rule, not been treated as citizens, and have been refused a share in the government of the community. Children are cared for and are protected, but political rights are denied them. Their status before the law is a peculiar one. The mentally defective, both in primitive communities and in developed ones, stand in a relation to the community peculiar to themselves. They are not excluded from it; they are accorded rights; but they are assigned in the community a place of their own. Wherever we look, we find inequality. The sharers in the social will do not share equally, nor do they share in the same way. This is true of communities of every description, but the differences are more marked in some than in others.

72. THE COMMUNITY AND THE DEAD.—It is not merely of the living human beings which compose a community that the social will takes cognizance. Other wills are made participants in the body of rights and duties peculiar to the community.

In many communities the dead are still counted among its members. They are conceived as affecting its welfare, and as demanding services from the living. Duties towards the dead are a well-recognized division of the sum of a man's obligations in communities the most diverse in their character. In some, they occupy a very prominent place; in no community are they wholly overlooked. A striking illustration of the recognition by the social will of the rights of the dead is to be found in the whole modern law of testamentary succession. The will expressed by a man while he is alive is given effect as though he were still in the flesh and insisted upon the fulfillment of his desire. It appears to work as a permanent factor in the community life, making its influence felt for generations. Witness its influence in charitable foundations, in the law of entail, and the like.

73. THE COMMUNITY AND THE SUPERNATURAL.—Nor is it merely in recognizing the wills of the dead that the social will extends its sphere beyond the community of living human beings. To primitive man, and to man far from primitive, his social environment has not seemed to be limited to the living and the dead who have, or who have had, an undeniable and unequivocal place in the community.

The part played in the life of man by supernatural beings of various orders has been a most significant one. Demons and gods, spirits of a lower or of a higher order, have occupied his mind and have influenced his actions. Such beings have been conceived to be, sometimes, malevolent and needing to be placated, sometimes, benevolent and fit objects of gratitude. Their wills man has regarded as forces to be taken into account, a something to which the individual and the community must adjust themselves.

Man's relation, or supposed relation, to such beings has been a source of classes of duties upon which great stress has been laid. The influence of this admission of supernatural beings into the circle of those directly concerned in the community life has found its expression in the organization of the state, in custom, in law, in public opinion. We know little of a community when we overlook this factor.

Between magic and religion it is not easy to draw a sharp line, especially when we view religion in the lower stages of its development. In both we have to do with what may be called the supernatural. Magic has been defined as the employment of mechanical means to attain the desired end. In religion, when it so far develops that its specific character seems clearly revealed, we have left the sphere of the mechanical.

The distinction between the mechanical and the spiritual is familiar to us in our dealings with our fellow-men. In such dealings we may employ physical force. On the other hand, we may appeal to their intelligence and their emotions, and thus influence their action. In so far as we do not make such an appeal, we deal with our fellows, not as though they belonged to our social environment, but to our physical.

At the lowest stages of his development, man does not distinguish clearly between persons and things. This means that he cannot distinguish clearly between his material environment and his social. But the distinction becomes gradually clearer, and it is, in the end, a marked one. Religion becomes differentiated from magic. To confound religion, in its higher developments, with magic is an inexcusable confusion.

74. RELIGION AND THE COMMUNITY.—The denotation of the term religion is a broad one, and there will probably always be dispute as to the justice of its extension to this or to that particular form of faith. But it seems clear that it is typical of religion to extend what may not unjustly be called the social environment of man.

Will is recognized other than the wills of the human beings constituting the community. To the part played by such wills a very great prominence may be given.

States may be theocratic, as among the ancient Hebrews; or church and state may share the dominion, or struggle between themselves for the supremacy, as in Europe in the Middle Ages; or the state may be theoretically supreme in authority and yet maintain and lend authority to a church. Even where church and state are, in theory, quite divorced—a modern conception—the church with its ordinances and prescriptions, its sacred days, its ceremonial, its educational institutions, remains a very significant factor in the social environment of man. Religious duties have at all times and in all sorts of societies been regarded as constituting an important aspect of conduct. They color strongly the *mores* of the community. Whole codes of morals may be referred to the teachings of certain religious leaders. They claim their authority on religious grounds.

The great significance of the role played by religion in the sphere of morals is impressed upon one who glances over the works of those writers who have approached the subject of ethics from the side of anthropology or sociology. A review of the facts has even tempted one of the most learned to seek the origin of morals almost wholly in religion. [64]

That religion should play an important part in giving birth to or modifying moral codes is not surprising. Man adjusts himself to his social environment as he conceives it. If the community of wills which he recognizes includes the wills of supernatural beings, it is natural that the social will which finds its expression in the organization of the state, in

---

[64] WUNDT, *Ethics*, Vol. I. "The Facts of the Moral Life"; see chapters ii and iii. English Translation, London, 1897.

custom, in law and in public opinion, should be modified by such inclusion.

Nor is it surprising that the supernatural element should, at times, dwarf and render insignificant the other elements which enter into the social will. It may seem to man the all-important factor in his life.

Within the human community some individuals count for much more than do others. There are those who scarcely seem to have any voice in contributing to the character and direction of the social will. Others are influential; and, in extreme cases, the wills of the few, or even that of a single individual, may be the source of law for the many. If men come to the conclusion that the weal and woe of the community are dependent upon the will of the gods, or of God, they will unavoidably give frank recognition to that will above others, and such recognition will dictate conduct. The gods of Epicurus, leading a lazy existence in the interstellar spaces, indifferent to man and in no wise affecting his life, could scarcely become the objects of a cult. But the God of the Mahometan, of the Jew, or of the Christian, is a ruler to be feared, loved, obeyed. His will is law, and is determinative of conduct.

75. THE SPREAD OF THE COMMUNITY.—So far I have been speaking of the community properly so called, of the single group of human beings living its corporate life. But such groups do not normally remain in isolation. As the isolation of the group diminishes, as contacts between it and others become more numerous and more important, the necessity of conventions controlling the relations of groups becomes more pressing.

This implies the development of a broader social will, inclusive of the social wills of the several communities. This social will may be very feeble, and the bond between men belonging to different communities may be a weak one; or it may be vigorous, and furnish an intimate bond. The savage, to whom those beyond the pale of his tribe or small confederation are mere strangers, and probably enemies, stands at the lower limit of the scale; the trader, to whom the stranger is co-partner in a mutually profitable transaction, stands higher; the Stoic philosopher, cosmopolitan in thought and feeling, rating the claims of kindred and country as less significant than the bonds which unite all men in virtue of their common humanity, marks the other extreme. The spread of the social will grows marked as man rises in the scale of civilization. Barriers are broken down and limits are transcended.

This broader social will, like the narrower, reveals itself in the organization of society. We find confederations of tribes or states; alliances temporary or relatively permanent. And the broader social will modifies customs, gives birth to systems of law, and encourages the development of an inclusive humanitarian sentiment.

It does not necessarily obliterate old distinctions. The family, neighborhood, kindred, have their claims even under the most firmly organized of states; but those claims are limited and controlled. Even so, the broader social will may come to regard states as answerable for their decisions. International law remains to the present day what has aptly been called a pious wish. But public opinion prepares the way for law; and all states, whatever be their real aims, now attempt to justify their actions by an appeal to the more or less nebulous tribunal of international public opinion. In this they recognize its claim to act as arbiter. Within the jurisdiction of a state, the motto, "my family, right or wrong," would not be a maxim approved in a court of justice. International law is made a mock of by the frank enunciation of the maxim, "my country, right or wrong." Hence, such frankness is, in international relations, not encouraged.

The more or less skillfully made appeal to the moral sense of mankind—to the broader social will as public opinion—implies a certain recognition of its authority, or, at least, of its influence. Whether this is a definite step toward the granting of a real authority to the broader social will, an authority which will curb impartially the selfishness of individual states, it remains for the future to decide.

PART VI

THE REAL SOCIAL WILL

CHAPTER XX

THE IMPERFECT SOCIAL WILL

76. THE APPARENT AND THE REAL SOCIAL WILL.—It is important to distinguish between the apparent and the real social will. We may begin by pointing out that the question "apparent to whom?" is a pertinent one.

The social will is brought to bear upon the individual through a variety of agencies. The family, the neighborhood, the church, the trade or profession, the political party, the social class—all these have their habits and maxims. They tend to mold to their type those whom they count among their members. The pressure which they bring to bear is felt as a sense of moral obligation. Naturally, individuals with different affiliations will be sensible of the pressure in different ways, and may differ widely in their conceptions of the obligations actually laid upon the individual by the will of the greater organism of which he is a part.

But even he who rises above minor distinctions and takes a broad view of society is forced to recognize that the distinction between the apparent and the real social will may be a most significant one.

We have found the expression of the social will in custom, law and public opinion. This is just; but the statement must be accepted with reservations.

There are instances in which neither the organization of the state, nor the laws according to which it is governed, can be considered as in any sense an expression of the social will. An autocracy, established by force, and ruling without the free consent of the governed, is an external and overruling power. It may be obeyed, but it is not consented to. Nor is any body of law or system of government imposed upon a subject people by an alien and dominant race a fair exponent of the social will of the people thus governed. Custom and public opinion are at variance with law. However just and enlightened the government, as judged from the standpoint of some other race or nation, its control must be felt as oppressive by those upon whom it is imposed. Traditions felt to be the most sacred may be violated; moral laws, as understood by those thus under dictation, may be transgressed by obedience to the law of the land.

Where custom, law and public opinion are more nearly the spontaneous outcome of the life of a community, they may with more justice be taken as expressions of the social will of that community as it is at the time. Yet, even here, we must make reservations.

The organization of a state represents rather the crystallized will of the past than the free choice of the present. To be sure, it is accepted in the present; but this is little more than the acquiescence of inertia. And public opinion may be at variance both with custom and with law long before it succeeds in modifying either. What is the actual social will of a community during the interval?

The past may be felt as exercising a certain tyranny over the present. That the present cannot be cut wholly loose from it is manifest, but how far should its dependence be accepted? In the past there have been historical causes for the rise of dictatorships, of oligarchies, of dominant social classes. The men of a later time inherit such social institutions, may accept them as desirable, or may feel them as instruments of tyranny. Shall we say that they represent the actual social will of the community until such time as they are done away with by a successful revolution? Or shall we say that they are in harmony with the apparent social will only, and really stand condemned?

77. THE WILL OF THE MAJORITY.—Our own democratic institutions rest upon the theory that the social will is to be determined by the majority vote. To be sure, we seem to find it necessary to limit the application of this doctrine, and to seek stability of government by fixing, in certain cases rather arbitrarily, the size of the majority that shall count. [65] But the doctrine, taken generally, does seem in harmony with the test of rationality developed above. [66] It aims at the satisfaction of many desires—at what may be termed satisfaction *on the whole.*

---

[65] See the Constitution of the United States, Article V.

[66] Chapter xvi.

Nevertheless, it is possible to question whether the vote of the majority represents, in a given instance, the actual will of the community.

No one knows better than the practical politician how the votes of the majority are obtained. No one knows better than he that, in the most democratic of communities, it is the wills of the few that count. The organization of a party, clever leadership, the command of the press, the catching phrases of the popular orator, the street procession, the brass band, the possession of the ability to cajole and to threaten—these play no mean role in the outcome, which may be the adoption of a state policy of which a large proportion of the majority voting may be quite unable to comprehend the significance. Shall we say, in such a case, that the will of the majority was for the ultimate end? Or shall we say that the vote was in pursuance of a multitude of minor ends, many of which had but an accidental connection with the ultimate end?

78. IGNORANCE AND ERROR AND THE SOCIAL WILL.—The apparent will of the community appears to be, in large measure, an accidental thing. That is to say, men will what they would not will were they not hampered by ignorance and error, and were they not incapable of taking long views of their own interests.

The decisions of the social will may be the outcome of ignorance and superstition.

Where it is thought necessary to punish the accidental homicide in order to appease the ghost of the dead man, which might otherwise become a cause of harm, the course of justice, if one may call it such, deviates from what the enlightened man must regard as normal. The belief that sin is an infection, communicable by heredity or even by contact, must lead to similar aberrations of primitive justice. Animals, and even material things, have, and not by peoples the most primitive, been treated as rational, responsible and amenable to law. This seems to do the brutes more than justice. On the other hand, the philosophical tenet of the Cartesians, which denied a mind to the brutes, resulted in no little cruelty. The treatment of drunkards, and of the mentally defective, has, at times, been based upon the notion that they are possessed by god or demon, and, hence, have a right to peculiar consideration, or may be treated with extreme rigor.

It is worth while to follow up the above reference to the Cartesians by a reference to St. Augustine. Trains of reasoning based upon theological or philosophical tenets have more than once given rise to aberrations of the moral judgment.

The intellectual subtlety of Augustine betrays him into magnifying to enormous proportions the guilt of the boyish prank of stealing green pears from the garden of a neighbor, inspired by the agreeable thought of the irritation which would be caused by the theft. The pears were not edible, and were thrown to the pigs, which circumstance seduces this father of the Church into the reflection that the sin must have been committed for no other end than for the sake of sinning. A greater crime than this he cannot conceive.

Many years after the event, in writing his Confessions, he expresses in unmeasured terms his horror of the deed, filling seven chapters [67] with his reflections and lamentations: "Behold my heart, O God, behold my heart, upon which thou hadst mercy when in the depths of this bottomless pit." "O corruption! O monster of life and depth of death! Is it possible that I liked to do what I might not, simply and for no other reason than because I might not?"

Saint as he was, Augustine would have made a sorry schoolmaster. It is evident that the enlightened mind cannot regard schoolboys as unique monsters of iniquity for making a raid on an orchard.

The community whose decisions are made under the influence of erroneous preconceptions undoubtedly wills, but its will is determined by the accident of ignorance. It is to be likened to the man who, in unfamiliar surroundings, takes the wrong road in his desire to get home. He chooses, but he does not choose what he would if he knew what he was about.

79. HEEDLESSNESS AND THE SOCIAL WILL.—Numberless illustrations might be given of the fact that, not merely ignorance and error, but also a short- sighted heedlessness plays no small part in introducing elements of the accidental and irrational into the social will. The man who spends freely with no thought for the morrow is not more irrational than the state that permits a squandering of its resources, and wakes up too late only to discover that it has lost what cannot easily be replaced.

The life of the community is a long one, and calls for long views of the interests of the community. These are too often lacking. Heedlessness and indifference are a fertile source of abuses. In which case, the will of the community resembles that of the impulsive and erratic man, who has too little foresight and self-control to consult consistently his own interests. We may say that he desires his own good on the whole, but we cannot say that he desires it at all times. Future goods disappear from his view. His choices clash. His actual will at any given moment appears to be the creature of accident. So it may be with the community.

---

[67] *Confessions*, chapters iv-x.

80. RATIONAL ELEMENTS IN THE IRRATIONAL WILL.—The actual social will, as revealed in custom, law and public opinion, often appears, thus, highly irrational, and we may be justified in distinguishing between it and the real will which we conceive of as struggling to get itself expressed. Nevertheless, in justice to custom, law and public opinion, we must look below the surface of things. Even where the decisions of the community seem most irrational, and where there appears to be little consciousness of the ends pursued by the real will, the discriminating observer may see that pure irrationality does not prevail. The individual may show by his actions that he has comprehensive ends, and may yet not be distinctly aware of them. So may a community of men.

"The true meaning of ethical obligations," says Hobhouse,[68] "—their bearing on human purposes, their function in social life—only emerges by slow degrees. The onlooker, investigating a primitive custom, can see that moral elements have helped to build it up, so that it embodies something of moral truth. Yet these elements of moral truth were perhaps never present to the minds of those who built it. Instead thereof we are likely to find some obscure reference to magic or to the world of spirits. The custom which we can see, perhaps, to be excellently devised in the interests of social order or for the promotion of mutual aid is by those who practice it based on some taboo, or preserved from violation from fear of the resentment of somebody's ghost." It is not wholly irrational that, in the laws of various peoples, an allowance should be made for the sudden resentment which flames up when wrong has been suffered, and that an offence grown cold should be treated more leniently than one which is fresh and the smart caused by which has not had time to suffer diminution. Society has to do with men as they are. It is its task to bend the will of the individual into conformity with the social will. That resentment for wrongs suffered is an important element in the establishment of order in the community can scarcely be denied, nor is it wholly unreasonable, men being what they are, for the community to make some concessions to the natural feeling of the individual. Moreover, the offender caught in the act is indubitably the real offender; and settled animosities are more injurious to the social order than are fugitive gusts of passion.

And if it is true that the arbitrary laws of hospitality, as recognized by some primitive and half-civilized communities, are reinforced by the superstitious fear of the stranger's curse, it is none the less true that they serve certain social needs. The fact that hospitality tends to decline when it becomes superfluous is sufficient to indicate its social significance.

Again, collective responsibility—the making of a man responsible for the delinquencies of those connected with him, even when he could in no way

---

[68] *Morals in Evolution*, New York, 1906, p. 30.

have prevented the evils in question—appears to modern civilized man, in most instances, [69] an irrational thing. Yet men are actually knit into groups with common interests and accustomed to cooperation. To treat them as wholly independent units, responsible only to some higher organization such as the state, is to overlook actual relationships which have no small influence in determining the course of their lives. Within each lesser group the members can and do encourage or repress given types of action beneficial or the reverse. Is it irrational for the larger group to set such influences to work by holding the lesser group responsible in its collective capacity? In China the principle has worked with some measure of success as an instrument of order for many centuries. In an enlightened society some better method of attaining order may obtain, but it would be a mistake to assume that there is nothing behind the principle of collective responsibility save the unintelligent attempt to satisfy resentment by striking indirectly at the offender through those connected with him, or the mental confusion that identifies the culprit, through mere association of ideas, with other members of the group to which he belongs.

81. THE SOCIAL WILL AND THE SELFISHNESS OF THE INDIVIDUAL.—There is, then, often some reason to be discovered even in what appears at first sight to be wholly irrational. But no small part of the irrationality of the actual social will must be set down, in the last instance, to that peculiar form of irrationality in the individual or in groups of individuals which we call selfishness.

That some degree of inequality should be necessary in communities of men, in view of the differentiation of function implied in cooperative effort, may be admitted. How far the inherited organization or the existing environment of a given community may make it necessary, in the interests of all, to grant a large measure of power or prerogative to a single individual, or to the few, is fair matter for investigation. But the most cursory glance at the pages of history, the most superficial survey of the present condition of mankind, must make it evident that a far-seeing and enlightened social will has not been the determining factor in bringing into existence many of the institutions which are accepted by the actual social will of a given epoch.

Neither Alexander the Great nor Napoleon can be regarded as true exponents of the social will. The rule of the oligarchy is based upon selfish considerations. The institution of slavery overrides the will of the bondsman in the interests of his possessor. The perennial struggle between the "haves" and the "have nots"—the rich and the poor—is, unfortunately,

---

[69] Only under normal conditions. We have recently had abundant opportunity to see that in time of war civilized nations have no scruples in making the innocent suffer with the guilty, or even for the guilty.

carried on by those engaged in it with a view to their own interests and not with a view to the good of society as a whole.

That those to whom especial opportunities are, by the accident of their position, open, or by whom special rights are inherited, should accept the situation as right and proper is not to be wondered at. All rights and duties have their roots in the past, and conceptions of what is feasible and desirable are always influenced by tradition. While from the standpoint of the real social will anomalous and accidental it is nevertheless psychologically explicable and natural that the mediaeval knight should be bound by the rules of chivalry only in his dealings with those of his own rank; that the murder of a priest should be regarded as a crime of a special class; that benefit of clergy should be extended to a limited number of those guilty of the same offence; that the lists of the deadly sins should, in an age dominated by the monastic idea, smack so strongly of the cloister.

Natural it is, and, perhaps, inevitable, that such expressions of the social will should make their appearance. They have their place in the historic evolution of society. But they betray the fact that man is imperfectly rational. They cannot be regarded as expressions of the permanent rational will which belongs to man as man.

CHAPTER XXI

THE RATIONAL SOCIAL WILL

82. REASONABLE ENDS.—We have seen in the chapter on "Rationality and Will," that we cannot consider a man rational unless his choices are harmonized and converge upon some comprehensive end. It has been hinted, furthermore, that not all comprehensive ends can be described as reasonable or rational.

A child may be consistently disobedient to its parents, and, given parents of a certain kind, it may find its life highly satisfactory. A man may consistently be a bad neighbor, and may harbor the conviction that, on the whole, he gains by it. A miser may be consistent; he may come to joy in denying himself luxuries and even comforts, repaid in the consciousness of an increasing store. The philosophical egoist may reason with admirable consistency, and may habitually act in accordance with his convictions, leading, for him, a very endurable life.

All these may be intelligent, even acutely intelligent, and may reason clearly and well. Nevertheless, men generally refuse to consider their behavior reasonable. There are ends which we regard as rational, and others which we condemn as irrational.

It is not enough, hence, that a man's volitions should be intelligently harmonized and unified. His will must be adjusted to ends which themselves can be judged rational.

And in deciding whether the ends he chooses are rational or not, we proceed just as we do in judging the rationality of his individual choices. If the latter are made in the light of information, if their significance is realized, if they converge upon some comprehensive end and do not merely clash and defeat one another, we have seen that they are made under the guidance of reason or intelligence. The individual volitions are congruous with the permanent set of the man's will. They are judged by their background, by their harmony with the "pattern" which is revealed in the man's volitional life.

Even so, each such volitional pattern, the harmonized and unified will of the individual as directed upon some comprehensive end, is judged to be rational or not according as it does or does not accord with the ends pursued by the social will. Individuals, whose wills are thoroughly unified and harmonized by the dominant influence of given chosen ends, may be thoroughly out of harmony with the chosen ends of the larger organism of which they are a part. They may be out of harmony with each other. Considered alone, each may display an internal order and unity. Taken together they may be seen to be in open strife.

We have found the social will to be something relatively permanent and moving with more or less consistency toward certain comprehensive ends. That the ends chosen by given individuals may be very much out of harmony with these is palpable. The deliberate idler, the whole-hearted epicure, the habitually untruthful man, the miser, the cold egoist—these and such as these are condemned in enlightened communities. Their lives do not help to further, but serve to frustrate, the ends approved by the social will. In so far they may be regarded as consistently irrational.

83. AN OBJECTION ANSWERED.—Consistently irrational! it may be exclaimed; how can that be? is not a far-sighted consistency the very mark of rational choice?

The difficulty is only an apparent one. Many forms of consistency may indicate a certain degree of rationality, and yet too slight a degree to win approval. There is such a thing as a narrow consistency. He who devotes his life to the purpose of revenge, may live consistently, but he loses much. A bitter and angry life is not a desirable thing, even from the standpoint of the individual.

But why should we limit ourselves to the standpoint of the individual, in judging of the rationality of ends? There are those to whom it appears self-evident that this should be done; those to whom it does not seem reasonable for a man to do anything by which he, on the whole, loses; those who deny the reasonableness of self-sacrifice in any form. This doctrine will be examined later. [70]

Here it is enough to point out that men do not actually limit the notion of rationality in this way. In every, even moderately, rational life some desires must be suppressed. All desires cannot be satisfied. Why should it not be regarded as rational and reasonable that, to attain the comprehensive ends of the social will, certain ends consistently chosen by certain kinds of individuals should deliberately be denied?

As a matter of fact, men generally do so regard it. They employ the terms rational and irrational, reasonable and unreasonable, to indicate the harmony or lack of harmony between the individual and the social will. We call the man unreasonable who insists upon having his own way regardless of his fellows; and this, even in instances in which his fellows cannot punish him for his selfish attitude.

It is not a matter of accident that this should be so. The analogy between the relation of separate volitions to the dominant ends which control action on the part of the individual, and the relation of the ultimate choices of individuals to the ends pursued by the social will, is a close one. In the well-ordered mind the clash of conflicting desires is reduced to a minimum. In a well-ordered community the conflict of individual wills is also reduced to a minimum. In each case, we are concerned with the work of reason, and judgments as to rationality and irrationality are equally in place.

84. REASONABLE SOCIAL ENDS.—The will of the individual, when

---

[70] See Sec 102 and 128.

affirmed to be rational or irrational, is, therefore, referred to the background of the social will. But the social will is more or less different in different communities, and in the one community at different stages of its development. Is there any measure of the degree of rationality of the social will itself? is there any standard to which its different expressions may be referred?

We may criticise a community as we criticise an individual man even when he is taken as abstracted from his social setting. The man's choices may be blind, conflicting, wayward, and ill-adapted to serve his interests taken as a whole. In the last chapter we saw that a community may resemble such a man. It may be ignorant, superstitious, short-sighted, and in conflict with itself. The social will as actually revealed may be an imperfect and inconsistent thing. Here enlightenment and inner harmonization are called for, to set the social will free.

But even where the will of a community is something more definite and consistent than this, it may be condemned by the moral judgment of the enlightened. An appeal may be made from the will of the community in the narrower sense to that of the larger community. The limits of nation, race and religion may be transcended, and we may appeal to humanity as such, refusing to recognize the will of any lesser unit as really ultimate. He who occupies the one standpoint is apt to speak of defending his legitimate rights, or of extending to subject races the blessings of civilization. He who takes his stand upon the other may talk of lust of dominion, or desire for economic advantage. The one may use the term righteous indignation; the other, the word anger. The moral judgment passed upon an act depends upon the concept under which men manage to bring it. What is approved by the tribal ethics may be abhorrent to the ethics of humanity.

But the larger social will, so far as it has gotten itself expressed at all, seems to remain something vague and indefinite. It is appealed to as rational; but how indicate clearly the end which it sets before itself and the obligations which it lays upon mankind?

The difficulty of describing in detail the ultimate ends of the real social will has led some writers to speak in terms of exaggerated vagueness. The mere idea in a man "of something, he knows not what, which he may and should become" can give little guidance to action; nor can one aim with much confidence at a goal of which "we can only speak or think in negatives." [71]

---

[71] *Prolegomena to Ethics*, Sec Sec 192, 172, 180. But GREEN is not always so indefinite. He is on the right track. He reverences the social will and the historical development of the social order.

But it is not necessary to speak in this way. We may form some conception of the real, rational social will, without being compelled to know all that man is capable of becoming and without being able to forecast the details of his environment in the distant future.

We may attain to our conception by determining clearly the nature of the aims man sets before himself in proportion to his growing rationality. We can see in what direction man moves as he develops and becomes enlightened. From this standpoint, the aims of the rational social will appear to be as follows:

(1) The harmonious satisfaction of the impulses and desires of man.

(2) Such an unfolding of his powers as will increase their range and variety, broaden man's horizon, and give him an increased control over erratic impulses.

(3) The bringing about of a social state in which the will of each individual within a community counts for something, and not merely the will of a chosen few.

(4) The broadening of the conception of what constitutes a community, so that ever increasing numbers are regarded as having claims that must be recognized.

(5) The taking into consideration of the whole of life; the whole life of individuals and of communities, so that the insistent present shall not be given undue weight, as against the future.

85. THE ETHICS OF REASON.—The doctrine of the Rational Social Will might very properly be called the Ethics of Reason. It is not to be confounded with the so-called "tribal" or "group" ethics. To be sure, it has to do with man as a social being; but this is characteristic of ethical systems generally. Man is a social being; he is one essentially, and not accidentally. That he should be a member of a tribe, or of any lesser group than the whole body of sentient and reasonable beings, may not unjustly be regarded as an historical accident, as a function of his position in the scale of development.

In judging the doctrine of the rational social will, bear in mind the following:

(1) It rests upon the basis of the impulsive and volitional nature of man.

(2) It recognizes reason in the individual, and declares that only so far as he is rational is he the proper subject of ethics at all. Erratic and uncontrolled impulse knows no moral law.

(3) It sees reason in the customs, laws and public opinion of the tribe or the state, while recognizing a higher tribunal before the bar of which all these are summoned.

(4) It appeals to the reason of the race—the reason appropriate to the race as enlightened and freed from the shackles of local prejudice and restricted sympathy.

(5) It recognizes that man can give expression to his nature, can satisfy his desires and exercise his reason, only as aided by his physical and social environment. It emphasizes the necessity of a certain reverence for the actual historical development of human societies, with their institutions. Such institutions are the embodiment of reason—not pure reason, but reason struggling to get itself expressed as it can. He who would legislate for man independently of such institutions has left the solid earth and man far behind. He is suspended in the void.

86. THE DEVELOPMENT OF CIVILIZATION.—Civilizations differ; some are more material, laying stress upon man's conquest of his material environment. Others exhibit a greater appreciation of idealistic elements, the pursuit of knowledge for its own sake, the cultivation of the fine arts, the development of humanitarian sentiment. For civilization in general it is not necessary to advance an argument. But there are elements in many civilizations which the thoughtful man may feel called upon to defend.

Civilization, taken generally, scarcely needs a labored justification because it is only in a civilization of some kind or other that we can look for a guarantee of the broad social will, for the reign of reason. Undeveloped man is at the mercy of nature; he is the sport of history. Where developed man can raise his voice, man possessed of power and capable of taking broad views of things, the rule of reason may be set up. A deliberate attempt may be made to recognize many wills, harmonize discords. Order may be brought out of chaos, and the limits of the realm within the borders of which order reigns may be indefinitely extended.

Such is the general ethical justification for the rise of a civilization. It is an expression of, and an instrument for the realization of, the broader social will. That a given civilization may be imperfect in both respects has been made clear in the last chapter. In the light of the general justification for civilization many questions may be raised touching this or that element in civilizations as we observe them.

Thus, it may be pointed out that as man progresses in civilization he calls into being a multitude of new wants, many of which may have to remain unsatisfied. [72] It may be asserted that literature, art and science are, in fact, cherished as though they were ends in themselves, and not means called into existence to serve the interests of man. Absorbing as it may be to him, how can the philologist prove that his science is useful to humanity either present or prospective? How shall the astronomer, who may frankly admit that he cannot conceive that nine tenths of the work with which he occupies himself can ever be of any actual use to anyone, justify himself in devoting his life to it? Shall a curiosity, which seems to lead nowhere, be satisfied? And if so, on what ground?

Moreover, every civilization recognizes that some wills are to be given a more unequivocal recognition than others. Inequality is the rule. A man does not put his own children upon a level with those of his neighbor. Even in the most democratic of states men do not stand upon the same level. In dealing with our own fellows we do not employ the same weights and measures as in dealing with foreigners. Who loses his appetite for his breakfast when he reads that there have been inundations in China or that an African tribe has come under the "protection" of a race of another color? The white man has added to his burden—the burden of economic advantage present or prospective—and we find it as it should be. Finally, when we bring within our horizon the "interests" of humbler sentient creatures, we see that they are unhesitatingly subordinated to our own. Some attention is paid to them in civilized communities. They are recognized, not merely by custom and public opinion, but, to some degree, even by law. Men are punished for treating certain animals in certain ways. But why? Have the animals rights? There is no topic within the sphere of morals upon which moralists speak with more wavering and uncertain accents. [73]

I know of no way in which such problems as the above can be approached other than by the appeal to reason, as reason has been understood in the pages preceding. The reign of reason implies the recognition of all wills, *so far as such a recognition is within the bounds of possibility*. The escape from chaos lies in the evolution of the enlightened social will. Man must be raised in the scale, in order that he may have control; control over himself, over other men, over the brutes. And he cannot rise except through the historical evolution of a social order. This implies the development of the capacities latent in man.

To decide that any of his capacities shall be allowed to remain dormant may threaten future development. To cut off certain arts and sciences as

---

[72] Compare chapter xxx, Sec 142.
[73] See chapter XXX, Sec 141.

not palpably serving the interests of man is a dangerous thing. To ignore the actual history of man's efforts to become a rational being, and to place, hence, all wills upon the one level, is to frustrate the desired end. It is not thus that the reign of reason can be established.

CHAPTER XXII

THE INDIVIDUAL AND THE SOCIAL WILL

87. MAN'S MULTIPLE ALLEGIANCE.—We have seen that each man has his place in a social order. This order is the expression and the embodiment of the social will, which accepts him, protects him, gives him a share in the goods the community has so far attained, recognizes his individual will in that it accords to him rights, and prescribes his course of conduct, that is, defines his duties or obligations.

The social will is authoritative; it issues commands and enforces obedience. With its commands the individual may be in sympathy or he may not. But upon obedience the social will insists, and it compasses its ends by the bestowal of rewards or the infliction of punishment. The moral law to which man thus finds himself subject is something not wholly foreign to the nature of the individual. It has come into being as an expression of the nature of man. That nature the individual shares with his fellows.

Obedience to the social will would be a relatively simple matter were that will always unequivocally and unmistakably expressed, and did all the members of a community feel the pressure of the social will in the same manner and to the same degree. But the whole matter is indefinitely complicated by what may be called man's multiple allegiance.

Organized societies do not consist of undifferentiated units. They are not mere aggregates, both are highly complex in their internal constitution. A conscientious man may feel that he owes duties to himself, to his immediate family, to his kindred, to his neighborhood, to his social class, to his political party, to his church, to his country, to its allies, to humanity. The social will does not bring its pressure to bear upon the man who holds one place in the social order just as it does upon him who holds another.

Nor are the injunctions laid upon a man always in harmony. The demands of family may seem to conflict with those of neighborhood or of profession; duties to the church may seem to conflict with duties to the state; patriotism may appear to be more or less in conflict with an interest in humanity taken broadly. That the individual should often approach in doubt and hesitation the decision as to what it is, on the whole, his duty to do, is not surprising. Nor is it surprising that individuals the most conscientious should find it impossible to be at one on the subject of rights and duties. Two men may agree perfectly that it is right to "do good," and be quite unable to agree just what good it is right to do now, or with whom one should make a beginning.

88. THE APPEAL TO REASON.—Were there no appeal save to the social will as it happens to make its pressure felt upon this person or that, in this situation or that, there could be no issue to dispute. Dispute would be useless and sheer dogmatism would prevail. But there is such an appeal and men do make it, where they are in any degree enlightened. It is the appeal to Reason.

He who says: "I have especial rights, just because I am Smith, and so has my father, because he is my father," has no ground of argument with Jones, who says: "I have especial rights because I am Jones, and so has my father, because he is my father." Upon such a basis, or lack of basis, all discussion becomes fatuous. But if Smith and Jones agree that duties to self should only within limits be recognized, and that duties to family have their place upon the larger background of the will of the state, they may, at least, begin to talk.

The multiple allegiance of the individual does not mean that a man is subject to a multitude of independent masters whose several claims have no relation to one another. An appeal may be made from lower to higher.

We have seen that, in the organization of a given society, the social will may be imperfectly expressed. It may come about that the place in the social order assigned to a man cramps and pains him, or forces him to exertions which seem intolerable. He may passively accept it, or he may set himself in opposition to the social will as it is, appealing to a better social will. The fact that an individual finds himself out of harmony with given aspects of the social will characteristic of his age and country is no proof that he desires to set himself up in opposition to the social will in general.

104

In a given instance, he may be, from the standpoint of existing law, a criminal. Yet he may reverence the law above his fellows. His aberrations need not be arbitrary wanderings, prompted by selfish impulses. He may leave the beaten track because he does not approve of it, which is a very different thing from disliking it. Some will judge him to be a pestilent fellow; some will rate him as a reformer, a prophet, perhaps a martyr. Neither judgment is of the least value so long as it reflects merely the tastes or prejudices of the individual. Each must justify itself before the bar of reason, if it would have a respectful hearing. A reason must be given for conservatism and a reason must be given for reform.

89. THE ETHICS OF REASON AND THE VARYING MORAL CODES.— Several advantages may be claimed for the ethical doctrine I have been advocating:

(1) It gives a relative justification to the varying moral codes of communities of men in the past and in the present. A code may, even when imperfect from some higher point of view, fit well a community at a given stage of its development. It may be a man's duty to obey its injunctions, even where they are not seen to be the wisest possible. One reason for bowing to custom is that it *is* custom; one reason for obeying laws is that they *are* laws. They embody the permanence and stability of the social will, and have a *prima facie* claim to our reverence.

(2) In recognizing the social will as something deeper and broader than the will of the individual, as having its roots in the remote past and as reaching into the distant future, it admits the futility of devising utopian schemes which would bless humanity in defiance of the actual expressions of the social will revealed in the development of human societies. The whim of the individual cannot well be substituted for the settled purpose of the community—a purpose ripened by generations of experience, and adjusted to what is possible under existing conditions.

(3) On the other hand, it distinguishes between lower and higher ethical codes, or codes lower or higher in certain of their aspects. It sets a standard of comparison; it recognizes progress towards a goal.

(4) And, in all this, it does not appear to decide *arbitrarily* either what is the goal of man's moral efforts or what means must be adopted to attain to it. It rests upon a study of man; man as he has been, man as he is, in all the manifold relations in which he stands to his environment, physical and social.

There are other ethical theories in the field, of course. Some of them are advocated by men of original genius and of no little learning. Some deserve more attention than others, but all should have a hearing, at least. A close scrutiny will often reveal that advocates of different theories are by no means so far apart as a hasty reading of their works would suggest. Writers the most diverse may assist one to a comprehension of one's own theory. Its implications may be developed, objections to it may be suggested, its strong points may stand revealed. By no means the least important part of a work on ethics is its treatment of the schools of the moralists. If it be written with any degree of fairness, it may contain what will serve the reader with an antidote to erroneous opinions on the part of the writer. To a study of the most important schools of the moralists I shall now turn.

PART VII

THE SCHOOLS OF THE MORALISTS

CHAPTER XXIII

INTUITIONISM

90. WHAT IS IT?—"We come into the world," said Epictetus, "with no natural notion of a right-angled triangle, or of a quarter-tone, or of a half-tone; but we learn each of these things by a certain transmission according to art; and for this reason those who do not know them do not think that they know them. But as to good and evil, and beautiful and ugly, and becoming and unbecoming, and happiness and misfortune, and proper and improper, and what we ought to do and what we ought not to do, who ever came into the world without having an innate idea of them? [74] Seneca adds his testimony to the self-luminous character of moral truth: "Whatever things tend to make us better or happier are either obvious or easily discovered." [75]

With the general spirit of these utterances the typical intuitionist is in sympathy, although he need not assent to the doctrine of innate ideas, nor need he hold that all moral truths are equally self-evident. There are intuitionists of various classes, and there are sufficiently notable differences of opinion. Still, all intuitionists believe that some moral truth, at least, is revealed to the individual by direct inspection (*intueor*), and that we must be content with such evidence and must not seek for proof. It

---

[74] *Discourses*, Book II, chapter xi, translation by GEORGE LONG.
[75] *On Benefits*, Book VII, chapter i.

may be maintained that our moral judgments—or some of them—are the result of "an immediate discernment of the natures of things by the understanding." and appeal may be made to the analogy furnished by mathematical truths. [76]

91. VARIETIES OF INTUITIONISM.—Forms of intuitionism have been conveniently classified as Perceptional, Dogmatic and Philosophical. [77] To this nomenclature it may be objected that the term "dogmatic" carries with it a certain flavor of disapprobation, and predisposes one to the assumption of a critical attitude, while the term "philosophical" has the reverse suggestion, and smacks of special pleading. While admitting that there is something in the objection, I retain the convenient terms, merely warning the reader to be on his guard.

(1) Perceptional Intuitionism falls back upon the analogy of perception in general. I seem to perceive by direct inspection that my blotter is green, and that my penholder is longer than my pencil. I do not seek for evidence; I do not have recourse to any chain of reasonings to establish the fact. And I am concerned here with facts, not with some general proposition applicable to many facts. Even so, I may maintain that, in specific situations, the rightness or wrongness of given courses of action may be perceived immediately.

He who accepts the spontaneous deliverances of his conscience, when confronted with the necessity of making a decision, as revelations of moral truth, may be called a perceptional intuitionist. The deliverances must, however, be spontaneous and immediate, not the result of reasoning. If a man reasons, if he falls back upon general considerations, if he looks into the future and weighs the consequences of his act, and, as a result, decides what he ought to do, he is no longer a perceptional intuitionist.

The perceptional intuitionist, consistently and unreservedly such, is rather an ideal construction than an actually existing person. Most men, on certain occasions, are inclined to say, "I feel this to be right, and will do it, although I cannot support my decision by giving reasons." Many men are, at times, tempted to maintain that a given course of action is evidently right and should be followed irrespective of consequences. But this is not the habitual attitude even of men very little gifted with reflection, and it is highly unsatisfactory to those who have the habit of thinking.

---

[76] This appeal has been made by famous intuitionists from the seventeenth century to the nineteenth— Cudworth, More, Locke, Clarke, Price, Whewell.

[77] SIDGWICK, The Methods of Ethics, Book I, chapter viii, Sec 4.

Primitive man supports his decisions by an appeal to custom. Civilized man turns to custom, to law, or to general principles of some sort, which he accepts as authoritative, and which he regards as having a bearing upon the particular instance in question. That individual decisions should be capable of some sort of justification by the adduction of a reason or reasons is generally admitted. No sane man would maintain the general proposition that the consequences of acts should be wholly disregarded in determining whether they are or are not desirable.

(2) Thus, Perceptional Intuitionism gives place to what has been called Dogmatic Intuitionism—to the doctrine that certain general moral rules can be immediately perceived to be valid. The application of such general rules to particular instances implies discrimination and the use of reason.

Here decisions are not wholly unsupported. Reasons may be asked for and given. In answer to the question: Why should I say this or that? it may be said: Because the law of veracity demands it. In answer to the question: Why should I act thus? it may be said: Because it is just, or is in accordance with the dictates of benevolence. The general rule is accepted as intuitively evident, but it is incumbent upon the individual to use his judgment in determining what may properly fall under the general rule.

But there are rules and rules. It is not easy to draw a sharp line between Perceptional Intuitionism and Dogmatic, just as it is not easy in other fields to distinguish sharply between knowledge given directly in perception, and knowledge in which more or less conscious processes of inference play a part. Do I perceive the man whom I see, when I look into a mirror, to be behind the mirror or in front of it? Do I perceive the whereabouts of the coach which I hear rattling by my window, or does reasoning play its part in giving me information? And if I follow my conscience in not withholding from the cabman the small customary fee in addition to his fare, am I prompted by an unreasoned perception of the rightness of my act, or am I influenced by general considerations—the thought of what is customary, the belief that gratuities should not be withheld where services of a certain kind are rendered, etc.?

Even so, it is difficult to draw a sharp line between Dogmatic Intuitionists and Philosophical, or to regard Dogmatic Intuitionists as a clearly defined class of any sort. A man may accept it as self-evident that a waiter should receive ten per cent of the amount of his bill; a woman may find it obviously proper that an old lady should wear purple. Those little given to reflection may accept such maxims as these without attempting to justify them by falling back upon any more general rule. We all find about us human beings who have their minds stored with a multitude of maxims not greatly different from those adduced, and who find them serviceable in guiding their actions. But thoughtful men can scarcely be content with such a modicum of reason, and they distinguish between ultimate principles and minor maxims which stand in need of justification by their reference to principles.

The intuitional moralists by profession draw this distinction. We find them setting forth as ultimate a limited number of ethical principles of a high degree of generality. It is obvious that, the more general the principle, the more room for conscious reasoning in its interpretation and application. The man to whom it appears as in the nature of things suitable that the waiter should receive his ten per cent is relieved from many perplexities which may beset the man who feels assured only of the general truth that it is right to be benevolent.

A glance at a few of the moralists who are treated in the history of ethics as representative intuitionists reveals that they are little in harmony as touching the particular moral intuitions which they urge as the foundation of ethics.

Thus, John Locke maintains that from the idea of God, and of ourselves as rational beings, a science of morality may be deduced demonstratively; a science: "wherein I doubt not but from self-evident propositions, by necessary consequences, as incontestible as those in mathematics, the measures of right and wrong might be made out to anyone that will apply himself with the same indifferency and attention to the one, as he does to the other of those sciences." [78]

Among Locke's self-evident propositions or moral axioms we find: where there is no property there is no injustice; no government allows absolute liberty; all men are originally free and equal; parents have the power to control their children till they come of age; the right of property is based upon work, but is limited by the supply of property left for others to enjoy. [79]

These axioms cannot be identified with Samuel Clarke's four chief rules of righteousness, which inculcate: piety toward God, equity in our dealings with men, benevolence, and sobriety. [80] Richard Price gives us still another choice, in dwelling upon our obligation as regards piety, prudence, beneficence, gratitude, veracity, the fulfillment of promises, and justice. [81] And Whewell, emulating the performance of Euclid, tried to build up a

---

[78] *Essay Concerning Human Understanding*, Book IV, chapter iii, Sec 18.
[79] See above, chapter iii, Sec 10.
[80] *A Discourse concerning the Unalterable Relations of Natural Religion*, Prop. I.
[81] *A Review of the Principal Questions and Difficulties in Morals*, chapter vii.

system of morals upon axioms embodying the seven principles of benevolence, justice, truth, purity, order, earnestness, and moral purpose.[82]

These moralists press the analogy of mathematical truth. It must be confessed, however, that a row of text-books on geometry, with so scattering and indefinite a collection of axioms, would do little to support one another; and little to convince us that they represented a coherent and consistent body of truth in which we might have unquestioning faith.

(3) It is not unnatural that some thoughtful intuitionists, dissatisfied with a considerable number of independent moral principles, should aim at a further simplification. Such a simplification Kant finds in the Categorical Imperative, or unconditional command of the Practical Reason: "Act only on that maxim whereby thou canst at the same time will that it should become a universal law." [83] And Henry Sidgwick, refusing to regard all intuitions as of equal authority, selects two only as ultimately and independently valid—that which recommends a far-seeing prudence, and that which urges a rational benevolence. [84] Those who make their ultimate moral rules so broad and inclusive base upon them the multitude of minor maxims to which men are apt to have recourse in justifying their actions. Whether their doctrine may be called philosophical in a sense implying commendation is matter for discussion.

92. ARGUMENTS FOR INTUITIONISM.—What may be said in favor of intuitionism?

(1) It may be urged that it is the doctrine which appeals most directly to common sense, and that it is found reasonably satisfactory in practice by men generally.

Intuition appears to be, in fact, man's guide in an overwhelming majority of the situations in which he is called upon to act. In the face of the concrete situation he *feels* that he should say a kind word, help a neighbor, stand his ground courageously, speak the truth, and a thousand other things which a moralist might, upon reflection, approve.

That he "feels" this does not mean merely that he is influenced by an emotion. We constantly employ the word to indicate the presence of a judgment which presents itself spontaneously and for which men cannot or do not seek support by having recourse to reasons.

---

[82] *The Elements of Morality*, Book III, chapter iv.
[83] *Fundamental Principles of the Metaphysic of Morals*, Sec 2.
[84] *The Methods of Ethics*, Book III, chapter xiii, Sec 3.

He who, without reflection, affirms, "this action is right," has framed a moral judgment. He has in a given instance distinguished between right and wrong, although he has not raised the general problem of what constitutes right and wrong. He has exercised the prerogative of a moral being, though not of a very thoughtful one.

We have seen above, that perceptional intuitionism tends to pass over into dogmatic intuitionism of some sort, even in the case of minds little developed. The egoistic rustic may defend his selfishness by citing the proverb, "my shirt is closer to me than my coat." If he does so, it means that a doubt has been suggested, a conflict of some sort called into being. Were such conflicts, causing hesitation and deliberation, of very frequent occurrence, life could scarcely go on at all. Conversation would be impossible were no word placed and no inflection chosen without conscious reference to the rules of grammar. No man could conduct himself properly in a drawing-room or at a table, were his mind harking back at every moment to the instructions contained in some volume on etiquette. He who must justify every act by reflection is condemned to the jerkiest and most hesitant of moral lives. Perceptional moral intuition must stand our friend, if there is to be a flow of conduct worthy of the name.

There are, however, occasions for checking the flow by reflection. Then men are forced to think, and we find them appealing to custom, citing proverbs, quoting maxims, taking their stand upon principles. Recourse may be had to generalizations of a very low or of a very high degree of generality.

But low or high, it is upon intuitions that men actually fall back in justifying their actions. Benevolence, justice, honesty, truthfulness, purity, honor, modesty, courtesy, and what not, are intuitively perceived to be right, and an effort is made to bring the individual act under some one of these headings. The mass of men, even in enlightened communities, do not feel impelled to justify these general moral maxims, to reduce them to a harmonious system, or to reconcile with each other the different lists of them which have been drawn up. They find it possible in practice to resolve most of their doubts by an appeal to this maxim or to that. From such doubts as refuse to be resolved they are apt to turn away their attention. But the moral life goes on, and to intuitions it owes its guidance.

As to the few who reduce the moral intuitions to a minimum, and, like Kant and Sidgwick, end with one or two ultimate intuitional moral principles, we may say that they, like other men, are compelled, in the actual conduct of life, to turn to intuitions of lower orders. All sorts of moral intuitions are actually found helpful by all sorts of men.

(2) To the minds of men differing in their education and traditions, and at different stages of intellectual and moral development, very different moral judgments spontaneously present themselves. It is not a matter of accident that this man may "feel" an action to be right, and that man may "feel" it to be wrong. There is evident adaptation of the judgments to history and environment. They spring into being because the men are what they are and are situated as they are.

It is this adaptation that renders the moral intuitions serviceable in carrying on the actual business of life. It is more complete, the less abstract the moral intuitions which come into play. Plato, who in his "Laws" enters very minutely into the question of the permissible and the forbidden in the life of the citizens of his ideal state, finds it necessary to leave some things to the judgment of the individual. Thus, he finds it impossible to determine exhaustively what things are, and what things are not, worthy of a freeman. He leaves it to the virtuous to give judgments "in accordance with their feelings of right and wrong." [85] The intuitions of the mediaeval saint, of the upright modern European, of the virtuous Chinaman, would have impressed him as without rhyme or reason. He appealed to the Greek gentleman, whose sense of propriety was Greek, and might be expected to be adjusted to the situation.

(3) The intuitive judgment of a sensitive moral nature may often be more nearly right than moral judgments based upon the most subtle of reasonings.

It is not hard to find, with a little ingenuity, apparent justification for actions which the consciences of the enlightened condemn at first sight. Scarcely any action may not be brought under some moral rule, if one deliberately sets out to do so. A narrow selfishness is defended as caring for one's own; a refusal of aid to the needy is justified by a reference to the evils of pauperization; patriotism becomes the excuse for hatred, wilful blindness and untruthful vilification. To the sophistries of those who would thus make the worse appear the better, the intuitive judgment of the moral man opposes its unreasoned conviction. That the conviction is not supported by arguments does not prove that it is not a just one.

93. ARGUMENTS AGAINST INTUITIONISM.—What may be urged against Intuitionism?

(1) It may be pointed out that such considerations as the above constitute an argument to prove the value of moral intuitions, and not one to prove

---

[85] Book XI; see the account of the occupations permissible to the landed proprietor.

the value of intuitionism as an ethical theory. That moral intuitions are indispensable may be freely admitted even by one who demurs to the doctrine that intuitionism in some one of its forms may be accepted as a satisfactory theory of morals.

(2) Perceptional Intuitionism, at least, cannot be regarded as embodying a rational theory or furnishing a science of any sort. Its one and only dogma must be that whatever actions reveal themselves to this man or that as right, are right, and there is no going behind the judgment of the individual.

Shall we say to men: "In order to know what is right and what is wrong in human conduct, we need only to listen to the dictates of conscience when the mind is calm and unruffled"? [86] As well say: "The right time is the time indicated by your watch, when you are not shaking it." If men are to keep appointments with each other, they must have some other standard of time than that carried by each man in his vest-pocket.

Perceptional Intuitionism ignores the fact that consciences may sometimes disagree, and that there may be a choice in consciences. The consistent perceptional intuitionist is, however, scarcely to be found, as has been said above; and we actually find those, some of whose utterances read as though the authors ought to be adherents of such a school, dwelling upon the desirability of the education of the conscience, i.e., upon the desirability of acquiring a capacity for having the right intuitions. In other words, they tell us to follow our noses—but to make sure that they point in the right direction. [87] In which case the determination of the right direction is not left to perceptional intuition.

(3) The Dogmatic Intuitionist has difficulties of his own with which to cope. It is not enough to possess a collection of valid and authoritative rules. The rules must be applied; there is room for the exercise of judgment and for the possibility of error. Error is not excluded even when the rule appears to be at only one or two removes from the individual instance; where the rule is one of great generality the problem of its application becomes correspondingly difficult. The interpretation of the rule is not given intuitively with the rule. This means that the rule must, in practice, be supplemented.

Always and everywhere, a straight line appears to be the shortest distance between two points. What is meant by shortness hardly seems to be

---

[86] THOMAS REID, *Essays on the Active Powers of Man*, v, Sec 4.
[87] See THOMAS REID, *Essays on the Active Powers of Man*, iii, Part 3, Sec 8.

legitimate matter for dispute. But the man convinced that he ought to pay his workman a fair wage, and that he ought to do his duty by his son, may be in no little perplexity when he attempts to define that fair wage or that parental duty. If he turns for advice to others, he will find that history and tradition, time, place and circumstance, very perceptibly color the advice they offer.

The application of the general rule is, hence, quite as important as the rule. There is no such thing as conduct in the abstract. Let us admit that benevolence is morally obligatory. How shall we be benevolent? Shall we follow Cicero, and give only that which costs us nothing? or shall we emulate St. Francis? The general rule may be a faultless skeleton, but it is, after all, only a skeleton, and it cannot walk of itself.

Again. The dogmatic intuitionist has quite a collection of rules by which he must judge of his actions. They are severally independent and authoritative. Suppose an act appears to be commanded by one rule and forbidden by another? Who shall decide between them? Prudence and benevolence may urge him in opposite directions. Benevolence and justice may not obviously be in harmony. The rule of veracity may seem, at times, to prescribe conduct which will entail much suffering on the part of the innocent. To what court of appeal can we refer the conflicts which may arise when ultimate authorities disagree? He who, in war time, can conscientiously shoot a sentry, but cannot conscientiously lie to him, may, later, have his misgivings, when the Golden Rule knocks at the gate of his mind.

(4) Nor does he leave all difficulties behind him, who abandons Dogmatic Intuitionism and takes refuge in Philosophical.

Kant's maxim needs a vast amount of interpretation. As it stands, it is little more than an empty formula. What I can wish to be the law of the universe must depend very much upon what I am. The lion and the lamb do not thirst for the same law. To the quarrelsome heroes of Walhalla a world of perpetual fighting and feasting must seem a very good world, in spite of knocks received as well as given. Kant's fundamental maxim scarcely appears to be a moral rule at all, unless we make it read: "Act on a maxim which a *wise and good man* can will to be a universal law." But how decide who is the wise and good man?

The philosophical intuitionist who accepts more than one ultimate moral rule must face the possibility that he will meet with a conflict of the higher intuitions to which he has had recourse. Shall his intuitions be those recommending a rational self-interest and a rational benevolence? Can he be sure that the two are necessarily in accord? Can there be a rational adjustment of the claims of each? Not if there be no court of appeal to which both intuitions are subject. [88]

Furthermore, between the philosophical and the dogmatic intuitionist serious differences of opinion may be expected to arise. He who makes, let us say, benevolence the supreme law naturally allows to other intuitions, such as justice and veracity, but a derivative authority. It appears, then, that there may be occasions on which they are not valid. To some famous intuitionists this has seemed to be a pernicious doctrine.

"We are," writes Bishop Butler, "constituted so as to condemn falsehood, unprovoked violence, injustice, and to approve of benevolence to some preferably to others, abstracted from all consideration, which conduct is likeliest to produce an overbalance of happiness or misery." [89]

Butler thought that justice should be done though the heavens fall; the philosophical intuitionist must maintain that the danger of bringing down the heavens is never to be lost sight of. But this doctrine that there are intuitions and intuitions, some ultimately authoritative and others not so, raises the whole question of the validity of intuitions. How are we to distinguish those that are always valid from others? By intuition? Intuition appears to be discredited. And if it is proper to demand proof that justice should be done and the truth spoken, why may one not demand proof that men should be prudent and benevolent? One may talk of "an immediate discernment of the nature of things by the understanding" in the one case as in the other. If error is possible there, why not here?

94. THE VALUE OF MORAL INTUITIONS.—It would not be fair to close this chapter on intuitionism, an ethical theory competing with others for our approval, without emphasizing the value of the role played by the moral intuitions.

They are the very guide of life, and without them our reasonings would be of little service. They should be treated gently, gratefully, with reverence. To them human societies owe their stability, their capacity for an orderly development, the smooth working of the machinery of daily life. Their presence does not exclude the employment of reasoning, but they furnish a basis upon which the reason can occupy itself with profit. They are a safeguard against those utopian schemes which would shatter our world and try experiments in creation out of nothing.

---

[88] With his usual candor, SIDGWICK admits this difficulty. He leaves it unresolved. See, *The Methods of Ethics*, in the concluding chapter.
[89] Dissertations appended to the "Analogy," II, *Of the Nature of Virtue*. Cf. DUGALD STEWART, *Outlines of Moral Philosophy*, Part 2, Sec 348.

Nevertheless, he who busies himself with ethics as science must study them critically and strive to estimate justly their true significance. He may come to regard them, not as something fixed and changeless, but as living and developing, coming into being, and modifying themselves, in the service of life. Does he dishonor them who so views them?

CHAPTER XXIV

EGOISM

95. WHAT IS EGOISM?—Egoism has been defined as "any ethical system in which the happiness or good of the individual is made the main criterion of moral action," [90] or as "the doing or seeking of that which affords pleasure or advantage to oneself, in distinction to that which affords pleasure or advantage to others." [91]

It may strike the average reader as odd to be told that such definitions bristle with ambiguities, and that it is by no means easy to draw a sharp line between doctrines which everyone would admit to be egoistic, and others which seem more doubtfully to fall under that head. "Happiness," "good," "advantage," "self," all are terms which call for scrutiny, and which set pitfalls for the unwary.

96. CRASS EGOISMS.—We may best approach the subject of what may properly be regarded as constituting egoism, by turning first to one or two "terrible examples."

No one would hesitate to call egoistic the doctrine of Aristippus, the Cyrenaic, the errant disciple of Socrates. He made pleasure the end of life, and taught that it might be sought without a greater regard to customary morality than was made prudent by the penalties to be feared as a

---

[90] *Encyclopedia Britannica*, 11th edition.
[91] *Century Dictionary.*

consequence of its violation. Where the centre of gravity of the system of the Cyrenaics falls is evident from their holding that "corporeal pleasures are superior to mental ones," and that "a friend is desirable for the use which we can make of him." [92]

The doctrine of the English philosopher, Thomas Hobbes, is as unequivocally egoistic.

"Of the voluntary acts of every man," he writes, [93] "the object is some good to himself;" and again, [94] "no man giveth, but with intention of good to himself; because gift is voluntary; and of all voluntary acts the object is to every man his own good."

He leaves us in no doubt as to the sort of good which he conceives men to seek when they practice what has the appearance of generosity. Contract he calls a mutual transference of rights, and he distinguishes gift from contract as follows:

"When the transferring of right is not mutual, but one of the parties transferreth, in hope to gain thereby friendship, or service from another, or from his friends, or in hope to gain the reputation of charity or magnanimity, *or to deliver his mind from the pain of compassion*, or in hope of reward in heaven, this is not contract but gift, free gift, grace, which words signify the same thing." [95]

There is a passage from the pen of the British divine, Paley, which appears to merit a place alongside of the citations from Hobbes, widely as the men differ in many of their views. It reads:

"We can be obliged to nothing but what we ourselves are to gain or lose something by; for nothing else can be a 'violent motion' to us. As we should not be obliged to obey the laws, or the magistrate, unless rewards or punishments, pleasure or pain, somehow or other, depended upon our obedience; so neither should we, without the same reason, be obliged to do what is right, to practice virtue, or to obey the commandments of God." [96]

---

[92] Diogenes Laertius, *Lives of the Philosophers,* "Aristippus," viii.

[93] *Leviathan,* Part I, xiv.

[94] *Ibid.* xv.

[95] *Ibid.* I, xiv. The italics are mine. It was thus that Hobbes accounted for his giving a sixpence to a beggar: "I was in pain to consider the miserable condition of the old man; and now my alms, giving him some relief, doth also ease me." *Hobbes,* by G. C. ROBERTSON, Edinburgh, 1886, p. 206.

[96] *Moral Philosophy,* Book II, chapter ii.

97. EQUIVOCAL EGOISM?—The above is unquestionably egoism. The man who accepts such a doctrine and consistently walks in the light must be set down as self-seeking. But self-seeking, as understood by different men, appears to take on different aspects. Shall we class all those who frankly accept it as man's only ultimate motive with Aristippus and Epicurus and Hobbes?

Thomas Hill Green writes: "Anything conceived as good in such a way that the agent acts for the sake of it, must be conceived as his own good." [97] The motive to action is, he maintains, always "some idea of the man's personal good." [98] He does not hesitate to say that a man necessarily lives for himself; [99] and he calls "the human self or the man" [100] a self-seeking ego, a self-seeking subject, and a self- seeking person. [101]

Were Green's book a lost work, only preserved to the memories of men by such citations as the above, the author would certainly be relegated to a class of moralists with which he had, in fact, little sympathy.

But the book is not lost, and by turning to it we find Green continuing the first of the above citations with the words: "Though he may conceive it as his own good only on account of his interest in others, and in spite of any amount of suffering on his own part incidental to its attainment." He is willing to grant the self-seeking ego an eye single to its own interests, but he is careful to explain that: "These are not merely interests dependent on other persons for the means to their gratification, but interests in the good of those other persons, interests which cannot be satisfied without the consciousness that those other persons are satisfied." [102]

When Hobbes gave an account of "the passions that incline men to peace,"[103] he made no mention of the social nature of man. That nature Green conceives to be so essentially social that the individual cannot disentangle his own good from the good of his fellows. To live "for himself," since that self is a social self, means to live for others. May this fairly be called egoistic doctrine?

98. WHAT IS MEANT BY THE SELF?—It is sufficiently clear that the happiness, or good, or advantage, or interests of the individual or self may

---

[97] *Prolegomena to Ethics,* Sec 92.

[98] Sec Sec 95, 97.

[99] Sec 138.

[100] Sec 99.

[101] Sec Sec 98, 100, 145.

[102] Sec 199.

[103] *Leviathan,* I, xiii.

mean many things. It is equally clear that in our interpretation of all such terms our notions of the nature of the self will play no inconsiderable role. What is the self?

In his famous chapter on the Consciousness of Self, [104] William James enumerates four senses of the word. With three of these we may profitably occupy ourselves here. He calls them the Material Self, the Social Self and the Spiritual Self.

The innermost part of the material self he makes our body, and next to it, in their order, he places our clothes, our family, our home, and our property. They contribute to our being what we are in our own eyes, we identify ourselves with them, and we experience "a sense of the shrinkage of our personality" when even the more outlying elements, such as our possessions, are lost. "Our immediate family," he writes, "is a part of ourselves. Our father and mother, our wife and babes, are bone of our bone and flesh of our flesh. When they die, a part of our very selves is gone. If they do anything wrong, it is our shame. If they are insulted, our anger flashes forth as readily as if we stood in their place."

It is obvious that the limits of the material self, as above understood, may be indefinitely extended. There are men who feel about their country as the average normal man feels about his home; and doubtless the suffering of a stray beggar tugged at the heart of St. Francis as the misfortune of wife or child does in the case of other men. How far abroad our "interests" are to be found, and just what "interests" we shall regard as intimately and peculiarly our own, depends upon what we are.

The Social Self James describes as the recognition a man gets from his mates: "We are not only gregarious animals, liking to be in the sight of our fellows, but we have an innate propensity to get ourselves noticed, and noticed favorably, by our kind." Men certainly regard their fame or honor as to be included among their interests, and they may value and seek to obtain the good opinion of a very little clique or of a much wider circle.

By the Spiritual Self is meant our qualities of mind and character—"the most enduring and intimate part of the Self, that which we most verily seem to be." Our interest in these it is impossible to overlook, and their cultivation and development may become a ruling passion.

James's illuminating pages make clear that he who speaks of the advantage or interest of the individual may have in mind predominantly any one of

---

[104] *Psychology,* New York, 1890, I, chapter x.

these aspects of the Self, or all of them conjointly. The Self as he conceives it may be a narrow one, or it may be a very broad one.

99. EGOISM AND THE BROADER SELF.—It may with some plausibility be maintained that he who lives for himself may not properly be regarded as an egoist and called selfish, if his Self is sufficiently expanded. May it not, theoretically, include as much of the universe as is known to man? And where can a man seek ends of any sort beyond this broad field? On this view, all men are, in a sense, self-seeking, but only those are reprehensibly self-seeking who have narrow and scanty selves.

But common sense and the common usage of speech do not sanction such statements as that a man necessarily lives for himself and that all men are self-seeking. It is justly recognized that some men with broad interests—of a sort—are self-seeking, and that some others with great limitations are not.

He who has property scattered over four continents and watches with absorbing interest all movements upon the political and economic stage may nevertheless be a thorough-going egoist. The breadth of his horizon will not redeem him. One may look far afield and live laborious days in the pursuit of fame, and be egoistic to the back-bone, although one's interests, in this case, include even the contents of the minds of generations yet unborn. One may forego many pleasures and concentrate all one's efforts upon the attainment of intellectual eminence or of a virtuous character, and yet seem to have a claim to the name of egoist.

That even the pursuit of virtue may take an egoistic turn has frequently been recognized: "Woe betides that man," writes Dewey, "who having entered upon a course of reflection which leads to a clearer conception of his own moral capacities and weaknesses, maintains that thought as a distinct mental end, and thereby makes his subsequent acts simply means to improving or perfecting his moral nature." [105] He characterizes this as one of the worst kinds of selfishness. The task set himself by the egoist who aims at outshining his fellows in an unselfish self-forgetfulness would seem to be a particularly difficult one; yet we have all met persons who appear to be animated by some such desire.

100. Egoism not Unavoidable.—On such cases as the above the common judgment can hardly be in doubt. But there are cases more questionable. Was Hobbes really self-seeking when he gave the sixpence to the old beggar? Is it egoism that leads the young mother to give herself the exquisite pleasure of feeding and caring for her babes? or that induces the

---

[105] *Ethics*, chapter xviii, Sec 3, p. 384.

patriot to die for his country? To be sure, both the babes and the fatherland may fall within the limits of the self, as the psychologist has broadly defined it.

But they fall within it only in a sense. No doctrine of the mutual inclusion of selves can obliterate the distinction between self and neighbor, and make my neighbor *merely* a part of myself. The common opinion of mankind is not at fault in basing upon the distinction between selves the further distinction between egoism and altruism. Whatever interests the egoist may have, his ultimate motive to action *cannot* be the recognition of the desire or will of another. Such can be the motive of the altruist.

Human motives are of many sorts, and just what they are it is not always easy to discover. Cornelia, in exhibiting her "jewels," may have been puffed up with pride. When Cyrano de Bergerac threw, with a noble gesture, his purse to the players, his "Mais quel geste!" reveals that he was a player himself and was "showing off." There may be spectacular patriots, who are willing to suffer the extreme penalty for the sake of a place in history. But all maternal affection is not identical with pride; all generous impulses cannot be traced to vanity; all patriotism is not spectacular; nor is the motive to the relief of suffering necessarily the removal of one's own pain. It is one thing to hire Lazarus not to exhibit himself in his shocking plight on our front porch, and it is a distinctly different thing to be concerned about the needs of Lazarus *per se.*

It is obvious, then, that it is only by a straining of language that one can say that man necessarily lives for himself, or is unavoidably self- seeking. He who makes such statements overlooks the fact that, even if is true that, in a sense, a man's self may be regarded as coextensive with all that interests him, it is equally true that different selves are mutually exclusive and that the good of one may serve as the ultimate motive in determining the action of another. The ethnologist is compelled to recognize altruistic impulses in men primitive and in men civilized: "Of the doctrine of self-interest as the primary and only genuine human motive, it is sufficient to say that it bears no relation to the facts of human nature, and implies an incorrect view of the origin of instinct." [106]

101. Varieties of Egoism.—The egoist may set his affections upon pleasure, and become a representative of Egoistic Hedonism, the variety of egoism normally treated as typical and made the subject of criticism in ethical treatises. But there is nothing to prevent him from making his aim, not so

---

[106] HOBHOUSE, *Morals in Evolution*, p. 16.

much pleasure, as self-preservation; or from taking as his goal wealth, power, reputation, intellectual or moral attainment, or what not. [107]

So long as the motives which impel him to get, to avoid, to be, or to do, something, do not include, except as means to some ulterior end, the desire or will of his fellow-man, there appears no reason to deny him the title of "Egoist." Nor need we deny him the title because he may be unconscious of his egoism. There are unconscious egoists who are wholly absorbed in the individual objects which are the end of their strivings. They may be quite unaware that they are ruled by self-interest, when it is clear to the spectator that such is the case. [108] But the philosophical egoist must rise to a higher plane of reflection.

There are, thus, egoisms of many sorts, and they may urge men to very different courses of conduct. Some of them may pass over more naturally than others into forms of doctrine which are not egoistic at all. He who aims at a maximum of pleasure for himself is likely to remain an egoist; he whose ambition is to be a patron of science or a philanthropist, may, it is true, remain within the circle of the self, but it is quite possible that his ulterior aim may come to be forgotten and his real interest be transferred to the enlightenment of mankind or to the relief of suffering.

It is especially worthy of remark that in judging a system of doctrine we must take it as a whole, and not confine ourselves to a few utterances of the man who urges it, however unequivocal they may appear when taken in isolation. He whose motive to action is always some idea of his own personal good is an egoist. But a philosopher may hold that human motives are always of this sort, and yet reveal unmistakably, both in his life and in his writings, that he is not really an egoist at all. In which case, we may tax him with more or less inconsistency, but we should not misconceive him.

102. THE ARGUMENTS FOR EGOISM.—So much for the forms of egoism. It remains to enquire what may be urged in favor of the doctrine, and what may be said against it.

(1) It has been urged that egoism is inevitable. This, to be sure, can scarcely be regarded as an argument that a man *ought* to be an egoist, for there seems little sense in telling a man that he ought to do what he cannot

---

[107] Thus, Hobbes made his end self-preservation; Spinoza takes much the same position; Nietzsche makes that which is aimed at, power.
[108] James, *Psychology*, Vol. I, chapter x, pp. 319-321; a baby is characterized as "the completest egoist."

possibly help doing. But the argument may be used to deter us from advocating some other ethical doctrine.

"On the occasion of every act that he exercises," says Bentham, "every human being is led to pursue that line of conduct which, according to his view of the case, taken by him at the moment, will be in the highest degree contributory to his own greatest happiness." [109]

From this we might conclude, not only that every man is an egoist, but also that every man is at all times a prudent and calculating egoist— which seems to flatter grossly the drunkard and the excited man laying about him in blind fury. But one may hold that egoism is inevitable without going so far. [110]

(2) The egoistic ideal may be urged upon us on the ground that it addresses itself to man as natural and reasonable.

Thus, the Cyrenaics saw in the fact that we are from our childhood attracted to pleasure, and, when we have attained it, seek no further, a proof that pleasure is the chief good. [111] Paley maintains that, when it has been pointed out that private happiness has been the motive of an act, "no further question can reasonably be asked." [112] Our citations from Hobbes and Bentham and Green reveal that these writers never think of giving reasons why a man should seek his own good.

And various moralists, who do not make self-interest the one fundamental principle which should rule human conduct, are evidently loath to make of it a principle subordinate to some other. Bishop Butler, who maintains that virtue consists in the pursuit of right and good as such, yet holds that: "When we sit down in a cool hour, we can neither justify to ourselves this nor any other pursuit till we are convinced that it will be for our happiness, or at least not contrary to it." [113] Clarke, who dwells upon the eternal and immutable obligations of morality "incumbent on men from the very nature and reason of things themselves" teaches that it is not reasonable for men to adhere to virtue if they receive no advantage from it. [114]

---

[109] *The Constitutional Code*. Introduction, Sec 2.

[110] Psychological Hedonism, the doctrine that "volition is always determined by pleasures or pains actual or prospective," need not be thus exaggerated. See SIDGWICK's *Methods of Ethics*, I, iv, Sec 1.

[111] *Diogenes Laertius*, II, "Aristippus," Sec 8.

[112] *Moral Philosophy*, II, Sec 3.

[113] *Sermon* XI.

[114] *Boyle Lectures*, 1705, Prop. I.

The moral here seems to be that, whatever else a man ought to do, he ought to seek his own advantage—real self-sacrifice cannot be his duty. This conviction of the unreasonableness of self-sacrifice reveals itself in another form in the doctrine that morality cannot be made completely rational unless a reconciliation between prudence and benevolence can be found; [115] and in the labored attempts to show that the good of the individual must actually coincide with that of the community. [116] It may be questioned whether the same conviction did not lurk in the back of the mind of that sternest of moralists, Kant, who denied that happiness ought to be sought at all, and yet found so irrational the divorce of virtue and happiness that he postulated a God to guarantee their union. [117]

Thus, moralists of widely different schools agree in recognizing that self-interest is a principle that should not be placed second to any other. The confessed egoist only goes a step further in recognizing it as a principle that has no rival. And that men generally are inclined to regard egoism as not unnatural seems evinced by the fact that for apparently altruistic actions they are very apt to seek ulterior egoistic motives, while, if the action seems plainly egoistic, they seek no further.

Does, then, anything seem more natural than egoism? and, if natural, may it not be assumed to be proper and right?

(3) Finally, it may be urged that he who serves his own interests at all intelligently has, at least, a comprehensive aim, and does not live at random. In so far, egoism appears to be rational in a sense dwelt on above;[118] it harmonizes and unifies the impulses and desires of the man.

103. THE ARGUMENT AGAINST EGOISM.—What may be said against egoism?

(1) Enough has been said above to show that egoism is not inevitable, but that men actually are influenced by motives which cannot be regarded as egoistic. It is, hence, not necessary to dwell upon this point.

(2) As to the naturalness of egoism. Both the professional moralist and the man in the street may hesitate to admit that a man should neglect his own

---

[115] SIDGWICK, *The Methods of Ethics*, concluding chapter, Sec 5.

[116] *E. g.* GREEN, *Prolegomena to Ethics*, Sec Sec 244-245. Aristotle tries to prove that he who dies for his country is impelled by self-love. He does what is honorable, and thus "gives the greater good to himself." *Ethics*, Book IX, chapter viii.

[117] *The Critique of the Practical Reason*, chapter ii.

[118] Sec. 55-56.

interests, and may find it natural that he should cultivate them assiduously. But it is only the exceptional man who maintains that he should have nothing else in view.

There are individuals so constituted that self-interest makes to them a peculiarly strong appeal. Others, more social by nature, may be misled by psychological theory to maintain that a man's chief and only end is his own "satisfaction." [119] Still others, realizing that both one's own interests and the interests of one's neighbor are natural and seemingly legitimate objects of regard, are perplexed as to the method of reconciling their apparently conflicting claims, and are betrayed into inconsistent utterances.

But it is too much to say that the professional moralist and the plain man normally regard pure egoism with favor and find it natural. In spite of our cynical maxims and our inclination to seek for ulterior motives for apparently altruistic acts, we abhor the thorough-going egoist, and we are not inclined to look upon the phenomena, let us say, of the family life, as manifestations of self-seeking.

It is worth while to remark that, even if the approach to the Cyrenaic ideal were so common as not to seem wholly unnatural, that would not prove that it ought to be embraced; it is natural for men to err, but that does not make error our duty.

(3) By the moral conviction of organized humanity, as expressed in custom, law, and public opinion, egoism stands condemned. Neither in savage life nor among civilized peoples, neither in the dawn of human history nor in its latest chapters, do we find these agencies encouraging every man to live exclusively for himself. Egoistic impulses are recognized, in that reward and punishment are allotted, but the end urged upon the attention of the individual is the common good, not his own particular good.

The social conscience has always demanded of the individual self-sacrifice, even to the extent of laying down his life, on occasion, for the public weal. And the enlightened social conscience does not regard a man as truly moral whose outward conformity to moral laws rests solely upon a basis of egoistic calculation. The very existence of the family, the tribe, the state, is a protest against pure egoism. Were all men as egoistic as Aristippus seems to have professed to be, a stable community life of any sort would be impossible.

(4) The argument that egoism is rational at least in so far as it introduces

---

[119] See below, chapter xxvi, 3.

consistency into actions and unifies and harmonizes desires and impulses deserves little consideration. Any comprehensive end will do the same, and many comprehensive ends may be very trivial. One may make it the aim of one's life to remain slender, or may devote all one's energies to the amelioration of the social position of bald-headed men. He who counsels deliberate egoism does not recommend it merely on the score that it leads to consistent action. He does it on the ground that the end itself appeals to him as one that ought to be selected and will be selected if a man is wise. That the interest of the individual is in this sense a matter of obligation, is something to be proved, not assumed.

104. THE MORALIST'S INTEREST IN EGOISM—It has been worth while to treat at length of egoism because the doctrine takes on more or less subtle forms, and its fundamental principle, self-interest, has a significance for various ethical schools which are not, or are not considered, egoistic. Men have been vastly puzzled by the moral claims of the principle of self-interest, both plain men and professional moralists.

That prudence is not the only fundamental virtue, most men would be ready enough to admit; but is it properly speaking, a virtue at all? *Ought* I, for example, to try to make myself happy? Suppose I do not want to be happy, what is the source of the obligation?

Butler tells me that interest, one's own happiness, is a manifest obligation;[120] Bentham, a writer of a widely different school, informs me that "the constantly proper end of action on the part of any individual at the moment of action is his real greatest happiness from that moment to the end of his life." [121] On the other hand, Hutcheson teaches me that I am under no obligation to be good to myself, although I am under obligation to be good to others: "Actions which flow solely from self-love, and yet evidence no want of benevolence, having no hurtful effects upon others, seem perfectly indifferent in a moral sense." [122] Which means that intemperance is blameworthy only so far as it is against the public interest.

May I, should I, on occasion, sacrifice myself? Thoughtful men generally recognize self-sacrifice, not only as possible, but as actual, and believe it to be at times a duty. But the moralist gives forth here an uncertain sound.

Self-interest and benevolence have been left to fight out their quarrel in a

---

[120] *Dissertation on the Nature of Virtue*, Sec 8; *Sermons* III and XI.
[121] BENTHAM, *Memoirs*, Vol. X of Bowring's Edition, Edinburgh, 1843, p. 560.
[122] *An Enquiry concerning Moral Good and Evil*, Sec 3, 5.

court without a judge to decide upon their conflicting claims; [123] self-sacrifice has been enjoined; [124] it has been declared impossible; [125] it has been denied that it can ever be a duty; [126] the kind of self-sacrifice in question has been regarded as significant. [127]

He who has rejected as unworthy of serious consideration the naive egoism of an Aristippus or an Epicurus is not on that account done with egoism, by any means. [128]

CHAPTER XXV

UTILITARIANISM

105. WHAT IS UTILITARIANISM?—The division of things desirable into those desirable in themselves, and those desirable for the sake of something else, is two thousand years old. Those things which we recognize as desirable for the sake of something else, we call useful.

What we shall regard as useful depends in each case upon the nature of the end at which we aim. If our aim is the attainment of pleasure, the preservation of life, the harmonious development of our faculties, or any other, we may term useful whatever makes for the realization of that end.

Hence, we can, by stretching the application of the word, call utilitarian any ethical doctrine which sets an ultimate end to human endeavor and

---

[123] See Sec 102, the citations from Butler and Clarke.

[124] KANT, see, later, chapter xxix.

[125] See, above, the position of Green, Sec 97; cf., below, Sec 126.

[126] FITE, *An Introductory Study of Ethics*, chapter vii, Sec 5.

[127] SIDGWICK, *The Methods of Ethics*, Introduction, Sec 4.

[128] The question of self-sacrifice recurs again in chapter xxvi, 3.

judges actions as moral or the reverse, according to their tendency to realize that end, or to frustrate its realization. As the ends thus chosen may be very diverse, it is obvious that widely different forms of utilitarian doctrine may come into being.

It is, however, inconvenient to stretch the term, "utilitarianism" in this fashion. Certain forms of doctrine which, in its wider sense, it would include, have come to be known under names of their own; and, besides, the especial type of utilitarianism advocated by Bentham and John Stuart Mill appears to have a claim upon the appellation which they set in circulation. Common usage has thus limited the significance of the word, and we naturally think of the doctrine of these men when we hear it uttered. It is in this sense that I shall use it.

"The creed which accepts as the foundation of morals, Utility, or the Greatest Happiness Principle," writes Mill, "holds that actions are right in proportion as they tend to promote happiness, wrong as they tend to produce the reverse of happiness. By happiness is intended pleasure, and the absence of pain; by unhappiness, pain and the privation of pleasure." This means, he adds, "that pleasure, and freedom from pain, are the only things desirable as ends; and that all desirable things ... are desirable either for the pleasure inherent in themselves, or as means to the promotion of pleasure and the prevention of pain." [129]

The pleasure here intended is not the selfish pleasure of the individual. Utilitarianism is not Cyrenaicism. The goal of the utilitarian's endeavors is the general happiness, in which many individuals participate. The moral rules which control and direct the strivings of the individual derive their authority from their tendency to serve this end.

106. BENTHAM'S DOCTRINE.—Most uncompromising is the utilitarianism set forth in the writings of Mill's master, that most benevolent and philanthropic of men, Jeremy Bentham. He is true to his principles and he makes no concessions.

He regards that as in the interest of the individual which tends to add to the sum total of his pleasures or to diminish the sum total of his pains. And he understands in the same sense the interest of the community. [130] That which serves that interest he sets down as "conformable to the principle of

---

[129] *Utilitarianism*, chapter ii. In the pages following, when I leave out a reference to pain in discussing the utilitarian doctrine, it will be for convenience and for the sake of brevity. The intelligent reader can supply the omissions.
[130] *Principles of Morals and Legislation*, chapter i, Sec 5.

utility." What is thus conformable he declares ought to be done, what is not conformable ought not to be done. Right and wrong he distinguishes in the same manner. "When thus interpreted," he insists, "the words *ought*, and *right* and *wrong*, and others of that stamp, have a meaning; when otherwise, they have none" [131]

Of differences in quality between pleasures Bentham takes no account. In his curious and interesting chapter entitled "Value of a Lot of Pleasure or Pain, how to be Measured," he enumerates the circumstances which should determine the value of a pleasure or a pain. They are as follows: [132]

1. Its intensity. 2. Its duration. 3. Its certainty or uncertainty. 4. Its propinquity or remoteness. 5. Its fecundity. 6. Its purity. 7. Its extent.

The first four of these characteristics call for no comment. By the fecundity of a pleasure Bentham understands its likelihood of being followed by other pleasures; by its purity, the likelihood that it will not be followed by pains. The characteristic "extent" marks off utilitarianism from egoism, for it has reference to the number of persons affected by the pleasure or the pain. The greater the number, the higher the value in question. The greatest number of pleasures of the highest value, as free as possible from admixture with pains, is the goal of the endeavors of the utilitarian. Naturally, when the interests of many persons are taken into account, the question of the principle according to which "lots" of pleasure are to be distributed becomes a pressing one. Bentham decides it as follows: "Everybody to count for one, and nobody for more than one." [133] In other words, the distribution should be an impartial one.

At first sight, this account of the relative desirability of pleasures and undesirability of pains seems sensible enough. Men do desire pleasure, and they undoubtedly approve the preference given to pleasures more intense, enduring, certain, immediate, fruitful in further pleasures, free from painful consequences, and shared by many, over those which have not these characteristics:

"*Intense, long, certain, speedy, fruitful, pure—*
　Such marks in *pleasures* and in *pains* endure.
　Such pleasures seek, if *private* be thy end:
　　If it be *public*, wide let them *extend.*

---

[131] *Ibid.*, i, 10.

[132] *Ibid.*, chapter iv.

[133] See the discussion of Bentham's dictum in its bearings on justice, J. S. Mill, *Utilitarianism*, chapter v.

Such *pains* avoid, whichever be thy view;
  If pains *must* come, let them *extend* to few." [134]

These mnemonic lines may well strike many readers as embodying a very good working rule of common-sense morality; as paying a proper regard to prudence and to benevolence as well. But there are passages in Bentham calculated to shake such acquiescence. He writes:

"Now pleasure is in *itself* a good; nay, even setting aside immunity from pain, the only good: pain is in itself an evil, and, indeed without exception, the only evil; or else the words good and evil have no meaning. And this is alike true of every sort of pain, and of every sort of pleasure." [135]

"Let a man's motive be ill-will; call it even malice, envy, cruelty; it is still a kind of pleasure that is his motive: the pleasure he takes at the thought of the pain which he sees, or expects to see, his adversary undergo. Now even this wretched pleasure, taken by itself, is good: it may be faint; it may be short; it must at any rate be impure: yet, while it lasts, and before any bad consequences arrive, it is as good as any other that is not more intense." [136]

Reflection upon such passages may well lead a man to ask himself:

(1) Is it, after all, the consensus of human opinion that pleasure is the only good and pain the only evil?

(2) Are some pleasures actually regarded as more desirable than others, solely through the application of the standard given above?

(3) Can the pleasure of a malignant act properly be called *morally* good at all?

107. THE DOCTRINE OF JOHN STUART MILL.—Bentham's purely quantitative estimate of the value of pleasures has aroused in many minds the feeling that he puts morality upon a low level. [137] Mill attempts an improvement upon his doctrine. "It is quite compatible with the principle of utility," he writes, "to recognize the fact that some *kinds* of pleasure are

---

[134] *Principles of Morals and Legislation*, chapter iv, i,

[135] *Ibid.*, chapter x, 10.

[136] *Ibid*, note.

[137] In justice to Bentham it must be borne in mind that his prime interest was not in ethical theory, but in legislative reform. His doctrine, such as it was, and applied as he applied it, was a tool of no mean efficacy. Bentham must count among the real benefactors of mankind.

more desirable and more valuable than others. It would be absurd that, while in estimating all other things quality is considered as well as quantity, the estimation of pleasures should be supposed to depend on quantity alone." [138]

Thus, Mill distinguishes between higher pleasures and lower, and he gives a criterion for distinguishing the former from the latter: "Of two pleasures, if there be one to which all or almost all who have experience of both give a decided preference, irrespective of any feeling of moral obligation to prefer it, that is the more desirable pleasure." He refers the whole matter to the judgment of the "competent;" and, in accordance with that judgment, decides that: "It is better to be a human being dissatisfied than a pig satisfied; better to be Socrates dissatisfied than a fool satisfied. And if the fool, or the pig, are of a different opinion, it is because they only know their own side of the question. The other party to the comparison knows both sides." [139]

That some pleasures may properly be called higher than others moralists of many schools will be ready to admit, but to Mill's criterion of what proves them to be higher they may demur. Of the delight that a fool takes in his folly a wise man may be as incapable as a fool is of the enjoyment of wisdom. With mature years men cease to be competent judges of the pleasures of boyhood. To each nature, its appropriate choice of pleasures. That human beings at a given level of intellectual and emotional development actually desire certain things rather than certain others does not prove that those things are desirable in any general sense. It does not prove that men *ought* to desire them. For that proof we must look in some other direction; and a critical scrutiny of the pleasures which moralists ancient and modern have generally accepted as "higher" reveals a common characteristic which explains their being thus classed together much better than the appeal to Mill's criterion. [140]

As has often been pointed out, Mill, while defending Utilitarianism, really passes beyond it, and his doctrine tends to merge in one widely different from that of Bentham. For the "Greatest Happiness Principle" he virtually substitutes the "Highest Happiness Principle." But he scarcely realizes the significance of his substitution, and he gives an inadequate account of the significance of higher and lower.

108. THE ARGUMENT FOR UTILITARIANISM.—We have seen above that Bentham maintains that such words as "ought," "right" and "wrong"

---

[138] *Utilitarianism*, chapter i.
[139] *Ibid.*
[140] See chapter xxx, Sec 142.

have no meaning unless interpreted after the fashion of the utilitarian. He admits that his "principle of utility" is not susceptible of direct proof, but claims that such a proof is needless. [141]

Accepting it as a fact revealed by observation that the actual end of action on the part of every individual is his own happiness as he conceives it, he appears to have passed on without question to the further positions, that the *proper* end of action of the individual is his own greatest happiness, and, yet, his *proper* end of action, as a member of a community, is the greatest happiness of the community. [142]

The second of these positions cannot be deduced from the first, nor can the third be inferred from the other two. Bentham appears to have taken the "principle of utility" for granted; but one coming after him and scrutinizing his work can scarcely avoid raising the question of the justice of his assumption. That happiness is the only thing desirable, and that the happiness of all should be the object aimed at by each, are propositions which seem to stand in need of proof.

Such proof Mill attempted to furnish. [143] He argues as follows:

"The only proof capable of being given that an object is visible, is that people actually see it. The only proof that a sound is audible, is that people hear it; and so of the other sources of our experience. In like manner, I apprehend, the sole evidence it is possible to produce that anything is desirable, is that people do actually desire it. If the end which the utilitarian doctrine proposes to itself were not, in theory and practice, acknowledged to be an end, nothing could ever convince any person that it was so. No reason can be given why the general happiness is desirable, except that each person, so far as he believes it to be attainable, desires his own happiness. This, however, being a fact, we have not only all the proof the case admits of, but all which it is possible to require, that happiness is a good: that each person's happiness is a good to that person, and the general happiness, therefore, a good to the aggregate of all persons. Happiness has made out its title as *one* of the ends of conduct, and, consequently one of the ends of morality." [144]

---

[141] Principles of Morals and Legislation, chapter i, 11.

[142] See the paper entitled "Logical Arrangements, Employed as Instruments in Legislation" etc., *Memoirs*, Bowring's Edition, Volume X, page 560.

[143] He does not regard his doctrine as provable in the usual sense; but he adduces what he regards as "equivalent to proof." *Utilitarianism*, chapter i.

[144] *Utilitarianism*, chapter iv.]

That happiness is the *only ultimate* end, Mill regards as established by the argument that other

things, for example, virtue, though they come to be valued for themselves, do so only through the fact that, originally valued as means to the attainment of happiness, they become, through association, valued even out of this relation, and thus treated as a part of happiness. [145]

The defects in Mill's argument have made themselves apparent, not merely to the opponents of utilitarianism, but even to its advocates. [146] We cannot say that things are desirable in any moral sense, simply because they are desired. In a loose sense of the word, everything that is or has been desired by anyone is desirable—it evidently can be desired. When we say no more than this, we say nothing. But when we call a course of action desirable we mean more than this; and we are compelled to admit that a multitude of desirable things are not generally desired. This is the burden of the lament of every reformer.

Furthermore, it does not appear to follow that, because his own happiness is a good to each member of a community, the happiness of all must likewise be a good to each severally. A community in which every man studies his own interest may conceivably be a community in which no man regards it as desirable to consult the public weal. That the general happiness is desirable, in a loose sense of the word, is palpable fact; it is obvious that it can be desired, for some persons do actually desire it. But that it is desirable in any sense cannot be inferred from the fact that all men desire something else, namely, their own individual happiness.

We must, then, look further for the proof of the utilitarian principle. Henry Sidgwick, that admirable scholar and most judicial mind, falls back upon certain intuitions which, he conceives, present themselves as ultimate and unassailable. He writes:

"Let us reflect upon the clearest and most certain of our moral intuitions. I find that I undoubtedly seem to perceive, as clearly and certainly as I see any axiom in Arithmetic or Geometry, that it is 'right' and 'reasonable' for me to treat others as I should think that I myself ought to be treated under similar conditions, and to do what I believe to be ultimately conducive to universal Good or Happiness."

And again: "The propositions, 'I ought not to prefer a present lesser good to a future greater good,' and 'I ought not to prefer my own lesser good to

---

[145] *Ibid.*

[146] SIDGWICK, *The Methods of Ethics*, Book III, chapter xiii, Sec 5.

the greater good of another,' do present themselves as self-evident; as much (e. g.) as the mathematical axiom that 'if equals be added to equals the wholes are equal.'" [147]

Whether these intuitions will be accepted as furnishing an indisputably sound basis for utilitarianism will depend upon one's attitude toward intuitions in general and the list of intuitions one is inclined to accept. It is significant that Sidgwick does not accept as self-evident such subordinate propositions as, "I ought to speak the truth." He regards their authority as derived from the Greatest Happiness Principle.

109. THE DISTRIBUTION OF HAPPINESS.—The man who accepts the Greatest Happiness Principle as the sole basis of his ethical doctrine is faced with the problem of its application in detail. The "greatest good of the greatest number" is a vague expression. What is properly understood by "the greatest number"? and upon what principle shall "lots" of happiness be assigned to each? Very puzzling questions arise when we approach the problem of the distribution of pleasures and the calculation of their values. Let us look at them.

I. Who should be considered in the Distribution?

(1) Shall we aim directly at the happiness of all men now living? or shall we content ourselves with a smaller number? Certainly, with increasing intelligence and broadening sympathies, men tend toward a more embracing benevolence.

(2) Shall we admit to the circle generations yet unborn? and, if so, how far into the future should we look?

(3) Should we make a deliberate attempt to increase the number of those who may share the common fund of happiness, by striving for an increase in the number of births? This end has been consciously sought for divers reasons. The ancestor-worship of China has made the Chinaman eagerly desirous of leaving behind him those who would devote themselves to him after he has departed this life. Nations ancient and modern have endeavored to strengthen the state by providing for an increase in its population. Shall a similar end be pursued for the ethical purpose of widening the circle of those who shall live and be happy? Most ethical teachers do not appear to have regarded this as a corollary to the doctrine of benevolence.

---

[147] *The Methods of Ethics*, concluding chapter, Sec 5, and Book III, chapter xiii, Sec 3.

(4) Shall we enlarge the circle so as to include the lower animals? As Bentham expressed it: The question is not, "Can they *reason*? nor, Can they *talk*? but, Can they *suffer*?" [148]

II. How should the "lots" of happiness be measured?

(1) Should everybody count as one, and nobody as more than one? in other words, should strict impartiality be aimed at?

Dr. Westermarck's striking reply to the argument for impartiality as urged by Professor Sidgwick has already been quoted. [149]

It must be confessed that to put one's parents, one's children, one's neighbors, strangers, foreigners, the brutes, all upon the same level, is contrary to the moral judgment of savage and civilized alike. It would seem contrary to the sentiments which lie at the root of the family, the community, and the state. Nor have we reason to look forward to any future state of human society in which such lesser groups within the broad circle of humanity will be done away with, though they tend to become less exclusive in their demands upon human sympathy.

(2) Suppose that the greatest sum of happiness on the whole could be best attained by an unequal distribution—by making a limited number very happy at the expense of the rest. Would this be justifiable? It would be in harmony with the Greatest Happiness Principle, though not with the principle of the greatest happiness equally shared.

III. The question of the distribution of happiness in the life of the individual is not one to be ignored. If we are concerned only with the quantity of happiness, may we not take as the ethical precept "a short life and a merry one"—provided the brief span of years be merry enough, and there be no objection to the choice on the score of harm to others?

This problem is closely analogous to that of the distribution of pleasures to those who compose the "greatest number" taken into account. There we were concerned with the shares allotted to individuals; here we are concerned with the shares assigned to the different parts of a single life. In the attempt to solve the problem, Bentham's criteria of intensity, certainty, purity, etc., might naturally be appealed to.

---

[148] *Principles of Morals and Legislation*, chapter xvii, Sec 4.
[149] See chapter v, Sec 16.] Let the reader glance at it again.

110. THE CALCULUS OF PLEASURES.—Nor are the problems which meet us less perplexing when we pass from questions of the distribution of pleasures to that of the calculus of pleasures. How are delights and miseries to be weighed, and reasonably balanced?

(1) Men desire pleasure, and they desire to avoid pain. The two seem to be opposed. But men constantly accept pleasures which entail some suffering, and they avoid pains even at the expense of some pleasure. Are, however, pleasures and pains strictly commensurable? How much admixture of pain is called for to reduce the value of a pleasure to zero? and how much pleasure, added to a pain, will make the whole emotional state predominantly a pleasurable one? A disagreeable taste and an agreeable odor may be experienced together, but they cannot be treated as an algebraic sum. If we do so treat them, we seem to fall back upon the assumption that the mere fact that the heterogeneous complex is accepted or rejected is evidence that its ingredients have been measured and compared. This is an ungrounded assumption.

(2) Undoubtedly men prefer intense pleasures to mild ones, and those long-continued to those which are fleeting. But what degree of intensity will overbalance what period of duration? Here, again, we appear to be without a unit of measure, both in the case of pleasures and of pains.

(3) Obviously, he who would distribute pleasures with impartiality must take into consideration the natures and capacities of the recipients. All are not susceptible of pleasure in the same degree, nor are all capable of enjoying the same pleasures. It is small kindness to a cat to offer it hay; nor will the miser thank us for the opportunity to enjoy the pleasures of liberality. The gift which arouses deep emotion in one man, will leave another cold. The diversity of natures would make the calculus of pleasures, in any accurate sense of the expression, a most difficult problem, even if such a calculus were admissible in the case of a single individual. [150]

III. THE DIFFICULTIES OF OTHER SCHOOLS.—It would be unjust to the utilitarian not to point out that those who advocate other doctrines must find some way of coping with the difficulties which embarrass him.

Thus, the egoist may ignore duties to others, but he cannot free himself from the problems of the distribution of happiness in his own life and of the calculus of pleasures. The intuitionist, who, among other precepts,

---

[150] This difficulty has not been overlooked by the Utilitarian, see BENTHAM, *Principles of Morals and Legislation*, chapter vi.

accepts as ultimate those enjoining upon him justice and benevolence, may well ask himself toward whom these virtues are to be exercised, and whether the claims of all who belong to the class in question are identical in kind and degree. If they are not, he must find some rule for estimating their relative importance. He who makes it his moral ideal to Follow Nature, to Strive for Perfection, or to Realize his Capacities, must determine in detail what conduct, self-regarding and other- regarding, the acceptance of such aims entails. Only the unreflective can regard the utilitarian as having a monopoly of the difficulties which face the moralist. The vague general statement that we should strive to render others happy—a duty recognized by men of very different schools— never frees us from the perplexities which arise when it is asked: What others? With what degree of impartiality? When? By what means? But that such questions can be approached by a path more satisfactory than that followed by the utilitarian, there is good reason to maintain. [151]

112. SUMMARY OF ARGUMENTS FOR UTILITARIANISM.—It is worth while to summarize what may be said for utilitarianism, and what may be said against it. It may be argued in its favor:

(1) That it appears to set as the aim of human endeavor, an intelligible end, and a fairly definite one. Everyone has some notion of what happiness means, and is not without ideas touching the way to seek his own happiness, or to contribute to that of others.

(2) The end is one actually desired by men at all stages of intellectual and moral development. Men are impelled to seek their own happiness, and there are few who do not feel impelled to take into consideration, to some degree, at least, the happiness of some others.

(3) The general happiness is not merely desired by some men, but it is felt to be *desirable;* that is, it is an end not out of harmony with the moral judgments of mankind. It makes its appeal to the social nature of man; it seems to furnish a basis for the exercise of benevolence and justice.

(4) The utilitarian's clear recognition of the general happiness as the ultimate end of human endeavor, and his insistence that institutions, laws and moral maxims must be judged solely by their fitness to serve as means to that end, have made him an energetic apostle of reform, and intolerant of old and passively accepted abuses. His insistence upon the principle of impartiality in the distribution of happiness has made him a champion of the inarticulate and the oppressed. Whatever one may think of his abstract

---

[151] See, below, chapter xxx, Sec Sec 140-142.

principles, the general character of the specific measures he has advocated must meet with the approval of enlightened moralists of very different schools.

113. ARGUMENTS AGAINST UTILITARIANISM.—Against utilitarianism as an ethical theory various objections have been brought or may be brought.

(1) Objection may be taken to the utilitarian assumption that the only ultimate object of desire is pleasure or happiness.

It was pointed out forcibly by Bishop Butler in the eighteenth century that men desire many things besides pleasure. Man's desires are an outcome of his nature, and that results in "particular movements towards particular external objects"—honor, power, the harm or good of another. [152] To be sure, "no one can act but from a desire, or choice, or preference of his own," but this is no evidence that what he seeks in acting is always pleasure. Particular passions or appetites are, Butler ingeniously argues, "necessarily presupposed by the very idea of an interested pursuit; since the very idea of interest or happiness consists in this, that an appetite or affection enjoys its object."

Here we find our attention called to a very important truth, the significance of which there is danger of our overlooking. Pleasure or happiness is not something that can be parcelled up and handed about independently of the nature of the recipient. It is not everyone who can desire everything and feel pleasure in its attainment. That the objects of desire and will are many, and that the strivings of conscious creatures have in view many ends, and vary according to the impulsive and instinctive endowments of the creatures in question, has been well brought out in the admirable studies of instinct which we now have at our disposal. The most ardent devotee of pleasure must recognize, that only certain pleasures are open to him; that, such as they are, they are a revelation of his nature and capacities; that pleasures, if sought at all, cannot be secured directly, but only as the result of a successful striving for objects not pleasures, which bring pleasure as their accompaniment. He who would have the pleasure of eating must desire food; and neither food, nor the eating of food, can be regarded as, *per se*, pleasure. The pleasure of the brooding hen is beyond the reach of man, who, however pleasure-loving, cannot desire to sit upon eggs, and so must forego the pleasure which, in the case of the bird, crowns that exercise.

Such considerations as the above have led some moralists to define, as the

---

[152] *Sermons*, Preface, Sec 29; cf. Sermon XI.

end of desire, not pleasure, but self-satisfaction. Every desire, it is pointed out, strives to satisfy itself in the attainment of its appropriate object. With the attainment of the object, the desire has produced its proper fruit and ceases to be. It is admitted that the satisfaction of desire is accompanied by pleasure, but it is denied that the pleasure may be properly called the object of the desire, or regarded as calling it into being: "The appetite of hunger must precede and condition the pleasure which consists in its satisfaction. It cannot therefore have that pleasure for its exciting object."[153]

At the same time it is conceded that the idea of a pleasure to be attained may "reinforce" the desire for an object, may "intensify the putting forth of energy," and may tend "to sustain and prolong any mode of action." [154] It is further conceded that pleasures may be consciously aimed at, but it is urged that this does not result in true self-satisfaction, and is evidence of the existence of unhealthy desires. [155]

The utilitarian is not wholly helpless in the face of such objections. He may argue that, if it is difficult to see how a pleasure which is the result of a desire may cause the desire, it is equally difficult to see how it may prolong, reinforce or intensify it. And he may maintain that, although the pursuit of pleasure, in certain forms, is calculated to defeat its own aim and is undoubtedly unhealthy, this need not be the case if one's aim be the true utilitarian one—the happiness of all. The direct attack upon his Greatest Happiness Principle which consists in the objection that, if pleasure is the only object of desire, a sum of pleasures, as not being a pleasure, cannot be desired,[156] he can put aside with the remark that no far-reaching and comprehensive aim can be realized at one stroke. I can desire a long and useful life; this cannot be had all at once. I can desire a long life full of pleasures; this cannot be enjoyed all at once either. But each can certainly be the object of desire.

But, when all is said, it remains true that the contention of those, who distinguish sharply between the satisfaction of desire and the attainment of pleasure, is of no little importance. It calls our attention to the following truths:

---

[153] GREEN, *Prolegomena to Ethics*, Book III, chapter i, Sec 161. See also Book II, chapter ii, Sec 131; Book III, chapter i, Sec Sec 154-160.
[154] *Prolegomena to Ethics*, Sec 161; DEWEY, *Ethics*, chapter xiv, Sec 1, p. 271; MCDOUGALL, *Social Psychology*, London, 1916, p. 43.
[155] *Prolegomena to Ethics*, Sec 158; DEWEY, *Ethics* p. 270.
[156] *Prolegomena to Ethics*, Sec 221.

(a) We have definite instincts and impulses which tend to satisfy themselves with their appropriate objects.

(b) At their first exercise, our aim could not have been the pleasure resulting from their satisfaction, for that could not have been foreseen.

(c) Although, after experience, the attainment of pleasure may come to be our aim in the exercise of many activities, and may often, as far as we can see, be a natural and not unwholesome aim; it is by no means evident that, even when we are experienced and reflective, the exercise of our faculties comes to be regarded *only* as a means to the attainment of pleasure.

(d) The hedonist, in maintaining that pleasure is the only ultimate object of desire, appears, thus, to be committed to the doctrine that the satisfaction of all other desires is subordinated to the satisfaction of the desire for pleasure. For this position he can furnish no adequate proof. Self-evident the doctrine is not.

(e) It is incumbent upon him, as a moralist, to prove, not merely that all other satisfactions are, but also that they *ought* to be subordinated to the satisfaction of the desire for pleasure. This he appears to assume without proof.

(2) We have seen above [157] that the fundamental principle of utilitarian hedonism, as against egoistic, namely, the making the Greatest Happiness of the Greatest Number the object of the endeavors of each individual, has not been satisfactorily established by leading utilitarians. Bentham assumes the principle; Mill advances a doubtful argument; Sidgwick falls back upon intuitions which all will not admit to be indubitable. To his assertion: "Reason shows me that if my happiness is desirable and a good, the equal happiness of any other person must be equally desirable," [158] the doubter may reply: Desirable to whom? to him or to me?

(3) Finally, it may be objected that the consistent utilitarian, in making pleasure, abstractly taken, the only ultimate good, and in regarding as the sole criterion of right actions their tendency to produce pleasure, really tears pleasure out of its moral setting altogether.

Thus Bentham's contention [159] that the pleasure a man may derive from the exercise of malice or cruelty is, "taken by itself," good—while it lasts, and before any bad consequences have set in, as good as any other that is

---

[157] See Sec 108.
[158] *The Methods of Ethics*, Book III, chapter xiv, Sec 5.
[159] Sec 106, above.

not more intense—derives what plausibility it has, from an ambiguity in the word "good." Pleasure, taken by itself, is undoubtedly pleasure, whatever be its source. To affirm this is mere tautology. And, if we chose to make "good" but a synonym for pleasure, we remain in the same tautology when we affirm that every pleasure is a good. But Bentham assumed that good in this sense and moral good are the same thing.

His assumption is not borne out by the moral judgments of mankind. Even a cursory view of those moral judgments as revealed in customs, laws and public opinion makes it evident that, under certain circumstances, pleasure is regarded as, from a moral standpoint, a good, and, under other circumstances, an evil. Torn out of its setting, it is simply pleasure, a psychological phenomenon like any other, with no ethical significance.

Take the case of the pleasure enjoyed by the malignant man. It may be intense, if he be peculiarly susceptible to such pleasure. The pain suffered by his victim may conceivably be less intense. Both may die before the "bad consequences," that is to say, other pains, arrive. There may be no spectators. Is, in such a case, the pleasure one to be called a "good"? Can it *be approved?* No reflective moralist would maintain that it can. Which means that the moralists, in all ages, have meant by "good" something more than pleasure, taken abstractly, and that Bentham's assumption may be regarded as an aberration.

114. TRANSFIGURED UTILITARIANISM.—It is possible to hold to a utilitarianism more circumspect and less startling than Bentham's. It is possible, while maintaining that pleasure is the only thing that an experienced and reasonable being can regard as ultimately desirable, to maintain at the same time that it is rash for any man to attempt to seek his own happiness, or to strive to promote the general happiness, without taking into very careful consideration the instincts and impulses of man and the nature of the social organization which has resulted from man's being what he is. One may argue that the experience of the race is, as a rule, a safer guide than the independent judgment of the individual; and that, in the secular endeavor to compass the general happiness, it has discovered the paths to that goal which may most successfully be followed. Thus, one may distrust Utopian schemes, recognizing the significance of custom, law, traditional moral maxims, and public opinion, and yet remain a utilitarian.

But he who does this must still answer the preceding objections. He must prove: (1) That pleasure is the only thing ultimately desirable; (2) that each is under obligation to promote the pleasure of all; (3) that its mere conduciveness to the production of a preponderance of pleasure makes an action right, even though the pleasure be a malicious one, as in the illustration above given.

Still, his doctrine has become less startling, and he has moved in the direction of a greater harmony with the moral judgments of men generally. The conduct he recommends need not, as a rule, differ greatly from that recognized as right by moralists of quite different schools.

Such a utilitarian may easily pass over to a form of doctrine which is not utilitarian at all. Thus, Sidgwick asks whether there is a measurable quality of feeling expressed by the word "pleasure," which is independent of its relation to volition, and strictly undefinable from its simplicity—"like the quality of feeling expressed by 'sweet,' of which also we are conscious in varying degrees of intensity;" and he answers: "For my own part, when the term (pleasure) is used in the more extended sense which I have adopted, to include the most refined and subtle intellectual and emotional gratifications, no less than the coarser and more definite sensual enjoyments, I can find no common quality in the feelings so designated except some relation to desire or volition." [160]

When we seek, then, to "give pleasure," are we doing nothing else than giving recognition to the desire and will of our neighbor? What has become of the Greatest Happiness Principle? Has it not dissolved into the doctrine of the Real Social Will?

CHAPTER XXVI

NATURE, PERFECTION, SELF-REALIZATION

I. NATURE

115. HUMAN NATURE AS ACCEPTED STANDARD.—The three doctrines, that the norm of moral action is to follow nature, that it is to aim at the attainment of perfection, and that it is the realization of one's capabilities,

---

[160] *The Methods of Ethics*, Book II, chapter ii, Sec 2, 4th Edition.
SIDGWICK never appreciably modified this opinion, which is most clearly expressed in the Edition quoted.

have much in common. They may conveniently be treated in the same chapter.

Early in the history of the ethics we find the moralist preaching that it is the duty of man to follow nature, and branding vice as unnatural and, hence, to be abhorred.

The word "nature," thus used, has had a fluctuating meaning. Sometimes the thought has been predominantly of human nature, and sometimes the appeal has been to nature in a wider sense.

Aristotle, who finds the "good" of man in happiness or "well-being," points out that this is something relative to man's nature. The well- being of a man he conceives as, in large part, "well-doing," and well- doing he defines as performing the proper functions of a man. [161] If we ask him what is proper or natural to man, he refers us to what man, when fully developed, becomes: "What every being is in its completed state, that certainly is the nature of that thing, whether it be a man, a house, or a horse." [162] He conceives man's nature, thus, as that which it is in man to become. Toward this end man strives; and it is this which furnishes him with the law of his action.

But, it may be asked, how shall this end be defined in detail? Individual men, who arrive at mature years, are by no means alike. Some we approve; some we disapprove. We evidently appeal to a standard by which the individual is judged. The appeal to the nature of man helps us little unless we can agree upon what we may accept as a just revelation of that nature— a pattern of some sort, divergence from which may be called unnatural, and is to be reprobated.

Neither Aristotle, nor those who, after him, took human nature as the moral norm, were without some conception of such a pattern. They kept in view certain things that men may become rather than certain others. They accepted as their standard a type of human nature which tends, on the whole, to realize itself more and more in the course of development of human communities. But as different human societies differ more or less in the characteristics which they tend to transmit to their members, in the kind of man whom they tend to form, we find the ideal of human nature, with which we are presented, somewhat vague and fluctuating. Different traits are dwelt upon by different moralists. Still, the appeals to human nature have a good deal in common; upon man's rational and social qualities especial stress is apt to be laid.

---

[161] *Nichomachean Ethics*, Book I, chapters iv, vii, viii.
[162] *Politics*, i, 2.

116. HUMAN NATURE AND THE LAW OF NATURE.—"Every nature," said Marcus Aurelius, [163] "is contented with itself when it goes on its way well; and a rational nature goes on its way well, when in its thoughts it assents to nothing false or uncertain, and when it directs its movements to social acts only, and when it confines its desires and aversions to the things which are in its power, and when it is satisfied with everything that is assigned to it by the common Nature."

In the last clause the Stoic turns from the contemplation of man's nature, taken by itself, and dwells upon the nature of the universe, which he conceives to be controlled by reason. He thus gains an added argument for the obligations laid upon man by his own nature. He writes:

"Every instrument, tool, vessel, if it does that for which it has been made, is well, and yet he who made it is not there. But in the things which are held together by Nature there is within and there abides in them the power which made them; wherefore the more is it fit to reverence this power, and to think that, if thou dost live and act according to its will, everything in thee is in conformity to intelligence." [164]

The law of man's nature is, thus, regarded as a part of the law of Nature—"We are all working together to one end, some with knowledge and design, and others without knowing what they do." [165] And, this being the case, man may take pattern, when he is inclined to fall below the standard of duty appropriate to him, by considering humbler creatures: "Dost thou not see the little plants, the little birds, the ants, the spiders, the bees working together to put in order their several parts of the universe? And art thou unwilling to do the work of a human being? And dost thou not make haste to do that which is according to thy nature?" [166] The delinquent is, hence, judged guilty, not merely of derogation from his high estate, but also of impiety. [167]

117. VAGUENESS OF THE LAW OF NATURE.—The question of the influence of religious belief upon a theory of morals I shall discuss elsewhere. [168] Here it is only necessary to point out that, if there is vagueness in the appeal to human nature, it can scarcely be dissipated satisfactorily by simply turning to Nature in a broader sense. Shall we, when in doubt as to human behavior, copy that of the brutes? The industry

---

[163] *Thoughts*, translated by George Long, viii, 7.
[164] *Ibid* vi, 40.
[165] *Ibid*, vi, 42.
[166] Ibid, v, 1.
[167] Ibid, ix, 1.
[168] See chapter xxxvi.

of some humble creatures it seems edifying to dwell upon; but from the fact that bees are stung to death by their sisters in the hive, or that the spider is given to devouring her mate, we can hardly draw a moral lesson for man.

The appeal to a Law of Nature so often made in the history of ethical speculation has furnished but a vague and elusive norm. He who makes it is apt to fall back upon the moral intuitions with which he is furnished, and to pack a greater or less number of them into his notion of Natural Law. [169]

In Cicero, Nature becomes fairly garrulous to man on all matters of deportment: "Let us follow Nature, and refrain from whatever lacks the approval of eye and ear. Let attitude, gait, mode of sitting, posture at table, countenance, eyes, movement of the hands, preserve the becomingness of which I speak." [170]

118. THE APPEAL TO NATURE AND INTUITIONISM.—The moralists who urge us to follow nature, whether human nature or Nature in a wider sense, we may, hence, regard as intuitionists of a sort. Those who emphasize human nature evidently depend upon their moral intuitions to give them information as to its characteristics. It is intuition that paints for them their pattern. They do not take man as they actually find him; they call for the suppression of some traits, and the exaggeration of others.

Nor are those who appeal to Nature in a wider sense less guided by moral intuitions. The appeal is never made without restrictions and limitations. No one dreams that the bird, the ant, the spider, the bee, can be regarded as satisfactory teachers of morals to human beings. Each may be occupied in putting in order its corner of the universe; but the order attained is not a human order, and there is in it much that is revolting to the moral judgments of mankind. Man must have a standard of his own. He listens to Nature only when she tells him what he already approves.

As a form of intuitionism the doctrine of following.. nature may be criticised in much the same way as other forms. One great merit it has. It calls attention to the fact that ethics is a discipline which has no significance abstracted from the nature of man. It appears absurd to say that man ought to do what it is not in man, under any conceivable circumstances, to do. And, like other forms of intuitionism, it has the merit

---

[169] See SIR HENRY MAINE'S fascinating chapters on the "Law of Nature," Ancient Law, chapters in and iv. The innumerable appeals to the Law of Nature contained in Grotius's famous work on the "Law of War and Peace" are very illuminating.

[170] De Officiis, i, 35, translated by Peabody.

of avoiding that short-circuiting which may easily prove seductive to the egoist or the utilitarian. He who accepts as his end either his own happiness or that of men generally may easily be induced to take short cuts to that end, and pay little attention to moral maxims as such. He may treat lightly that great system of rules and observances by which men are guided in their relations with one another, and which prevent human societies from relapsing into a chaos.

On the other hand, the follower of nature, like other intuitionists, may easily be thrown into perplexity by the fact that what seems to him natural, and, hence, right, may not be approved by other men. He cannot *prove* that he is right and they are wrong. He appears condemned to take refuge in subjective conviction, that is, in mere dogmatism.

II. PERFECTION

119. PERFECTION AND TYPE.—When we speak of a thing as more or less perfect, we commonly mean that it is more or less perfect in its kind. A good saw makes a poor razor; a good chair, a more than indifferent bed. A bee crushed by a blow, a bird with a broken wing, we regard as imperfect. But it scarcely occurs to us to ask ourselves whether the bee is more or less perfect than the bird, or the bird than the spider. Swift's Houyhnhnms at their best could not be either perfect horses or perfect men. They were creatures with a perfection of their own, and one appropriate to their hybrid nature.

To every creature its own perfection. This principle men seem to assume tacitly in their judgments. They set up a standard for each kind, and they conceive the individual to attain or to fall short, according to the degree of its approach to, or of its divergence from, the allotted standard.

If we take perfection in this sense—and we usually have no other sense in mind in our judgments of perfection—the doctrine that it is the whole duty of man to strive to attain to perfection is none other than the doctrine that it is his duty to follow nature, his proper nature as man. And any difficulties which may legitimately be urged upon the attention of the moralist who recommends the following of nature may with equal justice be urged upon the attention of him who exhorts us to aim at perfection.

Thus, if it is doubtful just what nature demands of us, it seems no less doubtful what obligations are laid upon us when we make perfection our goal. That goal cannot mean for each man simply the developing to the utmost of all the capacities which he possesses. There are men rich in the possibilities of sloth, of indifference to future good, of egoism, even of malignant feeling. Nor does the average man furnish the pattern of perfection. The perfectionist does not regard the average man as the embodiment of his ideal. He seeks to better him.

That, in striving to attain perfection, a man should remain a man, with essentially human characteristics, seems evident. But what sort of a man he should be is not as clear. Until we are in a position to give some reasoned account of what we mean by perfection as an ideal, and to show that it is a desirable goal for man, we appear to be setting up but a vague end for human endeavor, and to be assuming intuitively that it is a desirable end.

120. MORE AND LESS PERFECT TYPES.—So much for perfection as synonymous with the ideal human nature of which ancient and modern moralists have treated. It appears, however, possible to use the word "perfection" in a somewhat different sense.

Man is not merely man; he is a living being, and there are living beings of many orders. The plants, the simpler forms of animal life, the brutes which we recognize as standing nearer to us, and man may, from this point of view, be referred to the one series. Some members of this series we characterize as lower, and others we speak of as higher in the scale.

Now, such designations as higher and lower cannot be applied indiscriminately. There is little sense in the assertion that a bit of string is higher than a straight line, or a hat than a handkerchief. Some significant basis of comparison must be present. Things must be recognized as approximating to or diverging from an accepted standard in varying degrees.

Such a basis of comparison is present when some objects possess the same qualities in a more marked degree than do others. But this is not the only possible basis of comparison. We may assume that the possession of certain qualities marks a creature as higher, and that the creature which has them not, or has them imperfectly developed, thereby stamps itself as being of a lower order.

Something like this appears to determine our judgments when we assign to various creatures their place in the scale of living beings. We do not mean that the higher possess to a greater degree all the capacities possessed by the lower. Many things which the plant does man cannot do at all; and, among the animals, those which we recognize as higher may be lacking in many capacities present in a marked degree in the lower. In ranking one living creature as higher, and, thus, as more perfect, than another, we assume that the "nature" of the one, with its various capacities and lacks of capacity, is, on the whole, of more *worth* than the "nature" of another.

It might be maintained that, in his estimate of the worth of different kinds of beings man is influenced by his partiality for the distinctively human, rating creatures as lower or higher in proportion to their divergence from or approximation to his own type. Undoubtedly this plays a part in men's judgments. We are partial to ourselves. And yet judgments of perfection and imperfection cannot wholly be explained on this principle.

"I think we must admit without proof," writes Professor Janet, [171] a brilliant apostle of the doctrine of perfection, "that things are good, even independently of the pleasure which they give us, in themselves and by themselves, because of their intrinsic excellence. If anyone were to demand that I should prove that thought is worth more than digestion, a tree more than a heap of stones, liberty than slavery, maternal love than luxury, I could only reply by asking him to demonstrate that the whole is greater than one of its parts. No sensible person denies that, in passing from the mineral kingdom to the vegetable kingdom, from this to the animal kingdom, from the animal to man, from the savage to the enlightened citizen of a free country, Nature has made a continual advance; that is to say, at each step has gained in excellence and perfection."

One is naturally impelled to ask from what point of view things so disparate as the mineral, the plant, the brute, man, thought and digestion, liberty and slavery, can be compared with one another at all, and referred to any sort of a series. What is, in its essence, this excellence or perfection of which we have more shining evidence as we go up in the scale? Janet identifies it with intensity of being, with activity. The greater the activity, the greater the perfection.

To the identification of perfection and activity we may hesitate to assent. It does not seem clear that there is greater activity manifested in a snail than in a burning house, in maternal love than in furious hate, in quiet thought than in passion. Yet it seems significant that judgments of worth do not appear out of place in comparing such things.

121. PERFECTIONISM AND INTUITIONISM.—Taking into consideration all that is said above, it seems not unreasonable to conclude:

(1) That in speaking of the perfection of any creature we very often judge it

---

[171] The Theory of Morals, Book I, chapter iii, English translation, New York, 1883, p. 48.

only by the standard set by its own type. We regard it as a good specimen of its kind.

(2) But when we use perfection in a wider sense, we judge different types after the standard furnished by the distinctively human.

(3) And we take as our standard of the human the "pattern" man held in view by those who urge us to follow nature.

But why should this pattern man be assumed to be better or worthier than a man of a different sort? He who finds in him a greater exhibition of activity may with equal justice address to himself the question: Why is activity, in itself, of value? The one question, like the other, looks for its answer in the dictum of some intuition. What may be said for, and what against, intuitions, we have already considered. [172]

III. SELF-REALIZATION

122. THE SELF-REALIZATION DOCTRINE.—The ethical school which makes the realization of the capacities of the self the aim of moral action has for a generation, especially in England and America, had the support of many acute and scholarly minds. The doctrine, often spoken of as the Neo-Kantian or the Neo-Hegelian, may be said to be influenced by Kant, so far as concerns metaphysical theory, but its ethical character is more properly Hegelian and suggests in many particulars that great German philosopher's "Philosophy of Right."

We may conveniently take as the protagonist of the school the Oxford scholar, Thomas Hill Green, whose "Prolegomena to Ethics" has had, directly and indirectly, a powerful influence upon the minds of the men of our generation.

We find the doctrine of self-realization, as set forth by Green, to be as follows:

(1) In all desire some object is presented to the mind as not yet real, and there is a striving to make it real, and thus to satisfy, or extinguish, the desire. [173]

(2) Self-consciousness knits the desires into a system, and thus attains to

---

[172] See chapter xxiii

[173] Prolegomena to Ethics, Sec 131.

the conception of "well-being," which implies the satisfaction of desire in general, and not merely of this or that desire. [174]

(3) "Good" is that which satisfies some desire. Any good at which an agent aims must be his own good; and "true good" is nothing else than "permanent well-being." [175]

(4) A desire is determined by the nature of the creature desiring; man can attain satisfaction only in the realization of his capacities. His true good lies only in their complete realization—in his becoming all that it is in him to become. [176]

(5) But man is a social being, and has an interest in other persons than himself. Hence his complete self-satisfaction implies the satisfaction of his social as well as of his other impulses. That is, his true good includes the good of others. [177]

(6) We can only discover what our "capacities" are by observing them as so far realized, and thus gaining the idea of future progress. The ultimate end is unknown to us. [178]

(7) But we see enough to recognize that man's capacities can be realized, his self-satisfaction intelligently sought, only in a social state based upon the notion of the common good. The right reveals itself in the actual evolution of society. [179]

123. THE DOCTRINE AKIN TO THAT OF FOLLOWING NATURE.—The self- realization doctrine has much in common with the doctrine of following nature. Thus:

1. It evidently does not recommend the realization of all the capacities of the individual as such, but holds in view a "pattern" man.

2. This is social man, the true representative of human nature as conceived by the ancient Stoic. Green holds before himself "the ideal of a society in which everyone shall treat everyone else as his neighbor, in which to every rational agent the well-being or perfection of every other such agent shall

[174] Prolegomena to Ethics, Sec 128.

[175] Prolegomena to Ethics, Sec Sec 190, 92, 203.

[176] Prolegomena to Ethics, Sec Sec 171-2, 180.

[177] Prolegomena to Ethics, Sec Sec 199- 205.

[178] Prolegomena to Ethics, Sec 172.

[179] Ibid., Sec Sec 172-76, 205.]

be included in that perfection for which he lives." [180] The same thought was more pithily expressed by Marcus Aurelius in the aphorism that "what is good for the hive is good for the bee."

3. We find, too, the analogue of that wider appeal to nature which suffused the Stoic doctrine with religious feeling. In the above brief recapitulation of the steps in the self-realization doctrine I have omitted this aspect, as I wished to confine myself to the ethical doctrine pure and simple. But Green conceives of the Divine Consciousness as already having before it the consummation toward which man strives in his efforts at self-realization; he regards man as working toward the attainment of a Divine Purpose. The self-realizationist may prefer, sometimes, to use language more abstract. He may say: "Man's consciousness of himself as a member of society involves a reference to a cosmic order." [181] But the difference of language scarcely carries with it a substantial difference of thought. [182]

4. As the appeal to human nature, or to nature in a broader sense, left the norm for the guidance of human actions somewhat vague, so the appeal to the principle of self-realization seems to leave one without very definite guidance. There may easily arise disputes touching what capacities are to be realized, and in what degree.

124. IS THE DOCTRINE MORE EGOISTIC?—One difference between the principles of following nature, striving to attain to perfection, and aiming at self-realization seems to force itself upon our notice. On the surface, at least, the last doctrine appears to stand out as more distinctly egoistic. The very name has an egoistic flavor; the doctrine bases itself upon the satisfaction of desire; nor do its advocates hesitate to emphasize that the satisfaction sought is the satisfaction of the agent desiring. In the chapter on Egoism [183] I have cited some utterances which sound egoistic, and such citations might be multiplied.

Nevertheless, from this egoistic root springs a flower which disseminates the perfume of a saintly self-abnegation. How is this seeming miracle accomplished?

---

[180] Prolegomena to Ethics, Sec 205.
[181] MUIRHEAD, The Elements of Ethics, Book I, chapter in, Sec 10.
[182] Though the philosopher as such may shun the term 'God' on account of its anthropomorphic associations, and may prefer to speak of the 'conscious principle,' or of the 'universal self,' yet the latter has in substance the same meaning as the former." FITE, *An Introductory Study of Ethics*, chapter xiii, Sec 4.
[183] Chapter xxiv

The transition is brought about through a chain of reasoning which is subtle and ingenious in the extreme. Must we not admit that in all purposive action—the only action with which the moralist need concern himself—there is a striving to realize or satisfy desire in the attainment of some object? And if the desires of a mind or self converge upon some object, does not its realization imply the satisfaction or realization of the desires of that mind or self? Furthermore, if our desires have as their root our capacities—for we can desire nothing that it is not in us to desire—is not the realization of desire the realization of capacity? Does it not follow, hence, that every mind or self, in all purposive action, is striving, either blunderingly or with far-sighted intelligence, to attain to self-satisfaction, which means, to the realization of its capacities? Finally, as men are by nature social creatures, how can a man fully realize his capacities without becoming a truly unselfish being? Unselfishness appears to be the inevitable goal of the strivings for self-satisfaction of an unselfish self.

125. WHY AIM TO REALIZE CAPACITIES?—This reasoning appears highly satisfactory in two very different ways. It seems, on the one hand, to stop the mouth of the egoist, who insists that his own advantage is his only proper aim. It assures him that he is throughout seeking his own advantage, when he aims at self-realization. On the other hand, it assures the man to whom egoism appears repellant and immoral, that self-realization implies that one must love one's neighbor as oneself. The immemorial quarrel between self-love and benevolence appears to be adjusted to the mutual satisfaction of both parties.

Is the reasoning unassailable? There are two steps in it which appear to demand a closer scrutiny. One is the transition from desire to capacity; the other, the assumption that he who follows an unselfish impulse may properly be said to aim at self-satisfaction, and to exercise no self- denial.

As to the first. Our desires may have their roots in our capacities, but desires and capacities are, nevertheless, not the same thing.

Men do actually strive to realize their desires—a desire is nothing else than such a striving for realization or satisfaction. But it cannot be said that men generally strive to realize their capacities, except to the limited degree in which their capacities may happen to be expressed in actual desires. Capacities may lie dormant, and the man in whom they lie dormant need not on that account feel dissatisfied, as does the man whose desires are not realized. Self-realization, as understood by the school of thinkers which advocates it, implies much more than the satisfaction of desire. It implies the multiplication of desires and their satisfaction. On what ground shall we persuade the contented egoist, who has but a handful of commonplace desires and finds it possible to satisfy most of them, that it is better to call into being a multitude of wants many of which will probably remain unrealized? He may point out that the divine discontent is apt to leave the idealist and the reformer as lean as Cassius. All of which does not prove that the self-realizationist is not right in exhorting men to develop their capacities in the direction of the pattern which he holds in view; but it does seem to prove that the path to self-realization, in this sense, is not necessarily the path to self-satisfaction. "The good" has come to mean more than that which satisfies desire. How shall we persuade men that it is their duty to make this good their end?

126. THE PROBLEM OF SELF-SACRIFICE.—As for the second point. He who makes his moral aim self-satisfaction can scarcely be expected to advocate self-sacrifice.

Accordingly, we find among self-realizationists, a tendency to repudiate altogether what may properly be called self-denial. "Anything conceived as good in such a way that the agent acts for the sake of it," said Green, [184] "must be conceived as his own good." "A moment's consideration will show," writes Professor Fite, in his clear and attractive book, [185] "that, for self-sacrifice in any absolute sense, no ground of obligation is conceivable. Unless I am in some way interested in the object [186] whose attainment is set before me as a duty, it seems to be psychologically impossible that I should ever strive for it."

Now we do seem compelled to concede that, unless a man desires an end, he cannot will that end. Anything that is selected as an end, and striven for, must be desired. And the attainment of the end implies, of course, the satisfaction of that particular desire. But, admitting all this, is not the question left open whether some desires may not be sacrificed to others; and whether, indeed, a whole extensive system of desires may not, on occasion, be sacrificed to a single desire? In this case, may not the transaction properly be called self-sacrifice? Suppose the desire to serve one's neighbor, if satisfied, prevents the realization of a multitude of other desires of the same agent. Is it certain that its satisfaction does not imply self-denial?

127. SELF-SATISFACTION AND SELF-SACRIFICE.—The argument to prove that it is not really self-sacrifice may follow divers paths.

Thus, it may be argued that, since the proper end of a rational being is his own permanent good, the sacrifice of such goods as do not conduce to this end is not self-sacrifice. Sensual pleasures, the satisfaction of vanity or

---

[184] Prolegomena, Sec 92.
[185] An Introductory Study of Ethics, chapter viii, Sec 5.
[186] I.e., unless I desire the object.

ambition, the accomplishment of a vengeful purpose, an excessive preoccupation with one's own interests as contrasted with those of others— such things as these, it is claimed, do not permanently satisfy. That the so-called man of pleasure is a man upon whom pleasures pall, and that he who seeks too earnestly to save his own life is apt to lose it, has been reiterated by a long line of professional and lay moralists from Buddha to Tolstoi. The refuge from the discontent arising out of the attempt to quench one's thirst by sipping at transient delights has always been found in altruism under some guise. The self- realizationists may claim that certain things are given up in order that other things more permanently satisfying to the self may be attained, and may deny that this is any renunciation of self-satisfaction. [187]

Again. It may be argued that men's interests do not conflict as widely as is commonly supposed. To be sure, two men may have to struggle with each other for the pleasure of eating a given apple, of making a pecuniary profit, of obtaining a coveted post, of being the first authority in a given science or art, of securing the affections of a particular woman. Here one man's loss seems to be another man's gain. But two men may enjoy seeing a child eat an apple, or a deserving man profit, or their common candidate win the election, or their favorite artist honored, or their beloved nephew accepted by the lady of his choice. If one desires certain things, and certain things only, there seems no reason why one's desires should not be in harmony with those of others.

The things best worth having, it is claimed, do not admit of being competed for. [188] If my aim is unselfish devotion to humanity, how can I lose if my neighbor attains in the same running? Do virtuous men, in so far as they are virtuous, stand in each other's light? Are there not as many prizes as there are competitors? As long as I remain in this field I may seek self-satisfaction without scruple. I satisfy another's desire in satisfying my own. By benevolence I lose nothing.

The list of things which one may forego without self-sacrifice has been made a long one. Even the realization of capacities highly valued by cultivated men has been brought into it:

"No conflict," writes Professor Seth, [189] "is possible between the ends of the individual and those of society. The individual may be called upon to sacrifice, for example, his opportunity of esthetic or intellectual culture;

---

[187] GREEN, op. cit., Sec 176.

[188] GREEN, *Prolegomena to Ethics*, Sec Sec 244- 245.

[189] *A Study of Ethical Principles*, Part II, chapter ii, Sec 4, Edinburgh, 1911, p. 286.

but in that very sacrifice lies his opportunity of moral culture, of true self-realization."

128. CAN MORAL SELF-SACRIFICE BE A DUTY?—To this position one is tempted to demur until two questions have found a satisfactory answer:

1. Is it true that there is no sacrifice of self-realization or self- satisfaction, properly so called, where all other desires and impulses are sacrificed to the one desire to do right?

2. Is it not conceivable, at least, that obedience to an unselfish impulse may result even in the sacrifice of the opportunities of moral culture in general? Can it, then, be called self-realization?

Touching the first question it may plausibly be maintained that the desires of the self are many and various, and that the satisfaction of an altruistic impulse may imply the sacrifice of so many of them that the self may very doubtfully be said to attain to permanent satisfaction when the impulse is realized. Aristotle's hero, who, in dying for his country, chooses the more "honorable" for himself, [190] can hardly be said in that one act to have accomplished a state of permanent satisfaction or well-being for the self whose being was, in that act, brought to an abrupt termination. Certain Stoics seem to have taught that virtue is its own adequate reward and that nothing else matters; but this has not been the verdict of moralists generally. Paley, who writes like an unblushing egoist, [191] we may pass over; but even Kant, a thinker of a very different complexion, appears to regard the mere doing of a right act as not a sufficient reward for the doer. He looks for the act to be crowned with happiness in a life to come, thus saving it from being mere self- sacrifice.

The second question one approaches with some hesitation. "No moralist," writes Professor Sidgwick, [192] "has ever directed an individual to promote the virtue of others except in so far as this promotion is compatible with, or rather involved in, the complete realization of virtue in himself." It appears rash to admit to be a duty that which as high an authority as Sidgwick maintains no moralist has ever ventured to advise. Still, it is permissible to adduce an illustration taken from actual life, and to ask the reader to form his opinion independently.

A girl, anxious to provide her younger sister with a better lot, enters a factory and gives up her life to labor of a monotonous and mind-

---

[190] *Ethics*, Book IX, chapter viii, Sec 12.
[191] See Sec 96.
[192] *The Methods of Ethics*, Introduction.

destroying character, amid sordid and more or less degrading surroundings. The act is a heroic one, but is it clear that it conduces to the self-realization, not of the sister, but of the agent herself? The influence of surroundings counts for much. High impulses may, under such pressure, come to be repressed.

"Capacity for the nobler feelings," writes Mill, [193] "is in most natures a very tender plant, easily killed, not only by hostile influences, but by mere want of sustenance; and in the majority of young persons it speedily dies away if the occupations to which their position in life has devoted them, and the society into which it has thrown them, are not favorable to keeping that higher capacity in exercise. Men lose their high aspirations as they lose their intellectual tastes, because they have not time or opportunity for indulging them; and they addict themselves to inferior pleasures, not because they deliberately prefer them, but because they are either the only ones to which they have access, or the only ones they are any longer capable of enjoying."

In other words, one may put oneself into a situation in which self-realization appears to be made a most difficult and problematic goal. Nor does it seem inconceivable that one should do this for the sake of another's good. Hence, even if we restrict the meaning of the word "self- sacrifice" to the sacrifice of the "real" or moral self, the impossibility of self-sacrifice scarcely appears to have been proved; the impossibility of a conflict between the ends of the individual and of society does not appear to be indubitably established.

129. SELF-SACRIFICE AND THE IDENTITY OF SELVES.—Can it be maintained upon any other grounds than those adduced above? One line of argument remains open to us. We may maintain that, while two bodies are two because they occupy two portions of space, two minds, as not in space, cannot thus be held apart, and we may conclude that "the many individuals composing the race are not really many, but one." [194] I suppose that he who can take this position will find it natural to argue that any act which serves the interests of any self must be regarded as serving the interests of every self, and thus cannot be considered as sacrificing the interests of any self.

To these transcendental heights, however, comparatively few will be able to climb. To men generally it will still appear that Peter's love to Paul is not identical with Peter's love to Peter; and that Peter may act in such a way that, on the whole, he loses, while Paul gains. That the interests of Peter

---

[193] *Utilitarianism*, chapter iii.
[194] Fite, *An Introductory Study of Ethics*, chapter xii.

and Paul, as developed social beings and members of a civilized community, are less likely to be in conflict than those of their primitive cave-dwelling forerunners may be freely conceded. But from such relative harmony to a complete identity of interests seems a far cry.

130. QUESTIONS WHICH SEEM TO BE LEFT OPEN.—Evidently, the self-realization doctrine is a great advance upon the doctrine of following nature. The self-realizationist realizes that man's nature is in the making, and he is not blind to the difficulty of the task of determining just what the real demands of human nature are.

This leads to his laying much stress upon the gradual development of systems of rights and duties as they emerge under the actual conditions to which human societies are subjected in the course of their evolution. He reads history with comprehending eyes, and reverences the human reason as crystallized in social institutions. Hence, the divergence of the moral standards which obtain in different ages and among different peoples does not seem to him a baffling mystery. He can find a relative justification for each, and yet hold to an ideal in the light of which each must be judged.

It may be questioned, however, whether the edifice which he erects can be based wholly upon the appeal to the self which ostensibly furnishes the groundwork of the doctrine. We may ask whether such an appeal can:

(1) Prescribe to the individual in what measure his various capacities should be realized.

(2) Show that it is reasonable to awaken dormant capacities, and thus multiply desires.

(3) Justify social acts which certainly appear to be self-sacrificing, and which the moral judgments of men generally do not hesitate to approve.

CHAPTER XXVII

THE ETHICS OF EVOLUTION

131. THE SIGNIFICANCE OF THE TITLE.—The title, "The Ethics of Evolution," seems to assume that the evolutionist, frankly accepting

himself as such, must be prepared to join some school of the moralists different from other schools, and basing itself upon evolutionary doctrine.

That the ethical views of individuals and of communities of men may undergo a process of evolution or development is palpable. The ethical notions of the child are not those of the man, nor are the moral ideas of primitive races identical with those of races more advanced intellectually and morally.

But it is one thing to maintain that morals may be in evolution in individuals and in communities, and quite another to hold that the acceptance of the doctrine of evolution, broadly taken, forces upon one some new norm by which human actions may be judged. It was possible for as ardent an evolutionist as Huxley to hold that evolution and ethics are not merely independent, but are actually at war with one another, the competitive struggle for existence characteristic of the one giving place in the other to a new principle in which the rights of the weak and the helpless attain express recognition. [195] And Sidgwick, that clearest of thinkers, maintains [196] that we have no reason to assume that it is our duty as moral beings simply to accelerate the pace in the direction already marked out by evolution.

It should be remembered that the word evolution may be used equivocally. It is not evident that all evolution is in the direction of a life, brute or human, that we commonly recognize as higher. There is retrogression, as well as progress, where such retrogression is favored by environment. We may call this, if we please, *devolution*. Were the conditions of his life very unfavorable, man could not live as he now lives; and, indeed, were they sufficiently unfavorable—for example, if the earth cooled off to a certain point—he could not live at all, but would have to give place to a lowlier creature better fitted to the conditions. Must the man who foresees this end approaching strive to hasten its arrival, or should he oppose it? In a decadent society, to come nearer to the problems which concern us in ethics, must a man strive to realize the social will expressed in progressive decadence? Should he hasten the decline of the community?

That those who study man as a moral being, like those who study man in any of his other aspects, will be more or less influenced in their outlook by the broadening of the horizon which results from a study of what the students of the evolutionary process have to tell us, may be conceded. But when we admit this, we do not necessarily have to look for a new norm by

---

[195] HUXLEY, *Evolution and Ethics*, New York, 1894. See, especially, the *Prolegomena*.
[196] *The Methods of Ethics*, Book I, chapter vi, Sec 2.

which to judge conduct. We seem, rather, forced to ask ourselves how this broadening of the horizon affects the norms which have heretofore appealed to men as reasonable. To be sure, any evolutionist has, in the capacity of a moralist, the right to suggest a new norm. But, in that case, he must, like any other moralist, convince us that it is a reasonable one.

132. EVOLUTION AND THE SCHOOLS OF THE MORALISTS.—Those who have suggested the norms discussed above, no one would think of as greatly influenced in their ethical teaching by the doctrine of evolution. Locke, Price, Butler and Sidgwick; Aristippus and Epicurus; Paley and Hobbes; Bentham and Mill; Epictetus and Marcus Aurelius; Janet, Green, and the rest, no one would be inclined to class simply as evolutionary moralists. Some of them never thought of evolution at all. How would it affect their standards of right and wrong were evolution expressly taken into account? Would the standards have to be abandoned? Or would the men, as broader men, merely have to revise some of their moral judgments?

(1) It might be supposed that the acceptance of evolutionary doctrine would bring into being a grave problem for the intuitionist, at least. If the body and mind of man are products of evolution, must we not admit as much of man's moral intuitions? Then why not admit that these may be replaced some day by other moral intuitions to be evolved in an unknown future?

He who reasons thus should bear in mind that Sidgwick, who by no means repudiated the doctrine of evolution, was an intuitionist, and placed his ultimate moral intuitions on a par with such mathematical intuitions as that two and two make four. If all intuitions are a product of evolution, Sidgwick might claim that the moral intuitions he accepts fare no worse than those elementary mathematical truths which we accept without question and without reflection. And he might maintain that an appeal to evolution need cast no greater doubt upon ultimate moral truth than upon mathematical. If intuitionism in all its forms is to be rejected, it seems as though it must be done upon some other ground than an appeal to evolution.

(2) As to the egoist. It is not easy to see how the appeal to evolution need disconcert him. Should he be so foolish as to maintain that egoism is always, in fact, necessary and unavoidable on the part of every living creature, he might easily be refuted by a reference to the actual life of the brutes, where altruism can be shown to play no insignificant role. But if he simply maintains that the only *reasonable* principle for a man to adopt is egoism, he may continue to do so. He makes the self and its satisfactions his end. How can it concern him to learn how the self came to be what it is, or what it will be in the distant future? He panders to the present self; he

may assume that it will be reasonable to pander at the appropriate time to the self that is to be, whatever its nature.

(3) The utilitarian remains such whether he makes the greatest good of the greatest number to consist in pleasure or in some other end, such as self-preservation. Some utilitarians, who have been inclined to emphasize the good of man, rather than to extend even to the brutes the goods to be distributed, may be influenced to extend the sphere of duties, if they will listen to the evolutionist, who cannot well leave out of view humbler creatures. [197]

He may broaden his sympathies. But this need not compel him to abandon his fundamental doctrine.

(4) A very similar conclusion may be drawn, when we consider the influence of an acceptance of the doctrine of evolution upon those who would turn to man's nature, to perfection, or to self-realization, as furnishing the norm of human conduct.

A Marcus Aurelius could, with little reference to evolution, accept man's nature, or Nature in the wider sense, as marking out for man the round of his duties. A modern Darwinian might fall back upon much the same standard, while clearly conscious of the fact that man's nature is not something unchangeable, and while inclined to view Nature in general with different eyes from those of the Roman Stoic. No sensible evolutionist would maintain that a creature of a given species should act in defiance of all the instincts of creatures of that type, merely on the ground that species may be involved in a process of progressive development.

Nor need the perfectionist abandon his perfectionism in view of any such consideration. He who measures perfection by the degree of activity exercised in action, may admit that the coming man will be more perfect than it is possible for any man to be now; but that need not prevent him from holding that it is man's present duty to aim at the only perfection possible to him, he being what he is. Similar reasoning will apply to any other conception of perfection likely to be adopted, consciously or unconsciously, by any adherent of the school in question.

---

[197] "Thus we shall not go wrong in attributing to the higher animals in their simple social life, not only the elementary feelings, the loves and hates, sympathies and jealousies which underlie all forms of society, but also in a rudimentary stage the intelligence which enables those feelings to direct the operations of the animal so as best to gratify them." HOBHOUSE, *Ethics in Evolution*, chapter i, Sec 4.

As for the self-realizationist, a very little reflection seems sufficient to reveal that the maxim that it is man's duty to become all that it is in him to become is in no wise refuted by the claim that man may, in the indefinitely distant future, become much more than many people have supposed or now suppose.

(5) There remains the doctrine of the Rational Social Will as furnishing the norm of conduct. I have tried to show that this doctrine must rest upon broad views of man and of man's environment. It is the very essence of the rational will to take broad views, to consider the past, the present, and the future. Surely the adherent of this school may let the evolutionist work in peace, may thank him for any helpful suggestions he has to offer, and may develop his own doctrine with little cause for uneasiness at the thought that information given him may refute his fundamental principle.

However, it is not out of place for him to point out, if revolutionary measures of any sort are suggested by this or that evolutionist, that ethics is a discipline which is concerned with what men have to do, here and now. It must take into consideration what is advisable and feasible. Utopian schemes which break violently with the actual order of things and the normal development of human societies may be suggested by evolutionists, as they have been suggested by men who were not evolutionists at all. They are not to be taken much more seriously in the one case than in the other.

133. THE ETHICS OF INDIVIDUAL EVOLUTIONISTS.—Such considerations seem to make it evident that the acceptance of the doctrine of evolution should have no other influence upon us as moralists than that of making us take broad views of man and of his environment. It still remains to find a norm of conduct, and evolutionists, like other men, may develop ethical systems which are not identical. It is worth while here to touch very briefly upon the suggestions of one or two individual evolutionists. Those who speak of the ethics of evolution are very apt to have such in mind.

Thus, Darwin, whose study of the lower animals led him to believe that the social instincts have been developed for the general good rather than for the general happiness of the species, defines the "good" as "the rearing of the greatest number of individuals in full vigor and health, with all their faculties perfect, under the conditions to which they have been subjected." The "greatest happiness principle" he regards as an important secondary guide to conduct, while making social instinct and sympathy primary guides. [198]

---

[198] *The Descent of Man*, chapter iv, concluding remarks.

Spencer maintains that the evolution of conduct becomes the highest possible when the conduct "simultaneously achieves the greatest totality of life in self, in offspring, and in fellow-men." "The conduct called good," he writes, "rises to the conduct conceived as best, when it fulfills all three classes of ends at the same time." But life he does not regard as necessarily a good. He judges it to be good or bad "according as it has or has not a surplus of agreeable feeling." Hence, "conduct is good or bad according as its total effects are pleasurable or painful." [199]

To be sure, Spencer criticises the utilitarians, and thinks little of the Benthamic calculus of pleasures. He believes that we should substitute for it something more scientific, a study of the processes of life. In his earlier writings he appears to be largely in accord with the intuitionists in judging of conduct, regarding intuitions as having their origin in the experiences of the race. Nor does he ever seem inclined to break with intuitionism completely. But, as we have seen above (Sec 108), there appears to be nothing to prevent a utilitarian from being an intuitionist of some sort, as well.

Stephen, in his clear and beautifully written work on morals, also accepts the general happiness as the ultimate end of reasonable conduct; and he, too, criticizes the current utilitarianism. He writes: "This, as it seems to me, represents the real difference between the utilitarian and the evolutionist criterion. The one lays down as a criterion the happiness, the other the health of society." [200] By which, of course, he does not mean merely physical health, but such a condition of vigor and efficiency as carries with it a promise of continued existence and well- being in the future.

It is not necessary to multiply instances. It can readily be seen that all three of the writers cited are utilitarians, and the last two are what have been characterized as hedonistic utilitarians. That they suggest this or that means of best attaining to the desired goal does not put them outside of a school which embraces men of many shades of opinion.

---

[199] *The Data of Ethics*, chapter in, Sec Sec 8 and 10.
[200] *The Science of Ethics*, London, 1882, chapter ix, 12.

CHAPTER XXVIII

PESSIMISM

134. THE PHILOSOPHY OF THE PESSIMIST.—With philosophy in general this volume has little to do; but as pessimism is not the doctrine of normal men generally, but is apt to be identified in our minds with the teachings of certain of its leading exponents, it may be well to give, in briefest outline, the type of reasonings upon which the pessimist may take his stand.

Schopenhauer held that the one World-Will, which manifests itself in all nature, inorganic and organic, and is identical with the will of which each man is conscious in himself, is a "will to live." When the World- Will becomes conscious, as it does in man, the will to live is consciously asserted. But the will to live is essentially blind and unreasoning, or it would not do anything so stupid as to will life of any sort. He writes:

"Only a blind will, no seeing will, could place itself in the position in which we behold ourselves. A seeing will would rather have soon made the calculation that the business did not cover the cost; for such a mighty effort and struggle, with the straining of all the powers, under constant care, anxiety and want, and with the inevitable destruction of every individual life, finds no compensation in the ephemeral existence itself, which is so obtained, and which passes into nothing in our hands." [201]

The basis of all will, says Schopenhauer, is need, deficiency, and, hence, pain. He dwells at length upon the misery of life, and the desirability of a release from life. The refuge of suicide at once suggests itself, but is rejected by Schopenhauer on the ground that the destruction of the individual cannot prevent the One Will from manifesting itself in other individuals. Curiously enough he appears to approve of suicide by starvation, as indicating a renunciation of the will to live. But his general recommendation is asceticism, renunciation of the striving for pleasure,

---

[201] *The World as Will and Idea*, translated by HALDANE and KEMP, London, 1896. *On the Vanity and Suffering of Life*. Volume III, p. 390.

the voluntary acceptance of pain. Through this the Will is to be taught to apprehend its own nature, and, thus, to deny itself. How a general asceticism on our part will rob the one universal Will, revealed in the mineral, vegetable and animal worlds, of its nature, and still its strivings, the great pessimist does not indicate.

At this point, von Hartmann, who may fairly be called Schopenhauer's pupil, takes up the tale. He suggests that it is conceivable that a universal negation of the will may be obtained, if the preponderating part of the actual World-Will should come to be contained in the conscious minds that resolve to will no more. This he thinks may neutralize the whole, and put an end to existence, which is unavoidably an evil, and implies a preponderance of pain. [202]

135. COMMENT ON THE ETHICS OF PESSIMISM.—On the metaphysics of the pessimists I shall make no comment save that there appears to be here sufficient vagueness to satisfy the most poetical of minds. But the following points in the ethics of pessimism should be noted:

(1) Pleasure and pain are made the measure of the desirability or undesirability of existence.

(2) It is assumed that pleasure and pain are measurable; and that they may be quantitatively balanced against one another in such a way that this or that mixture of them may be declared by an enlightened man to be, on the whole, desirable or the reverse.

(3) It is claimed that the balance must necessarily incline to the side of pain, and hence, that life is not worth living.

(4) It follows from all this that it is our duty to aim, not necessarily directly, but in some manner, at least, at the destruction of life everywhere.

(5) I beg the reader to observe that the above doctrine rests upon assumptions which seem to be made without due consideration. Thus:

(a) It is by no means to be assumed without question that pleasure and pain alone are the measure of the desirable. They are not the only things actually desired; and, if we assert that they alone are desirable, we fall back upon a dubious intuition.

---

[202] *Philosophy of the Unconscious*, "Metaphysic of the Unconscious," chapter xiv.

(6) The quantitative relations of pleasures and pains are legitimate subjects of dispute, as we have seen in earlier chapters in this volume. When is one pleasure twice as great as another? How can we know that three pleasures counterbalance a pain? Is it by the mere fact that we *will* as we do, in a given instance? Then how prove that we will as we do, because of the equivalence of the pleasure to the pain?

(c) Who shall decide for us whether life is—not desired, it is admittedly that, as a rule,—but, also, *desirable*?

May the man who denies it rest his assertion upon such general considerations as that satisfaction presupposes desire, and that desire implies a lack, and, hence, pain? The famous author of "Utopia" pointed out long ago that the pains of hunger begin before the pleasure of eating, and only die when it does. Shall we, then, regard a hearty appetite as a curse, to be mitigated but not wholly neutralized by a series of good dinners?

To be sure, the pessimists do not depend wholly upon such general arguments, but point out in great detail that there is much suffering in the world, and that the fulfillment of desire, when it is attained, often results in disillusionment. But the fact remains that life, such as it is, is desired by men and other creatures generally; desired not as an exception, and under a misapprehension, but, as a rule, even by the enlightened and the far-seeing.

Is not the desirable what is desired by the rational will? We have seen that the rational social will does not aim at the suppression of desires generally, but only at the suppression of such desires as interfere with broader satisfactions. Viewed from this stand-point, the pessimist's "denial of the will to live" appears as an expression of the accidental or irrational will. It is not an expression of the nature of man, but of the nature of the pessimist.

(6) It is, perhaps, worth while to point out that there is nothing to prevent a given pessimist from being an intuitionist, an egoist, a utilitarian (of a sort), or an adherent of one of the other schools above discussed. He may assume intuitively that life is undesirable; in view of its undesirability he may act, either taking himself alone into consideration, or including his neighbor; he may invoke the doctrine of evolution; he may even, if he chooses, call it self-realization to annihilate himself, for he may argue that a will that comes to clear consciousness must see that it must be its own undoing. It is hardly necessary to point out, however, that the pessimist, as such, should not be in any wise confounded with the moralists discussed in the five chapters preceding.

166

CHAPTER XXIX

KANT, HEGEL AND NIETZSCHE

136. KANT.—-It is impossible, in any brief compass, to treat of the many individual moralists, some of them men of genius and well worthy of our study, who offer us ethical systems characterized by differences of more or less importance. When we refer a man to this or that school and do no more, we say comparatively little about him, as has become evident in the preceding chapters. As we have seen, it has been necessary to class together those who differ rather widely in many of their opinions. Here, I shall devote a few pages to three men only, partly because of their prominence, and partly because it is instructive to call attention to the contrast between them in their fundamental positions. I shall begin with Kant.

Kant held that the human reason issues "categorial imperatives," that is to say, unconditional commands to act in certain ways. The motive for moral action must not be the desire for pleasure, but solely the desire to do right.

He makes his fundamental rule abstract and formal: "So act that you could wish your maxim to be universal law." As no man could wish to be himself neglected when in distress, this law compels him to be benevolent, and a new form of the fundamental rule is developed: "Treat humanity, in yourself or any other, as an end always, and never as a means." [203]

Now Kant, although he maintains that it is not a man's duty to seek his own happiness—a thing which natural inclination would prompt him to do— by no means overlooks happiness altogether. He thinks that virtue and happiness together constitute the whole and perfect good desired by rational beings. The attainment of this good must be the supreme end of a will morally determined. [204] We are morally bound to strive to be virtuous ourselves and to make others happy.

Still, each man's happiness means much to him; and Kant, convinced that virtue *ought* to be rewarded with happiness, holds that our world is a

---

[203] *Fundamental Principles of the Metaphysic of Morals*, Sec 2.
[204] *Dialectic of the Pure Practical Reason*, chapter ii.

moral world, where God will reward the virtuous. If we do not assume such a world, he claims, moral laws are reduced to idle dreams. [205]

Such utterances as the last may well lead the utilitarian to question whether Kant was quite whole-hearted in his doctrine of the unconditional commands of the practical reason of man. They appear to be not independent of all consideration of human happiness.

I shall not ask whether Kant was consistent. Great men, like lesser men, seldom are. But, in order that the contrast between his doctrine and those of the two writers whom I shall next discuss may be brought out clearly, I shall ask that the following points be kept well in mind:

(1) Kant was an out-and-out intuitionist. He goes directly to the practical reason of man for an enunciation of the moral law.

(2) Moral rules of lesser generality, such as those touching benevolence, justice and veracity, he traces to the practical reason, making them independent of all considerations of expediency. Thus he defends the body of moral truth accepted by so many of his fellow-moralists.

(3) His "practical reason" speaks directly to the individual. Kant looked within, not without. We may call him an ethical individualist. Socrates, when on trial for his life, listened for the voice of the divinity within him. He needed no other.

137. HEGEL.—In strongest contrast to the individualism of Kant stands the doctrine of Hegel. To the latter, duty consists in the realization of the free reasonable will—but this will is identical in all individuals, [206] and its realization reveals itself in the customs, laws and institutions of the state. From this point of view the individual is an accidental thing; the ethical order revealed in society is permanent, and has absolute authority. It is true, however, that it is not something foreign to the individual; he is conscious of it as his own being. In duty he finds his liberation. [207]

But what is a man's duty? "What a man ought to do," says Hegel, [208] "what duties he should fulfill in order to be virtuous, is in an ethical community easy to say—the man has only to do what is presented, expressed and recognized in the established relations in which he finds himself."

---

[205] Ibid.

[206] *The Philosophy of Right*, Sec 209.

[207] *Ibid.*, Sec Sec 145-149

[208] *Ibid.*, Sec 150.

In other words, he ought to do just what his community prescribes! This seems, taken quite literally, a startling doctrine.

It would be a wrong to Hegel to take him quite literally, for he elsewhere[209] makes it plain that he by no means approves of all the laws and customs that have obtained in various societies. Still, he exalts the law of the state and regards any opposition to it on the authority of private conviction as "stupendous presumption." [210] This is a serious rebuke to the reformer. The individual must, according to Hegel, look for the moral law outside of himself—of himself as an individual, at least. He must find it in the State.

138. NIETZSCHE.—Again a startling contrast: after Hegel, Nietzsche—the voice of one crying in the wilderness, exquisitely, passionately, but scarcely with articulate scientific utterance. A prophet of revolt and emancipation; a cave-dweller, who would flee organized society and the refinements of civilization; the rabid individualist, to whom the community is the "herd," and common notions of right and wrong are absurdities to be visited with scorn and denunciation. He makes a strong appeal to young men, even after the years during which the carrying of one's own latch-key is a source of elation. He appeals also to those perennially young persons who never attain to the stature which befits those who are to take a responsible share in the organized efforts of communities of men.

With Nietzsche the man, his suffering life, and the melancholy eclipse of his brilliant intellect, ethics as science is little concerned. In Nietzsche the marvellous literary artist it can have no interest. These things are the affair of literature and biography.

Here we are concerned only with his contribution to ethics. Just what that has been it is more difficult to determine than would be the case in a writer more systematic and scientific. But he makes it very clear that he repudiates the morals which have been accepted heretofore by moralists and communities of men generally.

He confesses himself an "immoralist." He despises man as he is, and hails the "Superman," a creature inspired by the "will to have power" and free from all moral prejudices, including that of sympathy with the weak and the helpless.

"Full is the world of the superfluous," he sings in his famous dithyramb, [211]

---

[209] *Ibid.*, Introduction.
[210] Op. *cit.*, Sec 138.
[211] *Thus Spake Zarathustra, I, xi.* It is a pity to read NIETZSCHE in any translation. His diction is exquisite. But those who can only read him in

169

"marred is life by the many-too- many."... "Many too many are born; for the superfluous ones was the State devised."..."There, where the State ceaseth—there only commenceth the man who is not superfluous."

Man, says Nietzsche, should regard himself as a "bridge" over which he can pass to something higher. [212] Upon the fact that the Superman may have the same reason for regarding himself as a "bridge" as the most commonplace of mortals, and may begin anew with loathing and self-contempt, he does not dwell. Yet, as long as progress is possible, man may always be regarded as a "bridge." The reader of Nietzsche is tempted to believe that hatred and contempt must always be the predominant emotions in the mind of the "superior" man. Darwin, who knew much more about man and nature than did our passionate poet, was still able to regard man as "the crown and glory of the universe." Not so, Nietzsche.

Those who have read little in ethics are inclined to attribute to Nietzsche a greater measure of originality than he can reasonably claim. More than two milleniums before him, Plato conceived an ideal Republic in which moral laws, as commonly accepted, were to be set aside. Marriage was to be done away with; births were to be scientifically regulated; children were to be taken from their mothers; sickly infants were to be destroyed. In Sparta the committee of the elders did not permit the promptings of sympathy and the cries of wounded maternal love to influence the decision touching the life or death of the new-born.

Here was an attempt at bridge-building, but it was conceived as a scientific matter, to be taken in hand by the State, and for the good of the State. But Nietzsche would destroy the State. His Superman appears as individualistic as a "rogue" elephant, a few passages to the contrary notwithstanding. Are we to regard him as a mere lawless egoist, or as something more? We are left in the dark. [213] But we note that Nietzsche disagrees with most moralists, in that he refuses to regard Caesar Borgia as a morbid growth. [214] The Superman has always been with us, in somewhat varying types. From Alexander the Great to Napoleon, and before and after, he adorns the pages of history. Attila, among others, may enter his

---

English may be referred to the translations of his works edited by LEVY. New York, 1911.

[212] *Ibid.*, Prologue, and I, IV, XI, *et passim.*
[213] See the volume, *Beyond Good and Evil*, "What is Noble?" Sec 265.
[214] *Ibid., The Natural History of Morals*, Sec 197. DOSTOIEVSKY'S genius has portrayed for us an admirable Superman in the person of the Russian convict Orloff. See his *House of the Dead*, chapter v.

claim to consideration. It remains for the serious student of ethics to estimate scientifically his value as an ethical ideal, and to judge how far this type of character may profitably be taken as a pattern. Nietzsche stands at the farthest possible remove from Hegel. Does he, as an individualist, stand within hail of Kant? It scarcely seems so. When we examine Kant's "practical reason," in other words, the moral law as it revealed itself to Kant, we find that it had taken up into itself the moral development of the ages preceding. Kant's practical reason, his conscience, to speak plain English, was not the practical reason of, for example, Aristotle. The latter could speak of a slave as an "animated tool," and could believe there were men intended by nature for slavery. Kant could not. In theory an individualist, the Sage of Konigsberg stands, in reality, not far from Hegel. He does not break with the past. But Nietzsche is revolt incarnate.

PART VIII

THE ETHICS OF THE SOCIAL WILL

CHAPTER XXX

ASPECTS OF THE ETHICS OF REASON

139. THE DOCTRINE SUPPORTED BY THE OTHER SCHOOLS.—- I urge the more confidently the Ethics of Reason, or the Ethics of the Rational Social Will, because there is so little in it that is really new. It only makes articulate what we all know already, and strives to get rid of certain exaggerations into which many men who reason, and who reason well, have unwittingly fallen.

The fundamentals of the doctrine have been exhibited in Parts V and VI of this volume, and the exaggerations alluded to have been treated in Part VII. Hence, I may speak very briefly in indicating how the Ethics of Reason finds a many-sided support in schools which appear, on the surface, to be in the opposition.

It is evident, to begin with, that the Ethics of the Social Will cannot dispense with Moral Intuitions, but must regard them as indispensable; as, indeed, the very foundation of the moral life. That the individual may, and if he is properly equipped for the task, ought, to examine critically his own moral intuitions and those of the community in which he finds himself, and should, with becoming modesty and hesitation, now and then suggest an innovation, means no more than that he and the community are not dead, but are living, and that progress is a possibility, at least.

As for the Egoist, unless he is an absurd extremist, we must admit that he says much that is worth listening to. Was not Bentham quite right in maintaining that if all A's interests were committed to B, and all B's to A, the world would get on very badly? A charity that begins at the planet Mars would arrive nowhere. The Ethics of Reason has room for a very careful consideration of the interests of the self. But it may object to the position that the moral mathematician may regard as the only important number the number One.

With the Utilitarian our doctrine need have, as we have seen, no quarrel. Did not that learned, enlightened, and most fair-minded of utilitarians, Sidgwick, ultimately resolve the happiness which men seek into anything which may be the object of the mind in willing? Did not a critical utilitarianism resolve itself into the doctrine of the Rational Social Will? Why take less critical utilitarians as the only exponents of the school? Besides, is there any reason why the social will should be blind to the fact that men generally do desire to gain pleasure and to avoid pain? It is only the exaggeration of this truth that we need to combat.

To Nature, properly understood, we can enter no objection. Who objects to Perfection as a "counsel of perfection?" Can the Social Will object to a man's striving to Realize his Capacities—under proper control, and with a regard to others? The Pessimist is an unhealthy creature, and the Social Will represents normal and healthy humanity. Here we have disparity. But to Evolution our doctrine offers no opposition. It is only by a process of development that the Actual Social Will has come to be what it is; and the Rational Social Will looks to a further development under the guidance of reason.

The fact is that thoughtful men belonging to different schools tend to introduce into their statement of their doctrines modifying clauses; and in the end we find them not as far apart as they seemed at the beginning. The tendency is, I think, in the direction of the recognition of the Rational Social Will. This doctrine belongs to nobody in particular; it is the. common property of us all. It contains little that is startling.

140. ITS METHOD OF APPROACH TO PROBLEMS.—-He who looks to the Rational Social Will for guidance is given a compass which may be of no small service to him. For example:

(1) He will see that moral phenomena are not to be isolated. He will accept the historic order of society and judge man and his emotions and actions in the light of it. He will never feel tempted to say, with Bentham, that the pleasure which has its roots in malice, envy, cruelty, "taken by itself, is good." [215]

---

[215] *Principles of Morals and Legislation,* chapter x, Sec 10, note.

He will simply say, it is pleasure. That it is, of course; but he will maintain that nothing "taken by itself" is either good or bad, from the moralist's point of view. The cruel man may will to see suffering, and may enjoy it. The moral man may hold that the cruel man, his act of will, and his pleasure, should all be snuffed out, in the interest of humanity, as an unmitigated evil.

(2) The advocate of the Rational Social Will recognizes, as do many adherents of other schools, that the social will, as expressed at any given time, is only relatively rational; that men must live in their own day and generation, although they can, to some degree, reach beyond them; and that some differences of opinion as to the relative values of virtues, and the goodness of characters, are to be expected.

(3) Furthermore, he is in a position to explain how a man may be "subjectively" right and yet "objectively" wrong. The man's character may be such that it is, on the whole, to be approved by the Rational Social Will. He may be animated by the desire to adjust himself to that will. And yet, the accident of ignorance, the accident of prejudice not recognized by himself as such, may lead him to do what he thinks right and what those more enlightened recognize to be wrong.

141. ITS SOLUTION OF CERTAIN DIFFICULTIES.—Perhaps it would be better for me to give this section a heading more nearly like the last. I aim only to give the reader a point of view from which he can approach the problem of a solution.

Take the problem which has come up before in the form of the distribution of pleasures. [216] He who dwells, not so much upon pleasure, as upon the satisfaction of desire and will, must state it differently, but the problem is much the same. What degree of recognition should be given to the will of each individual, or to the separate volitions and desires in the life of the individual? Should everybody count for one? Should every desire or group of desires receive recognition? Is no distinction to be made in the intensity of desires? And how many individuals shall we include in our reckoning?

Light seems to be shed upon this complicated problem or set of problems when we hold clearly before ourselves what the task of reason is in regulating the life of man individually and collectively. Its function is to bring order out of chaos and strife; to substitute harmony and planfulness for accident; to introduce long views in the place of momentary impulses; to prevent the barter of permanent good for a mess of pottage.

---

[216] See Sec 109.

Reason must accept the impulses and instincts of man as it finds them, and do what it can with them. It cannot ignore them. Slowly, civilizations, to some degree rational, have come into being. In so far as they are rational, they are justified. Keeping all this in view we may say, tentatively:

(a) The principle, "everybody to count for one, and nobody for more than one," must be interpreted as an expression of the conviction that no will should be *needlessly* sacrificed.

Reason is bodiless, except as incorporated in human societies, and these must have their historic development. Can we do away with the special claims of family, of neighborhood, of the state? They have their place in the historic rational order. But the whispered "everybody to count for one" may help us to realize that such special claims cannot take the place of all others.

(b) Shall a deliberate attempt be made to enlarge the circle of those who are to share in the social will, not merely by diminishing the number of deaths, but by promoting the number of births? States have attempted it often enough. I can only say that, if this be attempted, it should not be attempted in ways that ignore the historical development of society, with its social and moral traditions.

(c) Why not justify our attitude toward the brutes by maintaining that they have, theoretically, rights to recognition, in so far as such recognition does not interfere with the rights of man in the rational social order? The brutes outnumber us, to be sure. We are in a hopeless minority. But were this minority sacrificed, there would be no rational social order at all—no right, no wrong; nothing but the clash of wills or impulses which reason now strives to harmonize as it can. [217]

(d) When we turn to the problem of the distribution of satisfactions in the life of the individual, we find ready to hand a variety of unwise saws—"A short life and a merry one," and the like.

How should the individual choose his satisfactions? Merely from the standpoint of the individual? What is *desirable*? Not *desired*, by this man or by that, but *desirable, reasonable*?

It is an open secret that the house of mirth lacks every convenience demanded of a permanent residence, and that those who breathlessly pursue pleasure are seldom pleased. Nor do men, when they stop to think, want their lives to be very short.

---

[217] See chapter xxi.

And, in any case, this question of the distribution of satisfactions in the life of the individual does not concern the individual alone. Is the man who wants a short life and a merry one an "undesirable" from the standpoint of the Rational Social Will? Then he should be suppressed. The manner of distribution of even his own personal satisfactions is not his affair exclusively. Every ordered society has its notions touching the type of man which suits its ends.

(e) But shall we, in making up our minds about the "satisfaction on the whole" which busies the rational individual or the rational community, take no account at all of the intensity of pleasures and of pains, the eagerness with which some things are desired and the feebleness of the impulsion toward others? May not the intense thrill of a moment more than counterbalance "four lukewarm hours?" Are we not, if we take such things into consideration, back again face to face with something very like the calculus of pleasures—that bugbear of the egoist and of the utilitarian?

It would be foolish to maintain that man, either individually or collectively, places all desires upon the same level. No man of sense holds that every desire should count as one. On the other hand, no man of sense pretends to have any accurate unit of measurement by which he can make unerring estimates of desirability.

Fortunately, he is not compelled to fall back upon such a unit. Even if he was born yesterday, the race was not. He is born into a system of values expressed in social organization and social institutions. It is the resultant of innumerable expressions of preference on the part of innumerable men. It is a general guide to what, on the whole, man wants.

It is, then, foolish for him to raise such questions as, whether it is not better to aim at intense happiness on the part of the few, to the utter ignoring of the mass of mankind. Such questions the Rational Social Will has already answered in the negative.

142. THE CULTIVATION OF OUR CAPACITIES.—Finally, we may approach the question whether it is reasonable to awake dormant desires, to call into being new needs; which, satisfied, may be recognized as a good, but which, unsatisfied, may result in unhappiness. [218]

A little cup may be filled with what leaves a big one half empty. It is easy to find grounds upon which to congratulate the "average" man. All the world caters to him—ready-made clothing is measured to fit his figure, and it is

---

[218] Compare chapter xxi, Sec 86.

sold cheap; the average restaurant consults his taste and his pocket; the average woman just suits him as a help-mate; he is much at home with his neighbors, most of whom diverge little from the average. Why strive to rise above the average—and fall into a divine discontent?

May one not say much the same of a community? Why should it strive to attain to new conquests, to awaken in its members new wants and strain to satisfy them? Does it seem self-evident that it is reasonable, in general, to multiply desires with no guarantee of their satisfaction?

I know no way of approaching the solution of this problem save from the standpoint of the Rational Social Will. We are confronted with the general problem of the desirability of civilization, with all that that implies. The life of man in some rather primitive societies has seemed in certain respects rather idyllic. The eating of the fruit of the tree, and the consequent opening of the eyes, has, time and again, seemed to result in disaster.

But was the idyllic life not an accidental thing, due to a fortuitous combination of circumstances, rather than to man's intelligent control of a larger environment? Civilization of some sort seems inevitable. Have we any other guarantee that we can make it, in the long run, rational, than a many-sided development of man's capacities? And must we not exercise a broad faith in the value of enlightenment, increase of knowledge, farsightedness, the cultivation of complex emotions, even at the risk of some waste of effort and some suffering to certain individuals?

Perhaps this is as good a place as any to say a word about the significance of the terms "higher" and "lower," when used in a moral sense. We have seen that John Stuart Mill made much of the distinction in his utilitarianism. Bentham appears to sin against the enlightened moral judgment in holding that, quantities of pleasure being the same, "push- pin is as good as poetry."

When we realize that the worth of things may be determined from the standpoint of the Rational Social Will, we can easily understand that some occupations and their accompanying pleasures should be rated higher than others, however satisfactory the latter may seem to certain individuals. It is not unreasonable to rate the pleasure of scientific discovery as higher than the pleasure of swallowing an oyster; and that, without following Bentham in falling back upon a quantitative standard, or following Mill in maintaining that pleasures, as pleasures, differ in kind. [219]

---

[219] See chapter xxv, Sec 107.]

CHAPTER XXXI

THE MORAL LAW AND MORAL IDEALS

143. DUTIES AND VIRTUES.—We saw, at the very beginning of this volume [220] that a single moral law, so abstractly stated as to cover the whole sphere of conduct, must be something so vague and indeterminate as to be practically useless as a guide to action. The admonition, "do right," does not mean anything in particular to the man who is not already well instructed as to what, in detail, constitutes right action. Nor do we make ourselves more intelligible, when we say to him "be good."

It seems to mean something more when we say "act justly" or "be just"; "speak the truth," or "be truthful." And the more we particularize, the more we help the individual confronted with concrete problems—the only problems with which life actually confronts us.

This is as it should be. Duties and virtues are expressions of the Rational Social Will, and that will is a mere abstraction except as it is incorporated, with a wealth of detail, in human societies. It would be hard for the small boy to classify, under any ten commandments, the innumerable company of the "don'ts" which he hears from his mother during the course of a week. He can leave such work to the moralist. But he is receiving an education in the moral law, as an expression of the social will, through the whole seven days.

If we wish, we can emphasize the *moral law*, and dwell upon the *duties* of man. On the other hand, we may lay stress upon the *virtues*, and point to *ideals*. The Greek made much of the virtues; the Christian moralist had more to say of man's duties. In the end, there need be little discrepancy in the results. I make the same recommendation, whether I say to a man, Speak the truth! or whether I say to him, Be truthful!

It may be claimed that shades of difference make themselves apparent, where one emphasizes the law and another points to an ideal. Perhaps they do, in most minds. It certainly sounds more conceited to say: "I am trying to be virtuous," than to say: "I am trying to do my duty." On the other hand, the admonition, "Be truthful," appears to leave one a little latitude.

---

[220] Chapter i, Sec 2.

We take the truthful man, so to speak, in the lump. If he has a strong bias toward truth-speaking, and is felt to be reliable, on the whole, it is not certain that we should rob him of his title on the ground of one or two lapses for which weighty reasons could be urged. The admonition: "Speak the truth!" seems more uncompromising; and yet he who prefers this legal form may maintain that it is a general admonition addressed to men of sense who are supposed to be able to exercise reason.

144. THE NEGATIVE ASPECT OF THE MORAL LAW.—Why does the Moral Law, on the surface at least, appear to be so largely negative? As we look back upon our early youth, our days appear to be punctuated with punishments. When we attain to years of discretion, this is not the case, with most of us, at least.

But when we turn to the law, in our own society or in others, we find prohibitions and penalties everywhere. Of rewards little is said. Is the social will meant to be chiefly inhibitory? Is it a check to the action of the individual?

(1) The negative aspect of the moral law is, to a considerable degree, an illusion. The social will takes us up into itself and forms us. In our early youth we are acutely conscious of the process. A vast number of the things a boy wants to do are things that do not suit the social will at all. He wants to break windows; he wants to fight other boys; he wants to be idle; his delight is in adventures not normally within the reach of, or suited to the taste of, the citizens of an ordered state. It is little wonder that the boy regards the moral law as a nuisance and the state as a suitable refuge for those suffering from senile decay.

There are individuals who scarcely get beyond this stage. They remain, even in their later years, at war with the state. From time to time, we seize them and incarcerate them. That the law *forbids* and *punishes*, they never forget. It is chiefly for such that the criminal law exists. They are in the state, but they are not of it. They have small share in the heritage of the civilized man.

For most of us there comes a time when most prohibitions are little thought of. It has been maintained, that the law is negative partly for the reason that positive duties are too numerous to be formulated. But how numerous are the things that ought not to be done which normal men never think of doing! At this moment, I could swallow a pen, taste the ink in the ink-well, throw my papers from the window, hurl the porcelain jar on the chimney-piece at the cat next door, swing on the chandelier. I am conscious of no constraint in not doing these things. Why? I have become to some degree adjusted to the type which the social will strives to produce.

(2) And, having become so far adjusted, I recognize that the social will is distributing rewards most lavishly. The whole organism of society is its instrument. Work is found for me, and I am paid for it. If I am industrious and dependable, I am recompensed. If I am truthful, I am believed, which is no little convenience. If I am energetic and persevering, I may grow rich or be elected to office. If I am courteous, I am liked and am treated with courtesy.

Every day I am paid, in the ordinary course of things, according to my deserts. Why should society work out an extraordinary system of rewards for those whom it is already rewarding automatically?

In some cases, recourse is had to extraordinary rewards. We give prizes to children in the schools; we give medals to soldiers for distinguished service; we confer honorary degrees upon men for a variety of reasons. In monarchical countries and in their colonies, the man who earns an extraordinary reward may even pass it on, in the shape of a title, to his descendants, as though it were original sin. But the giving of extraordinary rewards to all ordinary, normal persons would be too much.

The man who markedly offends against the moral law is not an ordinary, normal person. He is not adjusted to the social will. It is natural that he should attract especial attention. Thus the "Thou shalt not!" is given prominence. To this I might add, that punishments are cheaper and easier than extraordinary rewards. Pains are sharper than pleasures, and are easily inflicted.

(3) It is worthy of remark that, with the evolution of morality, it tends to become positive. The enlightened moral man recognizes, not merely the actual social will, but also the Rational Social Will. He may feel it his duty to do much more than society formally demands of him.

145. HOW CAN ONE KNOW THE MORAL LAW?—This question has already been answered in chapters preceding. Every man has three counsellors: (1) The "objective" morality of his community—custom, law, and public opinion, which certainly deserve to be taken very seriously; (2) his moral intuitions, which may be of the finest; and (3) his reason, which prevents him from making decisions without reflection.

Can a man who listens to these three counsellors be sure that he is right in a given decision? The sooner a man learns that he is not infallible and impeccable, the better it will be for him, for his neighbor, and for the world at large.

CHAPTER XXXII

THE MORAL CONCEPTS

146. GOOD AND BAD; RIGHT AND WRONG.—As a rule, men reflect little touching the moral terms which are on their lips every day. It is well worth while to take some of them up and to turn them over for examination.

We may use the terms "good" and "bad," "right" and "wrong," in a very broad sense. A "good" trick may be a contemptible action; the "right" way to crack a bank-safe may be the means to the successful commission of a crime. Evidently, the words, thus used, are not employed in a moral sense.

When we pass judgments from the moral point of view, we concern ourselves with men and with their actions, and measure them by the standard of the social will. Men and actions are "good," when they can meet the test. Actions are "right" or "wrong," when they are in accordance with the dictates of the moral law, or are at variance with them. That an act may be both right and wrong, when viewed from different standpoints, even on moral ground, we have seen in Chapter XXX. A man may mean to do right, and may, through ignorance or error, be guilty of an act that we condemn. To the intelligent, confusions are here unnecessary. But the history of ethics is full of confusions in just this field.

147. DUTY AND OBLIGATION.—Verbal usage sometimes justifies the use of one of these words, and sometimes that of the other. We say: I did my duty; we do not say: I did my obligation. But this is a mere matter of verbal expression, and we are really concerned with two names for the same thing.

(1) There has been much dispute as to whether the sense of duty or moral obligation can or cannot be analyzed. It has been declared unanalyzable and unique. Some think this a point of much importance which imparts a peculiar sacredness to the sense of duty.

There appears no reason why this position should be taken. No one has been able to analyze into its ultimate sensational elements the peculiar feeling one has when one is tickled. But this does not make the feeling sacred or awe-inspiring. The authority of the sense of duty must be looked for in another direction—and authority it has.

(2) I have spoken of the "sense" of duty. We all recognize that, when we are faced with a duty, a feeling is normally present. But the whole argument of this volume has maintained that man is not to be treated only as the subject of emotions. He is a rational being. In some persons feeling is very prominent; in others it is less so. It is quite conceivable that, in a given case, a man capable of reflection should recognize that he is confronted with a duty, and yet that he should feel no impulse to perform it. Did no one ever feel any such impulse, the whole system of duties, the whole rational order of society itself, would dissolve and disappear.

Fortunately, the normal man does feel an impulse to perform duties recognized as such. And in the case of those exceptional persons who do not, society strives to supply surrogates, extraordinary impulses based upon a system of rewards and punishments. This is a mere supplement, and could never keep alive a society from which the sense of duty had disappeared.

Duty *is* sacred. It is the very foundation of every rational society. It does not greatly concern ethics whether the impulse, which makes itself felt in men who want to do their duty, can or cannot be analyzed. But it is all-important that they should feel the impulse.

(3) Can a man do more than his duty? Is it the duty of everyone to be, not merely a good, average, honest, faithful, law-abiding citizen, but to go far beyond this and be conspicuously a saint?

It should be remembered that we are concerned with the connotation properly to be given to a word in common use.

A certain amount of goodness the social will appears to demand of men rather peremptorily. Its demands seem to vary somewhat with the exigencies of the times—for example, in peace and in war. It does not make the same demands of all men. From those to whom much has been given— wealth, education, social or political influence,—much is required. From certain persons it appears to be glad to get anything. If they keep out of the police-court, it is agreeably surprised.

I have no desire to dissuade anyone from the arduous pursuit of sainthood; but I submit that the word "duty," as sanctioned by usage, implies but a limited demand, and takes cognizance of character and environment. He who comes up to this moderate standard is not condemned; but he is free to go farther and to become as great a saint as he pleases. In which case, we admire him. Those who, in the past, have spoken of "counsels of perfection," have drawn upon a profound knowledge of human nature and of human societies.

148. REWARD AND PUNISHMENT.—We saw in the last chapter (Sec 144) that it is something of a criticism upon man and upon societies of men that extraordinary rewards have to be given and that punishments must be inflicted.

More attention has been paid to punishments than to rewards, and the question touching the proper aim of punishment in a civilized state has received much discussion. The study of the history of the infliction of punishment is suggestive, but it does not shed a clear light. The social will has not always been a rational social will, and some of its decisions may be placed among the curiosities of literature. Still, they may serve the purpose of the traditional "terrible example."

Should we, in punishing, aim at the prevention of crime? Are punishments to be "deterrent"? Under this head we must consider, not merely the criminal himself, but also those who are in more or less danger of becoming criminals, though they have, as yet, committed no known crime.

Should the aim of punishment be the reformation of the criminal?

Should we punish merely that "justice" be done? He who steals and eats fruit is visited with punishment, in the course of nature, if the fruit is unripe. But he suffers equally if he eats his own fruit, under like conditions. This seems a blind punishment. Should we visit pain upon him for the theft, merely because it is a theft, and without looking abroad for any other reason?

Light appears to be thrown upon these problems when we reflect that punishment is an instrument, employed by the Rational Social Will, in pursuance of its ends.

(1) It is desirable that men should be deterred from committing crime. If this cannot be done save by the infliction of punishment, then let men be punished. But be it remembered that punishment is a regrettable necessity, and that the occasions for the infliction of penalties may greatly be diminished by the amelioration of the organism of society. There is the born criminal, as there is the born inmate of an asylum for the insane. But there is also the manufactured criminal; the product of the slum, the victim of ignorance, the prey of the walking-delegate, the sufferer from over-work and undernourishment, the inhabitant of the filthy and overcrowded tenement, the man robbed of his self-respect, who has no share in the sweetness and light of civilization. A society that first manufactures criminals and then expends great sums in punishing them is, in so far, not rational.

(2) It is desirable that the criminal should be reformed and returned to society as a normal man. But this is not the one and only aim of the social will. The whole flock should not be sacrificed to the one black sheep, as some sentimental persons appear to believe. There is room here for the exercise of judgment and of some cool calculation.

(3) As for the demand that a given pain shall be inflicted for a given wrong done, irrespective of any gain to anybody, and irrespective of consequences,—it appears to carry one back to ancient and primitive law.

Undoubtedly many punishments have been inflicted in the past to satisfy the sense of resentment. [221] Undoubtedly the same is true of the present. Can anything be said in favor of this impulse? It plays no small part in the life of humanity.

We feel that a bad man *ought* to be punished. We harbor a certain resentment against him. The resentment of the individual for personal injuries we recognize to be wrong. It is not impartial, and it is apt to be excessive and unreasoning. Public order demands that it be refused expression.

But is the—we must admit, somewhat more disinterested—resentment of the community a rational thing? Have men, collectively, no whims, no prejudices? When a trial is deferred, and public indignation has cooled off, how do the chances of the prisoner compare with those he enjoyed just after the commission of the crime? And yet something may be said for public resentment. It has a certain driving-power. It may be questioned whether either our desire to deter men from crime, or our benevolent interest in the criminal, would be quite sufficient to enforce law, if all sense of resentment against the law-breaker were lacking. Its usefulness as an instrument of the social will appears to give it a certain justification. But it also suggests that even public resentment should not be given free rein.

Before leaving the subject of reward and punishment, it may be well to say a word touching our use of the terms *credit* and *discredit, merit* and *demerit.*

---

[221] It may be objected that we are not concerned here with resentment but with the satisfaction of "justice." Men's notions of the "justice" of punishments have been touched upon in chapter ii, Sec 4. Plato suggests, in his Laws, that the slave who steals a bunch of grapes should receive a blow for every grape in the bunch. This has an agreeably mathematical flavor of exactitude. But what shall be done to the man who steals half of a ham or a third of a watermelon?

We do not give a man credit for an action, we do not think of him as meritorious, merely because he has done right. Who thinks of praising the young mother for feeding and washing her first-born? Who shakes the hand of the Sunday-school teacher and congratulates him upon having stolen nothing for a week? But the waif from the gutter who wanders through a department-store and resolutely takes nothing, emerging exhausted with the struggle, we slap upon the back and call a little man.

Our notions of credit and merit are bound up with our notions of extraordinary rewards. The creditable action, the meritorious man, have a certain claim upon us, if only the claim of special recognition. Any man who makes a notable step forward deserves credit, whatever his actual position upon the moral scale. He who only "marks time" upon a relatively high level may be a good man, but we do not give him credit for the act normally to be expected of him. The recognition of merit is a part of the machinery of moralization.

149. VIRTUES AND VICES.—One swallow, said Aristotle, does not make a spring, nor does one happy day make a happy life. Elsewhere he draws our attention to the fact that one good action does not constitute a virtue.

We may define the virtues as those relatively permanent qualities of character which it is desirable, from the moral point of view, that a man should have. The vices are the corresponding defects. I shall not attempt to draw up a list of the virtues. For a variety of lists, exhibiting curious and interesting diversities, I refer the reader back to Chapter III, Sec Sec 9-11.

The Rational Social Will aims to build up a social order which shall do justice to the fundamental impulses and desires of man, a social and rational creature. The stones which it must build into its edifice are human beings. If the human beings are mere lumps of soft clay, incapable of holding their shape or of bearing any weight, the walls cannot rise. And a human being may be satisfactory in one respect, and far from satisfactory in another. No one of us is wholly ignorant of the qualities desirable in our building-material. Custom, law and public opinion are there to indicate what qualities have, in fact, proved, on the whole, not detrimental. Our intuitions help us in forming a judgment. Rational reflection is of service.

But one thing is very evident. Nowhere is it made clearer than in the study of the virtues and vices, that the moralist cannot consider the phenomena, with which he occupies himself, in a state of isolation.

Is courage a virtue? Is, then, the man who is willing to take the risk of breaking a bank, or holding up a stage-coach, in so far virtuous? Is perseverance a virtue? Is, then, the woman, who holds out to the bitter end in her desire to have the last word, in so far virtuous? Is justice a virtue? Then why not be virtuous in demanding the pound of flesh, if it is the law—as it once was?

Certain qualities of character have been recognized as, *on the whole*, and *generally*, serviceable to the social will. But a man is not a quality of character, and qualities of character are sometimes gathered into strange bundles. It is of men that the state is composed; of thinking, feeling men. We cannot isolate qualities of character, and assess their value in their isolation.

150. CONSCIENCE.—We are all forced to recognize that conscience has its dual aspect. It is characterized by *feeling*; and the feeling is seldom blind, or, at least, wholly blind; conscience implies a *judgment* that something is right or wrong.

(1) The feeling is, to be sure, very often in the foreground. Those who say, "My conscience tells me that this is wrong," often mean little more than, "I feel that it is wrong."

But the word "feeling" is an ambiguous one. It is used to cover all sorts of intuitive judgments as well as mere emotions. The man who takes the time to reflect upon his feeling of the rightness or wrongness of an action can often discover some, perhaps rather vague, reason for his feeling proper.

(2) In other words, he may come upon an intuitive judgment. And the thoughtful man who talks about his conscience is rarely satisfied with a blind intuition; he wants to be sure he is right, and he thinks the whole matter over.

(3) The feeling and the judgment are not necessarily in accord. The feeling may lag behind an enlightened judgment. On the other hand, the feeling of repugnance to acting in certain ways may be a justifiable protest against a bit of intellectual sophistry.

(4) So much ought to be admitted by everyone who holds that conscience may be blunted or may be enlightened. Consciences vary indefinitely. Some we set down as hopelessly below the average; others we reverence as refined and enlightened. The social worker makes it his aim to "awaken" conscience, to cultivate it, to bring it up to a high standard. No practical moralist regards the conscience of the individual as something which must simply be left to itself and treated as sacred, no matter what its character.

(5) The above sufficiently explains some of the puzzles which confront the man who reverences conscience and yet studies the consciences of his

186

fellow-men. He finds that the individual conscience is not an infallible guide-post pointing to right action; that it is not a perfect time- keeper, in complete accord with the watches of other men.

"It's a turrible thing to have killed the wrong man," said the conscience-stricken illicit distiller in his mountain fastness. "I never seen good come o' goodness yet; him as strikes first is my fancy," said the dying pirate in "Treasure Island." Augustine, passing over much worse offences, exhausts himself in agonies of remorse over a boyish prank. [222] Seneca draws up a list of the most horrifying crimes, and decides that ingratitude exceeds them all in enormity. [223]

(6) It appears to be quite evident that consciences ought to be standardized, and that the standard should be made a high one. The true standard is the one set by the Rational Social Will. It is as much a duty to have a good conscience as it is to obey the conscience one has.

CHAPTER XXXIII

THE ETHICS OF THE INDIVIDUAL

151. WHAT IS MEANT BY THE TERM?—Men collected into groups and organized in various ways we call states, and we treat a state as a unit. We look upon it as having rights and as owing duties both to individuals and to other states. There are individuals whom we are apt to regard as representatives of the state; as instruments, rather than as men— executive officers, legislators, official interpreters of its laws, whether good or bad. For states and their representatives we often have especial moral standards, differing more or less from those by which we judge human beings merely as human beings. It is with the morality of the latter that I am here concerned.

---

[222] See chapter xx, Sec 78.
[223] *On Benefits*, i, 10.

To be sure, all human beings are to be found in states, or in that rudimentary social something which foreshadows the state. To talk of the morality of the isolated individual is nonsense. Morality is the expression of the social will; and if we think of even Robinson Crusoe as a good man, it means that we apply to him social standards. Had he not been moralized, he would have killed and eaten Friday, when the latter made his appearance.

We must, then, take the individual as we find him in the state, but it is convenient to consider his morality separately from the ethics of the state, its institutions and its instruments.

152. THE VIRTUES OF THE INDIVIDUAL.—What moral traits have we a right to look for in the individual man? What sort of a man is it his duty to be?

Evidently, men's duties must vary somewhat according to the type of the society to which they belong, and to their definite place in that society. Still, certain general desirable traits of character unavoidably suggest themselves. To attempt a complete list seems futile, but the most salient have been dwelt upon by the moralists of many schools, and for centuries past.

Does it not appear self-evident that a man should be law-abiding, honest, industrious, truthful, and capable of unselfishness? Should he not have a regard for his health and efficiency? Should he not aim to develop his capacities, and in so far to diminish the dead mass of ignorance and bad taste which weighs down society?

Of marital fidelity, with all that that implies—personal purity, the good of one's children, a fine sense of loyalty—it is scarcely necessary to speak. No man, betrothed or married, can be sure that he will not meet tomorrow some woman whom the unprejudiced would judge to be more attractive than the one to whom he has bound himself. Shall he remain unprejudiced—a floating mine, ready to explode at any accidental contact? Away with him! He has, in the eyes of the scientific moralist, "too much ego in his cosmos." Those babble of "affinities" who know little, and care less, about the long and arduous ascent up which mankind has toiled, in the effort to attain to civilization.

And what shall we say of such things as religious duties, of cheerfulness, of good manners, of personal cleanliness? Of religious duties I shall speak elsewhere. [224] As to cheerfulness and good manners, it is only necessary to

---

[224] Chapter xxxvi.

reflect upon the baleful influence exercised upon the young—who have here my entire sympathy—by a bilious and depressing piety, or by those who are rudely and superciliously moral.

Cleanliness deserves some special attention, on account of the fact that it has perplexed even thoughtful scholars to discover why society has come to regard it as a duty at all. [225] That, if society does regard cleanliness as important, it should be the duty of the individual to keep himself and his house clean presents no problem. He has no right to make himself gratuitously offensive, and gratuitously offensive he will be, if he is a dirty fellow. But why does anyone object to his being a dirty fellow? The prejudice in favor of cleanliness does not appear to be universal—witness the Eskimo and various other peoples.

We have learned that the social will has its foundation in the fundamental impulses and instincts of man. An admirable scholar has suggested that the ultimate root of the regard for cleanliness which more or less characterizes civilized societies may be traced to some such primitive and inexplicable impulse to cleanliness as we observe, for example, in the cat.[226] It must be admitted that it is far more marked in the cat than in the human being. A kitten is much more fastidious than is a baby, and a grown cat would tolerate no powder or rouge.

But, assuming that such an instinct exists, even in weak measure, it might easily develop with the development of society. And, as man is a rational being, capable of discovering a connection between cleanliness and hygiene, the duty of cleanliness would acquire a new authority. Dirt becomes no longer merely distasteful; it is recognized as a danger.

153. CONVENTIONAL MORALITY.—There are virtues—taking the traits of character indicated by the names broadly and loosely, and making allowance for all sorts of variations within wide limits—which appear to be recognized as such very generally. Bishop Butler regarded justice, veracity and regard to common good as valued in all societies. Certainly they have served as expressions of the social will in many societies, ancient and modern, primitive and highly civilized.

We have seen that the forms under which they appear are not independent of the degree and kind of the development of the society we may happen to

---

[225] The chapter on cleanliness by Epictetus is a homily, and not a philosophic argument. See, *Discourses*, Book IV, chapter xi.
[226] WESTERMARCK, *Origin and Development of the Moral Ideas*, chapter xxxix.

be contemplating. [227] And we have realized that man is born into a world of ready-made duties which are literally forced upon his attention. He finds himself a member of a family, somebody's neighbor, a resident in a town or village, allotted to a social class, an employer or an employee, a citizen of a state. Justice, veracity and a regard for common good appear to have their value in all these relations; but the manner of their interpretation is not independent of the relations, and the relations with their appropriate demands are relatively independent of the individual will. One cannot ignore these demands and fall back, independently, upon metaphysical theory. Aristotle's claim that a man cannot be unjust to his own child, because the child is a part of himself, and a man cannot be unjust to himself, [228] excites our curiosity. It does not elicit our approval.

It is because the vast majority of our duties are so unequivocally thrust upon us that I have been able to touch so lightly, in the last section, upon the duties of the individual. Why dilate upon what everybody knows? Is it not enough to set him thinking about it?

And, in helping him to think, the reference to the virtue of cleanliness has its value. Cleanliness is prized by those who know little of hygiene. If a society cannot be happy without cleanliness, for whatever reason, is it not the duty of the individual to be clean? But *how* clean should he be?

There are virtues—I use the word here broadly to cover approved habits— which seem to have a very direct reference to chronology and geography. They are *conventional virtues*; they suit a given society, and satisfy its actual social will. A Vermont housekeeper in an *igloo* would be an intolerable nuisance. Imagine an unbroken succession of New England house-cleanings with the inhabitants of the house sitting in despair in the snow outside.

Those who live north of the Alps are sometimes criticized for dipping Zwieback into their tea. Those who live south of the Alps eat macaroni in ways revolting to other nations. A very pretty Frenchwoman, devouring snails after the approved fashion of the locality, has driven me out of an excellent restaurant. And the world opens its eyes in wonder when it sees the well-bred Anglo-Saxon dispose of his asparagus.

There is a little-recognized virtue called toleration. St. Ambrose was a wise man when he advised St. Augustine to do, when in Rome, as the Romans do. Of course, he did not mean this to apply to robbery or to murder. He was giving an involuntary recognition to the doctrine that there are

---

[227] See chapter ii.
[228] *Ethics*, Book V, chapter vi, Sec 7.

conventional virtues, worthy of our notice, as well as virtues of heavier caliber and wider range.

CHAPTER XXXIV

THE ETHICS OF THE STATE

154. THE AIM OF THE STATE.—He who has resolved to devote but a single chapter to the Ethics of the State must deliberately sacrifice nine-tenths, at least, of the material—some of it very good material, and some of it most curious and interesting—which has heaped itself together on his hands in the course of his reading and thinking. I have resolved to write only the one chapter. The State is the background of the individual, the scaffold which supports his moral life. Without it, he may be a being; but he is scarcely recognizable as a *human* being. It has made the individual what he is, and it is the medium in which he can give expression to the nature which he now possesses.

Plato maintains that the object of the constitution of the state is the happiness of the whole, not of any part. [229] Aristotle, in his "Politics," maintains that it is the aim of the state to enable men to live well. Sidgwick defines politics as "the theory of what ought to be (in human affairs) as far as this depends on the common action of societies of men." [230] We may agree with all three, and yet leave ourselves much latitude in determining the nature of the organization of, and the limits properly to be set to the activities of, the State as such. Shall the State only strive to repress grave disorders? or shall it take a paternal interest in its citizens, making them virtuous and happy in spite of themselves?

---

[229] *Republic*, II. It must be borne in mind that both Plato and Aristotle had the Greek prejudice touching citizenship. Their "citizenship" was enjoyed by a strictly limited class.
[230] *The Methods of Ethics*, chapter ii.

191

155. ITS ORIGIN AND AUTHORITY.—In Parts III to VI we have seen how and upon what basis the State has grown up. It is an organism, something that lives and grows. It is not a machine, deliberately put together at a definite time by some man or some group of men. The "social contract" fanatic may have read history, but he has not understood it. Of psychology he has no comprehension at all.

Herodotus, at some of whose stories we smile, was a wiser man. He writes: "It appears certain to me, by a great variety of proofs, that Cambyses was raving mad; he would not else have set himself to make a mock of holy rites and long-established usages. For, if one were to offer men to choose out of all the customs in the world such as seemed to them the best, they would examine the whole number, and end by preferring their own; so convinced are they that their own usages far surpass those of all others." [231]

This may be something of an over-statement, for men in one state have shown themselves to be, within limits, capable of learning from men in another. But only within limits. Those things which give a state stability—and without stability we are tossed upon the waves of mere anarchy—have their roots in the remote past. Strip a man of his past, and he is little better than an idiot; strip men within the State of their corporate institutions and ideals, of their loyalties and emotional leanings, and we have on our hands a mob of savages, something much below the tribe proper, knit into unity of purpose by custom and tribal law.

The State has its origin in man as a creature desiring and willing, and at the same time endowed with reason. Its authority is the authority of reason. Not reason in the abstract, with no ground to stand upon, and no material for its exercise; but reason as incorporate in institutions and social usages; reason which takes cognizance of the nature of man, and recognizes what man has already succeeded in doing.

Where shall we look for a limit to the authority of the State? Surely, only in the Reason which makes it possible for the State to be. The State must not defeat its own object.

156. FORMS OF ORGANIZATION.—The special science of politics enters in detail into the forms of organization of the State. The ethical philosopher must content himself with certain general reflections. Everyone knows that States have been organized in divers ways; and that

---

[231] *The History of Herodotus*, Book III, chapter xxxviii, translated by GEORGE RAWLINSON, London, 1910.

their citizens, under much the same form of political organization, have been here happy and contented, and there in a state of ferment. The form of government counts for something; but its suitability to the population governed, and the degree of enlightenment and discipline characteristic of the population, count for much more. It is not every shoe that fits every foot, and there are feet that are little at home in shoes of any description.

Monarchies of many sorts, aristocracies, oligarchies, democracies, even communisms, have been tried; and all, save the last, have managed to hold their own with some degree of success.

It is easy to bring objections against each form of government, just as it is easy to say something specious in its favor.

Are the eldest sons of a few families peculiarly fitted by nature to be governors of the State? Look at history, and wake up to common sense. Of the divine right of kings I shall not speak, for the adherents of the doctrine are in our day relegated to museums of antiquities. And have the members of aristocracies been carefully bred with a view to their intellectual and moral superiority, as we breed fine varieties of horses and dogs? Have those who have had their share in oligarchies been peculiarly wise and peculiarly devoted to the common good? The communist makes two fatal mistakes. He shuts his eyes to history, and he overlooks the fact that there is such a thing as human nature.

There remains democracy. Of this, Herodotus, already quoted as a man of sense, has his opinion. He makes a shrewd Persian, in a political crisis, thus address his fellow-conspirators:

"There is nothing so void of understanding, nothing so full of wantonness, as the unwieldy rabble. It were folly not to be borne, for men, while seeking to escape the wantonness of a tyrant, to give themselves up to the wantonness of a rude unbridled mob. The tyrant, in all his doings, at least knows what he is about, but a mob is altogether devoid of knowledge; for how should there be any knowledge in a rabble, untaught, and with no natural sense of what is right and fit? It rushes wildly into state affairs with all the fury of a stream swollen in the winter, and confuses everything. Let the enemies of the Persians be ruled by democracies; but let us choose out from the citizens a certain number of the worthiest, and put the government into their hands." [232]

To be sure, we, who belong to a modern, enlightened democracy, would resent being called "a rude unbridled mob," and being likened to the

---

[232] *Op. cit.* Book III, chapter lxxxi.

populace of ancient Persia. But those of us who reflect recognize the dangers that lurk in the "psychology of the crowd"; and we are all aware that, after a popular vote, it is quite possible to discover that few, except a handful of office-holders, have gotten anything that they really want. Democracy is not a panacea for all political evils, and there are democracies of many kinds.

Still, when all is said, it seems as though the Rational Social Will, the ultimate arbiter of every moral State, should give its authority to a democratic form of government, rather than to another form. Every individual will has a *prima facie* claim to recognition.

But the Rational Social Will can never forget that human nature is in process of development, and that each nation, at a given time, is a historical phenomenon. The Rational Social Will is too enlightened to drape an infant in the raiment appropriate to a college graduate. It is only an intemperate enthusiasm that is capable of that.

157. THE LAWS OF THE STATE.—The State allots to individuals, and to the lesser groups of human beings, of which it is composed, *rights*, and it prescribes to them *duties*. Upon its activities in this sphere I can touch only by way of illustration, and for the sake of making clear the nature of the functions of the State.

(1) To whom shall the State grant a share in the formulation and execution of its laws? Once, in communities very enlightened, in their own peculiar way, women, children, slaves, mechanics, petty traders, and hired servants were deemed quite unfit to be entrusted with such responsibilities. [233]

With us, the position of woman has changed. Slavery, in a technical sense, has been abolished. The mechanic and the petty trader are much in evidence at "primaries." Hired servants are by some accused of being tyrants. Children, and defectives who are grossly and palpably defective, we bar from elections, and we also reject some criminals.

The times have changed, and our notions of the right of the individual to an active share in the State have changed with them. The expression of the social will has undergone modification, and I think we can say that it is, on the whole, modification in the right direction.

To be sure, the court of last resort is the *Rational* Social Will. What is best for the State, and, hence, for those who compose it? What is practicable in

---

[233] See ARISTOTLE'S *Politics*.

the actual condition in which a given state finds itself at a given time? It seems too easy a solution of our problems to seek dogmatic answers to our questionings by having recourse to the "natural light," that ready oracle of the philosopher, Descartes.

(2) There are certain classes of rights which civilized states generally guarantee to their citizens with varying degrees of success. They make it the duty of their citizens to respect these rights in others.

(a) The laws protect life and limb. Much progress has been made in this respect in the last centuries past. I own no coat of mail; and, when I walk abroad, I neither carry a sword nor surround myself with armed retainers.

(b) They protect private property. To be sure, the "promoter" may prey upon my simplicity; and the state itself does not recognize that I have any absolute right to my property, any more than it recognizes that I have an absolute right to my life.

It may send me into the trenches. It may take from me what it will in the form of taxes. It may even forbid me to increase my income by using my property in ways which will make me insupportable to my neighbors. But it will not allow my neighbor, who is stronger than I, to take possession of my house without form of law. It will even allow me to dispose of my property by will, after my death.

I suggest that those, to whom this right appears to be rooted in the very nature of things, and not to be a creation of the State, called into being at the behest of the social will in a certain stage of its development, should read and re-read what Sir Henry Maine has to say about testamentary succession, in his wonderful little book on "Ancient Law." [234]

The State has not always treated a man as an individual, directly and personally responsible to the state. It has treated him as a member of a family or some other group; a being endowed, by virtue of his position, with certain rights, and burdened with certain duties. A being who, when he drops out of being, is automatically replaced by someone else who is clothed upon with both his rights and his responsibilities.

Our conceptions have changed. The lesser groups within the State have to some degree lost their cohesion, and the bond between the individual, as such, and the state has been correspondingly strengthened. But many traces of the old conception make themselves apparent. The law compels

---

[234] See chapters vi and vii.

me to provide for my wife and children; and, if I die intestate, the law by no means assumes that my property is left without a claimant.

Have we been moving in the right direction, as judged by the standard of the Rational Social Will? We think so. But it is well to bear in mind what Herodotus said about the madness of Cambyses, and the prejudice men have in favor of their own customs. No state is a mere aggregate of unrelated individuals. Men are set in families, and the State seems to be composed of groups within groups. How far the State should recognize the will of the individual, as over against the claims of the lesser groups to which he may belong, is a nice question for the Rational Social Will to settle.

(c) The law must regulate marriage and divorce. Matters so vital to the interests of society cannot be left at the mercy of the egoistic whims of the individual. But to what law shall we have recourse? It seems highly irrational to have forty-eight independent authorities upon this subject within the limits of a single nation. And, if we turn the matter over to the churches, we discover that we have committed it to the care of one hundred and eighty, or more, sects. Add to this, that a state of any sort cannot be set upon its feet without some difficulty, while any enterprising man or woman can call a sect into existence any day. There is a new adherent for sectarian eccentricities born every minute. Surely, here is a field for the activities of the Rational Social Will.

(d) To paternalism of some sort the modern State, as law-giver, seems hopelessly pledged. If we ignore this we are simply closing our eyes. The State seems to be justified in educating its citizens, in protecting children and women against exploitation, in protecting the working classes, in stamping out infectious diseases. We are not even allowed to expectorate when and where we will, a privilege enjoyed by the merest savage.

(e) In one respect the paternalism of our own State has lagged behind that of certain others. We do little to secure to a man a decent privacy, or to safeguard his personal dignity. The newspaper reporter is allowed to rage unchecked, to unearth scandals in private families, and to cause great pain by printing the names of individuals.

I have known, in Europe, a man, after a difference of opinion touching the ventilation of a railway carriage, to break a window with his elbow and to apply to his fellow-passenger an offensive epithet. The court made him pay a dollar and a half for breaking the window and six dollars for giving himself the pleasure of being insulting.

Which was the greater offense? Herodotus would expect this question to be answered in accordance with the prejudices of the person giving the answer.

158. THE RIGHTS AND DUTIES OF THE STATE.—The State evidently has rights over its citizens, and may enforce these rights through the infliction of punishment. It as evidently has duties. A given state may not be answerable to any actual given power. Our own State is in such a position at the present time—there is no other state strong enough to call it to account.

But this does not free it from duties. No state is anything more than a brute force, except as it incorporates, in some measure, the Rational Social Will. And states that fall far short, as judged by this standard, may overstep their rights and ignore their duties, whether they are dealing with individuals or with other states.

In punishing, the State should punish rationally. [235] And it should not demand of its subjects what will degrade them as moral beings. "We all recognize," said a pure and candid soul, "that a rightful sovereign may command his subjects to do what is wrong, and that it is then their duty to disobey him." [236]

But how discover what demands are just? It is the whole argument of this volume that no man should venture an opinion upon this subject without having come to some appreciation of what is meant by the Rational Social Will. Man, his instincts, the degree of his intelligence and self- control, the history of the development of human societies, cannot be ignored. It is the weakness of good men, endowed with a high degree of speculative intelligence, to construct Utopias, and to tabulate the "rights of man," or, as Bentham well expressed it, to make lists of "anarchical fallacies." [237] Thus, some may, with Plato and Aristotle, advocate infanticide. The Greek city-state was a crowded little affair, and in danger of over-population. Some may propose radical measures to increase the population. To France and Argentina, in our day, such an increase appears highly desirable. May any and every method be embraced which seems adapted to avert a given evil or to attain to a desired end? It is instructive to note that Francis Galton, the father of "eugenics," proposed to leave morals out of the question as "involving too many hopeless difficulties." [238] But do men live well who leave morals out of the question?

---

[235] See chapter xxxii, Sec 148.

[236] Sidgwick, *Methods of Ethics*, III, vi.

[237] See *Works*, Bowring's Edition, Volume II.

[238] Encyclopedia Britannica, 11th edition, article, "Sociology."

The man who falls back upon intuition alone, in his advocacy of the abolition of capital punishment, may be expected to maintain next that a state, in going to war, should stop short at the point where the lives of its citizens are put in jeopardy. Why kill a good man, when it is wrong to kill a bad one?

It must be admitted that the State and its representatives enjoy some rights and duties not accorded to individuals. The State may condemn men to death or to imprisonment; it may take over property; it may make itself a compulsory arbiter between individuals. On the other hand, its representatives are not always as free as are private persons. The individual, if he is a generous soul, may freely forego some of his advantages and may seek only a fair fight with an opponent. It is doubtful whether the duty the State owes to its citizens permits of chivalry. Certainly strong states do not hesitate to attack weak ones; nor do many hesitate to combine against one, on the score of fair play. And a private man may temper justice with mercy in ways forbidden to a judge.

CHAPTER XXXV

INTERNATIONAL ETHICS

159. WHAT IS MEANT BY THE TERM.—I am almost tempted to avoid the discussion of this thorny subject by simply referring the reader to what has been said already on "The Spread of the Community," and developed in the chapters on "The Rational Social Will" and "The Individual and the Social Will." [239]

He who confines himself to generalities avoids many difficulties and can assure himself of the approval of many. Who, condemns justice and humanity in the abstract? Who can wax eloquent in his condemnation of

---

[239] See Sec 75 and chapters xxi-xxii.

freedom? Who finds the Christian Church on his side, when he advocates rapacity and the oppression of the helpless, without entering into details?

On the other hand, who wishes to view his country with a cold impartiality, and to place its interests exactly on a par with the interests of other lands? Who, save the Chinaman himself, thinks it as important that a Chinaman should have enough to eat as that an American or an Englishman should? Was not the turpitude, that excluded the Chinaman from Australia, traced to the two deadly sins of undue diligence and sobriety? [240] As for freedom, men of certain nations regard it as the highest virtue to be willing to die for it—their own freedom, be it understood,—while they regard the same desire for freedom on the part of their colonists as a moral obliquity to be extirpated, root and branch.

That the historian and the sociologist should find much to say touching the relation of nations to each other and to subject peoples goes without saying. But the cynic may maintain with some plausibility that the moralist's chapter on International Ethics must be as void of content as the traditional chapter on "Snakes in Ireland." In this the cynic is wrong, as usual; but it is instructive to listen to him, if only that we may intelligently refute him.

It is not always easy for an individual to determine just what he owes to his family, to his neighbors, or to his country. Is it surprising that it should be difficult for men to determine just what one country, or what one race, owes to another? This is the subject of international ethics. He who treads upon this ground should walk gingerly, and not feel too sure of himself. But there is no reason why the moralist should not put upon paper such reflections as occur to him. He cannot say anything more devoid of reason than much that is said by others.

The great Grotius, in writing on international law, in the seventeenth century, drew his illustrations chiefly from Greeks and Romans long dead. He had much more recent material ready to hand. But he well knew that he, who would induce another to give him calm and dispassionate attention, must not begin by treading on the toes of his listener. I shall strive to profit by his example. It is best to say only what each man can apply to his neighbor. We are all sensitive in this field.

160. OUR METHOD OF APPROACH TO THE SUBJECT—We have seen (Sec 80) that rational elements are to be found even in the irrational will, if one will look below the surface.

---

[240] Encyclopedia Britannica, 11th edition, article, "Australia."

Is it rational for the mother to place before all else the interests of the hairless, toothless and, apparently, mindless little creature that she clasps to her breast? The very existence of society depends upon her having the feeling that prompts her to do it. Is it rational to favor one's neighbor, to be proud of one's native town, which may be a poor sort of a town? Is it rational to be patriotic, even when one's state is not much of a state?

We have seen that the Rational Social Will incorporates itself in societies very gradually, and that it draws into its service lesser groups of many descriptions. He who detaches himself from these lesser groups is not a man. He is the mere outline of a man—the "featherless biped" of the philosopher. It is not of such that a state can be made.

It is the duty of the state to prevent a man from shrinking into being the mere member of some lesser group, but it is not its duty to obliterate what is human in him. And the Rational Social Will must see to it that he does not, on the other hand, forget, in a blind and irrational patriotism, that he is a human being with a capacity for human sympathies—sympathies extending far beyond the limits of any state. Except when they are under the influence of strong passion, I think we may say that men in civilized states, at least, have already shown themselves amenable to the influence of the Rational Social Will in this direction. It must be confessed that that influence has, as yet, been limited.

The approach to the subject of international ethics must lie in the recognition that men are set in families, in neighborhoods, in towns or cities, in states; and are yet human beings with a capacity for respecting and loving those who belong to none of these particular organizations. My advice to the man who wishes to abuse his fellow-man is to do it quickly, and before he is acquainted with him. If he gets to know him well, he will probably find something lovable in him, and he will lose the pleasure of being malicious.

161. SOME PROBLEMS OF INTERNATIONAL ETHICS.—The man who reads history finds, sometimes, things to inspire him; and sometimes, things that are depressing. He sees that the family must expand into the clan, that the clan must come into contact with others, that the state must rise, and that some interrelation of states is an inevitable necessity. He sees that man's increase in insight, in diligence, in enterprise, must make him reach out and trade with his fellow-man.

He sees also conquest, with the subjugation of peoples; he sees trade extended by force, and under the smoke of cannon; he sees a peaceful economic penetration, which ends in protectorates and annexations, in defiance of the will of those who do not want to be either protected or annexed.

What is rational is real, and what is real is rational, said Hegel. [241] He further maintained that civilized nations may treat as barbarians peoples who are behind them in the "essential elements of the state"; and also that, in a given epoch, a given nation is dominant, and "other existing nations are void of right."

Hegel has long been dead, and is turned to dust. He always was as dry as dust, even when he was alive, but he was a great man. But the famous Englishman, Sir Thomas More, wrote more engagingly; and does he not tell us, in his "Utopia," that any nation's holding unused a piece of ground needed for the nourishment of other people is a just cause of war?

Such doctrines should be most comforting to us Americans. They appear to teach us that we are, at present, the chosen people; that the rights of other peoples are as the rights of the Hivites, the Hittites, and all the rest; that we are justified in taking what we please, for who is there to withstand us?

Yet ethical Americans shake their heads over such philosophies, and some of them even speak slightingly of philosophers. This, in spite of the fact that great men seldom talk pure nonsense, except when carried away by excitement, as all men may be, at times. If what they say sounds to us wholly unmeaning, it is probable that we have not fully understood the voice that speaks within them. What can be said in their defense? and what can be said in, at least, partial defence of the actual historical procedure of the nations? They have not been wholly composed of criminals, and they must possess at least the rudiments of a moral sense.

(1) We have seen that the state maintains its right as against those who belong to it by controlling, not by destroying, the lesser groups which exist within the state. Such a control appears to be demanded by the Rational Social Will, but it often frustrates the will of the individual.

(2) We have seen that the spread of the community is inevitable, and that, in the interests of rationality, it is desirable.

(3) We have seen that, even in the family, all the members are not equally free agents. The small boy is not consulted touching the amount of his punishment, nor can he dictate where it shall be laid on. And the state does not give to all the individuals in it equal political rights, nor guarantee to them an equal share of influence. This is desirable, on the whole, in the interests of the whole, but grave abuses may easily come into being.

---

[241] *The Philosophy of Right*, Preface, and see Sec Sec 351 and 347.

(4) We have seen that the greater whole guarantees to individuals rights, and assigns to them duties. In so far as it is rational, it cannot do this arbitrarily. To have recourse to metaphysical abstractions is futile. Shall we say, without hedging, that a man has a right to the fruits of his labor, or that first occupation gives a right to the soil? Then, shall the man who is too weak to work be refused a right to the ownership of a coat? Or must the discoverer of a continent prove a real occupancy, by performing the ridiculous task of the abnormal center of the mythical mathematical infinite circle, by being everywhere at the same time?

(5) We have seen that the human community, taking the words in a broad sense, will spread, and already has spread, beyond the limits of several nationalities. It is in the interest of human society that it should do so. It is rational, in the sense of the word everywhere used in this book. But the nations continue to exist, and they often cultivate selfishly national interests. So do families cultivate selfishly family interests. So does the egoist selfishly dig about and fertilize the number One.

(6) It requires little acuteness to see that some communities of men are miserable exponents of the social will. They are deplorably governed. Read Slatin's fascinating book, "Fire and Sword in the Soudan,"—it is better than any novel,—and ask yourself what becomes of the social will or of rationality of any sort under the rule of a Mahdi. Is it not the duty of the nations to combine and to relieve suffering humanity?

(7) There are theorists who maintain that, in the nature of things, the soil belongs to nobody. We find, in the actual state of things, it usually belongs to somebody, unless it is so poor that it is not worth owning at all. But it may belong to somebody who can make little more use of it than an infant can of a gold watch. A handful of Indians, wandering over a great tract of country in which they chase game in the intervals of time during which they chase and scalp one another, may have an immemorial, although unrecorded, title to the land.

Shall they be permitted to keep back settlers from more or less civilized and densely populated countries? Settlers eager to cultivate the land and to make it support many, where before it supported few, and supported those few miserably?

And shall the natural resources of great regions of the earth be permitted to lie fallow merely because the actual inhabitants are too ignorant and too indolent to want to produce anything and to trade? He who finds his happiness in idleness, bananas, and black wives who can be beaten with impunity, has little interest in international traffic, with such blessings as it is supposed to bring.

The world is filling up. The losses due to war and pestilence, said no less an authority than Darwin, are soon made up. There is something terrifying in what the very modern science of geography has to tell us about the rapidity with which the remaining part of the earth's surface, available for the nourishment of man, is being exhausted. What problems will face the Rational Social Will in the none too distant future?

162. THE OTHER SIDE OF THE SHIELD.—We have seen that something can be said for the philosopher. The Rational Social Will does not appear to give carte blanche to the man who wishes to remain ignorant, idle, cut off from the family of the nations, the possessor of great tracts of land which he will not develop, the cruel oppressor of such as he finds within his power. It tends to deal with him, wherever it finds him, as an enlightened nation treats the idle, the vicious and the irresponsible within its own borders.

Undoubtedly civilization has made some advance in the course of the centuries. When the world is at peace, the stranger is not normally an outlaw. I have sojourned in the cities of many of the nations of Europe and have made excursions into Africa and Asia. Nowhere have I been compelled to ask for the protection of an American consul. It has been recognized that I had rights, although an American. And the ability to sign my name has procured me a supply of money.

Notwithstanding all this, it is depressing to read of the dealings of the nations with each other, and with backward peoples—who have been well defined as peoples who possess gold-mines, but no efficient navy. Is it not generally taken for granted that it is the duty of more powerful and more enlightened nations to take the backward nations in hand, to exploit their resources, and, incidentally, to exploit *them*?

Not that international law has not counted for something. To be sure Hegel reduced it to the level of "a good intention," [242] but it has counted for something. Descartes and Spinoza could, with impunity, be heretics in little Holland. Switzerland has for centuries been the refuge of the oppressed. But we cannot forget that our highest authority, Captain Mahan, declared, in 1889, that certain rights of neutrals were "forever secured," [243] and he has since stood revealed as a false prophet, a mere man making a guess. International law is a capital thing—when it is not put under a strain, and when no nation is too powerful.

---

[242] *The Philosophy of Right*, Sec Sec 330-333.

[243] *The Influence of Sea Power upon History*, Boston, 1908, chapter ii, p. 84.

The depressing thing is that rapacity and oppression become glorified, when the cloak of patriotism is thrown over their shoulders. I drew my illustrations in the last section from wild Indians and from African savages. But there are nations in all stages of their development. How "backward" must a nation be to give us the right to rule over it by force? No people were more ingenious than the ancient Romans in finding plausible reasons for the wars which it pleased them to wage. This has never been a lost art. Men's enemies are, like the absent, always in the wrong; and those are apt to become enemies, in whose defeat some substantial advantage is to be looked for.

163. THE SOLUTION.—The very title seems a presumption. Who may dogmatize in matters so involved? I make no pretentions to giving a clear vision of "yonder shining light," but I venture to hint at the general direction in which one is to seek the little wicket gate.

The only ethical solution of our problem appears to lie in the frank recognition of the fact that the groups of men, called nations, may be as brutal egoists as are individual persons, and in the earnest attempt to avoid the baleful influence of such egoism.

Man *is* his brother's keeper. But that does not give him the right to keep his brother in chains, nor to use him for selfish ends. This is as true of nations as it is of individuals, of families, of religious orders, or of unions, whether of employers or of employees.

It is certainly true of nations. It is only as having a place in, and as being an instrument of, the great organism of humanity aimed at by the Rational Social Will, that the individual, the family, the tribe, the nation, have any ethical justification for being at all. Sometimes it is very profitable for the individual, or for some group of human beings, to disallow this obligation to be moral. We treat the individual as a robber; why not admit that there are robber nations?

I feel like reiterating that it is a great thing to be young; to live in that Golden Age in which one still believes what one sees in print, and still is moved by the honeyed words of statesmen. When one is old, and has enjoyed some breadth of culture, one has read the newspapers of many lands, and has met a certain number of statesmen, usually with a start of surprise.

It is borne in upon one—a matter touched upon in the last chapter—that it appears to be generally accepted that the state and its representatives may adopt a peculiar variety of ethics. Certainly statesmen feel justified in doing for their country what they, as gentlemen, would never dream of doing for themselves. They talk of justice, when they would scoff at such justice within the borders of their own states; they talk of humanity, and they have in mind the economic advantage of their own peoples; they speak of protection and Christianization, when they mean economic exploitation or strategic superiority. As for truth, the less said about that subject the better.

I know of only one way in which the determination of a nation to aid in the general realization of the Rational Social Will can be tested. Does it, in dealing with other nations, civilized or backward, propose what is palpably to its own advantage, or is it evidently disinterested? It is thus that we judge a man, when we wish to fix his ethical status; it is thus that the Rational Social Will judges a nation. The language in which the proposals are made is a matter of no moment. It may fairly be called professional slang, and can quickly be acquired, even by men of mediocre intelligence, in any diplomatic circle.

164. THE NECESSITY FOR CAUTION.—Shall a man, then, eschew patriotism, and become a citizen of the world, as though he were a Stoic philosopher? By no means. As well eschew the family or the neighborhood. But let him not, in his patriotism, forget that he is a man. Here, as everywhere, he is called upon to exercise judgment. This is a burden which he can never throw off. He must pay the penalty of being a rational human being. As an instrument of the Rational Social Will the state must be kept up. It is his duty to see that it is done. His cat has an easier task; she may sleep her life away in peace.

We hear much of the brotherhood of man and of artificial barriers. The barriers are not all artificial, and they cannot be swept away with a gesture.

Races and peoples are formed upon the model of their own immemorial past. They have their institutions, their traditions, their loyalties, their standards of living. What is tolerable to one man is wholly intolerable to another. To compel men to live together in intimacy, when centuries of training have made them antipathetic, is sheer cruelty.

Men may be brothers, but there are big brothers and little brothers. I do not refer to physical bulk. I refer to the development of intelligence, to the degree and kind of culture, which has been attained. There are little brothers still at the stage of development at which it is natural for human beings to drool. Shall we have them sit up to the table and serve them with the complete dinner, enlivening it with intellectual conversation?

Between incontinently doing this, and relegating the little brothers to a nursery where they will be treated with cruelty and starved in our interests, some persons seem to think there is no middle course. In their enthusiasm for humanity, they forget that the brotherhood of man may be made as ridiculous as the eight-hour day. Between eight hours of the creative work of a Milton and eight hours of the dawdling done by a lazy housemaid, there is no relation save that both may be measured by a clock.

These enthusiasts forget much. Men are not alike; they do not want to be alike; they do not want to live together in close intimacy, when they have little in common; they reverence different things; as a rule, they would rather be somewhat unhappy after their own fashion, than be happy under compulsion, after the fashion of someone else.

We have, thus, on the one hand, the enthusiasts who would at once sound the trump and announce the millenium, feeding the lion and the sucking calf out of the same dish and on the same meat. We have, on the other, those who are eager to take on their shoulders the white man's burden—to enclose in a coop, as if they were chickens, the greater part of the human race, allaying the discontent of the imprisoned by pointing out to them that, although their freedom of movement is limited, they are growing fat, and that they should show their gratitude by laying eggs.

Surely, there must be some middle course. Patience and caution are virtues. Surely, it is possible to accept the existing organism of society, to love one's country, and yet to strive to respect the freedom of others. It is not easy for a true patriot to do this, but it seems to be what the Rational Social Will demands of him.

The moralist who reads history carefully is not wholly discouraged. He may look forward to some time, in the more or less distant future, when there may be a union of the nations in the interests of all men; when the gross egoism of the hypertrophied patriot may be curbed; when the mellifluous language of the statesman may mean more than did the pious letter which Nero wrote to the Roman Senate, after he had murdered his mother.

CHAPTER XXXVI

ETHICS AND OTHER DISCIPLINES

165. SCIENCES THAT CONCERN THE MORALIST.—There are certain sciences that the Moralist must lay under contribution very directly, and yet he seems to be able to make little return to those who cultivate them, at least in their professional capacity.

He must ask aid from the biologist, the psychologist, the anthropologist. They help him to a comprehension of what man is; and, hence, of what it is desirable that man should strive to do. But these men seldom come to the moralist for advice. They appear to be able to work without his help.

There are, however, other sciences in which the moralist feels that he has more of a right to meddle, however independent they may regard themselves.

Take, for example, politics or economics, or the very modern and rudimentary science of eugenics. The man who cultivates political science may know much more than do most moralists about states and their forms of organization; about legislative, executive and judicial functions; about the probable effects of the centralization or decentralization of authority; about what may be expected, in a given case, from a restriction or extension of the franchise; about the creation and maintenance of a military establishment and the building up of an efficient civil service. The economist may be a monster of learning and a master in ingenuity on all problems touching the creation and distribution of wealth.

But the political scientist and the economist, however able, share our common humanity. A man's outlook is more or less apt to be bounded by the limits of the science of his predilection. The several sciences, broader or more specialized, rest, in the minds of most men, upon foundations which are taken for granted. It is too much to expect that every sermon should begin as far back as the Garden of Eden. "Practical" politics and economics do not, as a rule, go so far back.

The transition from practical politics and economics to ethical problems may be made at any time. No man was shrewder than Machiavelli, and the moral sense of mankind has rebelled against him and made him a byword.

A state, desirous of maintaining itself, may palpably violate in its institutions, inherited from the past, a social will grown more rational, more conscious of its rights and more articulate. Then the appeal is made to right and justice in other than the traditional forms. It may, in a given instance, be wrong to create wealth; existing forms of its distribution may be iniquitous. The ultimate arbiter in all such matters must be the Ethical Man.

Human society is indefinitely complex. Many specialists must occupy themselves with its problems. A technical question in this field may always be carried over to moral ground. He who undertakes to make this transition without having made a fairly thorough study of ethics appears to be working in the dark. His assumptions have been questioned, or have been abandoned. Who shall furnish him with a new basis for his special science?

Ethics is a basal science. It justifies, or it refuses to justify, those specialists who concern themselves with men in societies. It is a very old science and has interested men vastly. I have spoken above of eugenics as a new science. Only in its modern form is it new. Plato cultivated it intemperately when he wrote his "Republic"—but he saw that his "Republic" would not do, and he wrote his "Laws." He stood condemned by Ethics.

Usually men who occupy themselves seriously, and in a broad way, with man in society, have adopted, consciously or unconsciously, some ethical doctrine. But this is often done without due consideration, and without a sufficient knowledge of what has been said by the great thinkers of the past. It is for this reason that I have treated at such length in this volume of the schools of the moralists.

166. ETHICS AND PHILOSOPHY.—It should be observed that in developing the Ethics of the Rational Social Will, or the Ethics of Reason— the doctrine advocated in this volume—I have not depended upon a particular philosophy.

I see no reason why a Realist or an Idealist, a Monist or a Dualist, one who holds to an immediate perception of an external world or one who regards our acquaintance with it as a matter of inference, should refuse to go with me so far. Nor do I see any reason why a believer in God, one who bows at the shrine of Mind-Stuff, or one who refuses to commit himself at all upon such matters, should enter a demurrer. The Parallelist and the Interactionist, however widely they differ touching the relation of mind and body, may here fall upon one another's necks and shed tears of brotherly affection.

That it is proper for the philosopher to interest himself in ethics, I have maintained. [244] He is supposed to be a critical and reflective man, and to take broad views of human affairs. Such views are needed when one comes to the study of ethics.

I am forced to admit that some philosophers, when they have written on ethical subjects, have said certain things to which the critical moralist cannot readily assent. He who maintains that certain human intuitions— which it may even appear impossible to reconcile with each other—are inexplicably and infallibly authoritative, seems to leave us without so much as the hope of ever attaining to ultimate rationality. [245]

And there are philosophers who would persuade us that, unless we accept all the religious or theological doctrines which have appeared to them acceptable, we rob man of every incentive for being moral at all. If God is not going to repay him with interest for the pains which he gives himself, does he not play the part of a dupe in being good? We have seen that this was palpably the position of Paley. [246] If God will not reconcile, ultimately, benevolence and self- interest, proclaimed Reid, man "is reduced to this miserable dilemma, whether it is best to be a fool or a knave." [247] Some of the utterances of Kant and of Green seem to point in the same direction, but both have made it abundantly plain that they, personally, and whatever their intellectual perplexities, were moved by something much higher than egoism. [248]

I mean to say very little about philosophy in this volume. I wish to keep to ethics, a science old enough and strong enough to stand upon its own feet. But it would be wrong not to underline one or two points in this connection, if only to obviate misunderstanding:

(1) There is nothing wrong in a man's wishing to earn the heaven in which he believes. It is not wrong for him to wish to be happy on earth and in the body. But if the desire for his own happiness, either here or hereafter, is the *only* motive that can move him, he is not a good man. Prudence may be a virtue, generally speaking; but it is no substitute for benevolence. The

---

[244] See chapter vi, Sec 18.

[245] See chapter xxiii.

[246] Chapter xxiv, Sec 96.

[247] *Essays on the Active Powers of Man*, Essay III, Part III, chapter viii. It would be absurd to believe that either Paley or Reid lived down to the level of his doctrine. Both were very decent men, and capable of disinterestedness.

[248] See chapters xxiv, Sec 97; xxvi, 3; and xxix.

man who is *only* prudent is no fit member of any society of rational beings anywhere.

(2) Men are often better than their words would indicate. Paley talks as if he were a cad; Reid flounders; Kant, noble as are many of his utterances, sometimes gives forth an uncertain sound. Yet no one of these men was personally selfish.

And yet all of these men assumed that morality is endangered unless there is a God to repay men for being good. Why did they insist so strenuously upon this, and incorporate it into their philosophy? We must, I think, go beneath the surface to find the real reason; and when we have discovered it, we cannot regard them in an unfavorable light.

They felt, I believe, that good men *ought* to be made happy; that this is rational, if anything is. So far, they are quite in accord with the doctrine of the Rational Social Will. And they saw no other way of guaranteeing a complete rationality than in holding to a theistic philosophy.

(3) This means that their real motives were not selfish and personal. This is admirably brought out when we turn to Green. It is too much to expect that many of my readers have read his "Prolegomena to Ethics," which is repetitious, tedious, and rather vague, though it is inspired by a fine spirit and has the great merit of having influenced, directly or indirectly, a number of able writers to produce excellent works on ethics. [249]

Green dwells, with infinite repetition, upon the presence in man "of a principle not natural," which is identical in all men, and which, in some way that he does not explain, holds the world of our experiences together, being itself not in time or in space. The disciple of Paley or Reid or Kant will search his pages in vain for any indication that this "principle" performs or can perform any of the functions of the God believed in by the above-mentioned philosophers. Nevertheless, it is the source of an ardent inspiration to Green, who relieves the baldness of the appellation "principle," by calling it, sometimes, "self- consciousness," sometimes, "reason." It does not appear to promise Green anything, so his devotion to it may be regarded as disinterested. However, he owes to it inspiration.

Philosophers find their inspiration in very different directions. The philosopher, as such, sometimes rather objects to the word, "God." [250] But he may feel much as men generally feel toward God, when he contemplates

---

[249] I need only to refer to the text-books by Muirhead, Mackenzie, Dewey and Fite.
[250] See chapter xxvi, Sec 123, note

his "Conscious Principle," or his "Idea," or the "Substance" which he conceives as the identity of thought and extension, or, for that matter, "Mind-Stuff" or the "Unknowable." That other men may not see that he has anything in particular to be inspired about, or that he can hope for anything in particular for himself or for other men, does not rob him of his inspiration, and that may affect his life deeply.

It is, hence, not a matter of no importance to ethics what manner of philosophy it pleases a man to elect. One's outlook upon the great world may repress or may stimulate ethical strivings, may narrow or may broaden the ethical horizon. It is something to feel, even rather blindly, that one has a Cause. For myself, I think it is better to have a Cause that seems worth while, even when rather impartially looked at. But, of this, more in the next section.

(4) Whatever one thinks of such matters, it is well to come back to the fact that, nevertheless, ethics stands upon its own feet. Even if Paley, and Reid, and Kant, and Green, and many others, are in the wrong, the doctrine of the Rational Social Will stands sure. It is wrong to be selfish; it is wrong to be untruthful; it is wrong to be unjust. It is wrong for individuals, and it is wrong for nations. The man, or the group of men, that does wrong, is irrational. It stands condemned.

167. ETHICS AND RELIGION.—I regret having to speak, in this book, about religion at all, just as I regret having to refer to the philosophers. But it would be folly to omit all reference to religious duties. They have played quite too important a part in the life of the family, of the tribe, of the state; and that not merely here and there, but everywhere, in societies of all degrees of development, in recent centuries and in times of a hoary antiquity. Those interested in the classics have read the remarkable little book, "The Ancient City," by Fustel de Coulanges. As schoolboys we were brought up on the pious Aeneas. All Christians have some knowledge of the theocratic state of the Hebrews, and we know something of the history of Christian Europe. The anthropologist gives us masses of information touching the religious duties of all sorts and conditions of men.

There are those who rid themselves easily of the problem of religious duties. They simply deny that there are any. And there are those—the classes overlap—who easily shuffle off duties to the family and to the state. They regard it as their function to ignore and to destroy.

(1) I cannot think the matter is so simple. There always have been religious duties generally recognized, as a matter of fact. The boldest and most gifted of thinkers, who have not hesitated to call into being Utopian schemes for an ideal state, such men as Plato and More, have thought that the ideal state must have a religion. And the modern scientist has gravely

raised the question whether the state can maintain itself, if all religious beliefs, with their inspirations and their restraints, die out. [251]

The moralist, who accepts religious duties, has a difficult task. It is not enough for him to say that men have religious duties "in general," just as it is not enough for him to say that they have political duties "in general." On the other hand it would be the height of presumption for him to endeavor to tell every man what he should do in detail. He does not feel it his duty to tell every man whom he should marry, or for whom he should vote at each election. Still, it does seem as though the moralist ought to do more than tell a man vaguely that he has religious duties.

(2) Why not follow the analogy suggested by duties to the family, the neighborhood, the state?

States have their religions, sometimes unequivocally and unmistakably, and sometimes not so palpably. The religion of a people has, as a rule, its roots far back in the history of that people. Its religion has influenced in many subtle ways its institutions, its emotions, its habits, its whole outlook upon life.

Even where, as with us, state and church have been, in theory, wholly sundered, there has been no question, up to the present, of the disappearance of a religion. The United States has been regarded as a Christian nation, inspired by ideals and addicted to customs only explicable by a Christian past.

The fact that it is so is somewhat obscured to us. For this there are two causes. The first is, that the American, who is a freeman, possesses and exercises a fatal ingenuity in the creation of a multitude of sects out of practically nothing. Still, most of these sects have more in common than some of their adherents suppose. They spring, as a rule, from a Christian root. The second is, that our land has been the goal of the greatest migration ever recorded in human history. Most of those who have come to us have, so far, come from nations in some sense Christian, but they have brought with them very diverse traditions, and some appear to object to traditions altogether.

Nevertheless, I think we may be called a Christian nation, and if we follow the analogy above suggested—that of the relations of men to the state and to lesser organisms within the state—it would appear that it is the duty of an American to recognize himself as a Christian rather than as a Mahometan or a Pagan. If he does recognize this, he will feel himself under

[251] McDougall, *Social Psychology*, chapter xiii.

certain obligations which are independent of his personal tastes and proclivities.

(3) For one thing, he will recognize that a religion is not a thing to be stripped off and drawn on as one changes a suit of clothes.

A woman may regret that her infant has red hair. She will not, on that account, as a rule, exchange him surreptitiously for another. Men do not commonly repudiate their fathers because they are not rich or are growing old. A good citizen may regret that his country has seen fit to enter into a given war, but he will not, therefore, give aid or comfort to the enemy.

He who is capable of lightly repudiating his religion resembles the man who is capable of discarding his wife, when he sees the first grey hair. Those who do such things are apt to be men who fill their whole field of vision with their rights, and can find no place there for their duties. Nor should it be overlooked that the man, who is capable of lightly discarding his wife, is the man as capable of supplying her place with a worse. Even so, he who easily throws off his religion is usually the man who easily replaces it with some superstition, scientific or merely whimsical, at which other men wonder.

Men lament sometimes over the fact that the task of the foreign missionary is a hard one. Were it really an easy one, there would be no stability in human societies, for there would be no stability in human nature. The man of light credulity is the man who easily takes on new faiths; not the man to whom tradition and loyalty mean something.

(4) It seems to follow, as a corollary, that the religion in which a man has been brought up has the first claim upon him. I accept this without hesitation.

But this does not mean that the claim is in all cases final and valid.

There may be cases in which it seems to be the duty of a man to leave his wife, to disinherit a child, to transfer his allegiance from one state to another. Such cases are recognized as justifiable by men who are thoughtful and disinterested. But the same men also recognize that, were such disruptions of the bonds which unite men in communities the rule and not the exception, it would mean the destruction of the community. Similarly, it may become the duty of a man to transfer his allegiance from one church to another.

Are not religions, rationally compared, of different values? Have there not

213

been religions indisputably on a moral level lower than that of the community which they represent? Undoubtedly.

And there have been governments so bad that the only refuge has seemed to lie in revolution. It should be remembered, however, that revolutions can be resorted to too lightly; and that evolution, where possible, is preferable to revolution, whether in things secular or in things religious. It is always easier to tear down than it is to build up. Nor does anyone, save the anarchist, tear down through wanton love of destruction. Even he is apt to feel called upon to give some sort of a vague excuse for his violence.

It will be observed that I have all along spoken, not merely of religion, but of the Church. I have done this because religion is a social phenomenon. It has its institutions, and cannot live without them.

It cannot be denied that individual philosophers have evolved religious philosophies; it cannot be denied that solitary individuals, as such, have felt religious emotions. How much of this is due to the fact that there have been religions and churches, I do not believe that they themselves have realized.

But, if religion is to be a vital force of any sort in a state, holding up ideals and stimulating the emotion that helps to realize them, it must be incorporated in an institution or in institutions. You cannot remove the rose and keep the perfume. Even the memory of it tends to vanish. A religious man without a church is like a citizen without a state. A citizen without a state is a man who makes the effort to keep step, and to walk in single file, all alone.

(5) Having said so much for Religion and for the Church, it is right that I should refer to some things that may be said on the other side.

It may be claimed that men of science have a tendency to turn away from religion and to grow indifferent to or to deny religious duties. In this there is some truth, although notable exceptions to the rule may be cited.

But I have known many men of learning in two hemispheres, in some cases rather intimately. With the utmost respect for their learning and for their mental ability, I am still bound to say that I have found them quite human. Some of them—among the greatest of them—have been so absorbed in their special fields of investigation, that they have not merely given scant attention to religion and to religious duties, but have done scant justice even to their own family life or to the state. And all have not been equally broad men, capable of seeing clearly the part which religion has played in the life of humanity.

To this I must add that the impartial objectivity with which the scholar is supposed by the layman to view things is something of a chimera. In saying this I criticize no one more severely than I criticize myself. This may be taken as my apology for the utterance. Have we not seen, not many years since, that, in the feeling aroused by an international conflict, some scores of great scholars on the one side found it possible to write and to sign a series of statements diametrically opposed to a series drawn up and signed by some scores of equally famous scholars on the other? Was either group walled in hopelessly by sheer ignorance? It is easy to take lightly matters about which one does not particularly care.

There is another objection brought against religion and the church which seems to be more significant. Is there not a danger that an interest in these may hamper freedom of thought and encourage an undue conservatism?

It should be borne in mind that religion and the church are not the only forces that make for conservatism. Family affection is conservative; the law is conservatism itself, and men feel that it should not be lightly tampered with. How impartial and how ready to introduce innovations should men be in any field? Changes of certain kinds, though they may have no little bearing upon our comfort, do not threaten the existence of either state or church. Could someone devise a scheme by which the periodical visits of the plumber could be avoided, we should all welcome it, and have no fear of the consequences.

Other innovations may bring in their train consequences more momentous. What men deeply care about, they cling to, and the question which confronts us is a very broad one. Does humanity, on the whole, gain or lose by a given degree of conservatism? An increase of knowledge is by no means the only thing that makes for civilization. Men may be highly enlightened, and yet rotten to the very core. How much of the ballast of conservatism and of loyalty to tradition is it well to throw overboard in the interest of accelerated motion? Those who, in our judgment, throw overboard much too much we have taken to deporting.

(6) Here it will very likely be objected: In all this you are advocating sheer Pragmatism! Are we to accept God and look for a life to come, extending the spread of the community after the fashion suggested in Chapter XIX, and broadening the outlook for a future and more perfect rationality, for no better reason than that it is our whim? Shall we *believe* and join ourselves with other *believers*, for no better reason than that something happens to tempt our will?

I beg the reader, if he will be just to my thought, to follow me here with close attention.

168. ETHICS AND BELIEF.—Under this heading I must call attention to several points.

(1) I deny that I advocate Pragmatism at all. The views which I advocate are so many thousand years older than Pragmatism, that it seems unjust to them, at this late date, to compel them to take on a new name, and to be carried about in swaddling clothes in the arms of the philosophers, after they have been functioning as adults in human communities from time immemorial.

(a) That abounding genius and most lovable man, William James, realizing, as many lesser men did not realize, that the truth contained in such views was in danger of being lost sight of by many, wrote, with characteristic vivacity and unerring dramatic instinct, the little volume called "Pragmatism." It is with no lack of appreciation of the services he has rendered, that I venture to call attention to the fact that he has, in certain respects, failed to do justice to those views.

(b) Pragmatism has received attention partly on account of the exaggerations of which it has been guilty. These have repelled some men of sober mind. It appears to be maintained that we can play fast and loose with the world, and make it what we will. I have criticized this elsewhere,[9] and shall not do so now. I shall only say here that I do not believe that so able a man of science as William James meant all that he said to be taken quite literally. He was gifted with a sense of humor. This, some lack.

(c) Men of genius are apt to be strongly individualistic and impatient of restraints. We have seen that there is such a thing as a public conscience and a private conscience. The latter is only too often a whimsical thing. Pragmatism appears to teach that any individual, as such, has a moral right to adopt any hypothesis live enough to appeal to his individual will. One has only to call to mind the extraordinary assortment of guests collected by Signer Papini in his novel pragmatic "hotel." [252] Can such, by any human ingenuity, be moulded into anything resembling an orderly community?

(d) In a later work, Professor James, realizing that religion and theology are not identical, and strongly desirous of promoting religion, deals severely with theology and the theologians. [253]

One truth has been seen, but has not another been treated with some

---

[252] *Ibid.*

[253] *Varieties of Religious Experience*, Lecture xviii.]

injustice? Is it not inevitable that reflective men, who cherish beliefs, should endeavor to give a more or less clear and reasoned account of them? What degree of success is to be looked for, and what emphasis should be laid upon such attempts, are questions which will probably divide men for a long time to come.

(2) Hence, I do not advocate Pragmatism at all, but I agree with it in so far, at least, as to recognize that belief is a phenomenon which concerns the will. That it is so is a commonplace of psychology; and it was recognized dimly long before the psychologist, as such, came into being.

That it is so is rather readily overlooked where the evidence for certain beliefs is undeniable and overpowering. I seem forced to believe that I am now writing. I do not seem forced in a similar manner to accept a particular metaphysical doctrine or a given system of theological dogma. Intelligent men appear to be able to discuss such matters with each other and to agree to disagree. If they are tolerant, they can do this good-temperedly. It is worth while to keep several points clearly in mind:

(a) Beliefs are not a matter of indifference. Some evidently lead to palpable and speedy disaster. If I elect to believe that I can fly, and leave my window-sill as lightly as does the sparrow I now see there, it is time for my friends to provide me with an attendant.

Other beliefs are not of this character. And that they will lead to ultimate disaster of any sort to myself or to others seems highly disputable.

(b) What may be called scientific evidence may be adduced for different beliefs with varying degrees of cogency. Hegel tries to distinguish between the authority of the state and that of the church by attributing to the former something like infallibility. He maintains that religion "believes," but that the state "knows." [254]

We have had abundant reason to see that the state does not *know*, but *believes*, and that it is very often mistaken in its beliefs. Nevertheless, it does its best to keep order, to be as rational as it can, and to look a little way ahead. I think it ought to be admitted that it concerns itself with matters more *terre-a-terre* than does the church; and that it ought not to be taken as a general truth that the state should take its orders from the church. It has to do with matters which, like our daily bread, must be assured, if certain other matters are to be considered at all. In so far Hegel was right. There are those who forget this, and talk as if metaphysical

---

[254] The Philosophy of Right, Sec 270.

systems and religious beliefs should be forced upon men in spite of themselves, either by sheer force of windpower or with the aid of the police.

To this it may be added that beliefs range from an unshakable and unthinking conviction to that degree of acquiescence which can scarcely be distinguished from mere loyalty. It remains to be proved that the latter may not come under the head of belief, and is something to be condemned. [255]

(c) Beliefs, being phenomena which concern the will, are at the mercy of many influences. Is there any scientific evidence open to the parallelist in psychology which is not also open to the interactionist? Is the conviction that one's country is in the right a mere matter of scientific evidence? Are the enlightened adherents of a given sect wholly ignorant of the tenets and of the arguments of another?

I maintain that tradition and loyalty have their claims. They are not the only claims that can be made, but they are worthy of serious consideration. Man is man, whether he is dealing with things secular or with things religious.

To see that such claims are recognized everywhere we have only to open our eyes. It is absurd to believe that all the adherents of a political party are influenced only by the logical arguments published in the newspapers. A newspaper that lived on logic alone would starve to death. It is ridiculous to believe that all the members of a church are induced to become such only by the arguments of the theologians, many of which arguments the mass of the members are not in a position to comprehend at all.

And learned men are men, too. The philosopher who really kept himself free from all prepossessions would, if he did much serious reading, probably epitomize in his own person a large part of the history of philosophy, falling out of one system and into another, like an acrobat. But he is usually caught young and influenced by some teacher, or he is carried away by some book or by the spirit of the times. As he is not an abnormal

---

[255] More than thirty years ago, while I was the guest of Henry Sidgwick at Cambridge, England, I asked him how it was that he, the President of the British Society for Psychical Research, had never, in his presidential addresses, expressed a belief in the phenomena investigated. He answered that if the word "belief" were taken broadly enough to express a willingness to look into things, he might be said to believe. No more candid soul ever breathed.

creature, he acts like other men, becoming an adherent of a school, or, if he is ambitious, starting one.

(d) We have seen that the individual has duties toward the state. We have also seen that the state has duties toward the individual. The state should not make it practically impossible for him to be a loyal citizen. A somewhat similar duty appears to be incumbent upon the church.

A church that forces upon all of its members, as a condition of membership, intricate and abstract systems of metaphysics; a church that does not teach good-will toward men, but makes walls of separation out of slight differences of opinion; a church that lags behind the moral sense of the community in which it finds itself; a church that starves the religious life; these, and such as these, must expect to lose adherents. It is not that men reject them; it is that they reject men.

Those who read history have no reason to think that men, except here and there and under exceptional circumstances, will cease to regard religious duties as duties. I have not ventured to offer any detailed solution of the problem of loyalty to the church. But neither have I ventured to offer any detailed solution of the problem of loyalty to the state. In the one case, as in the other, I suggest as guides tradition, intuition and reflective reasoning. I can only counsel good sense and some degree of patience. It may be said: You do not solve the difficulty for the individual. I admit it. Such difficulties every thinking man must meet and solve for himself.

169. THE LAST WORD.—Those persons, whether students, or teachers, who dislike this final chapter, may omit it, without detriment to the rest of the book. The doctrine of the Rational Social Will is not founded upon this chapter. The latter is a mere appendix.

I regret that, in a work in which I have wished to avoid disputation, I have felt compelled to touch upon religious duties at all. But they have played, and still play, so significant a role in the history of mankind, that the omission could scarcely have been made. You are free to take them or leave them; but you are not free to take or leave the Rational Social Will as the Moral Arbiter of the Destinies of Man.

NOTES

1. CHAPTERS I TO III.—The notes in a book of any sort are rarely read, except by a few specialists, and by them not seldom with a view to refuting the author. I shall make the following as brief as I may. But I do wish to give some of my readers—all will not be equally learned—an opportunity to get acquainted with a few books better than this one. This first note is not addressed to the learned, and some will find it superfluous.

I intend to mention here a handful of books which any cultivated man may read with profit, and re-read with profit, if he has already read them. They can be collected gradually at a relatively slight expense, and it is a pleasure to have them in one's library. The list may easily be bettered, and may be indefinitely lengthened. I mention only books for those who are accustomed to do their reading in English.

It is hardly necessary to say that I do not advise all this reading in connection with the first three chapters of this book. But, as those chapters are concerned with the accepted content of morals as recognized by individuals and communities, I have a good excuse for bringing the list in here. Many other good books, not in the list, are referred to later in the volume, in other chapters.

It is very convenient to have within one's reach some such book as Sidgwick's *History of Ethics*. The only fault to find with Sidgwick is that he has made his book too short, and has not given enough references. But he is admirably fair and sympathetic, as well as clear and interesting.

He, who would dip more deeply into the Greek moralists, can read the accounts of the ancient egoists, Aristippus and Epicurus, in the *Lives of the Philosophers* by that entertaining old gossip, Diogenes Laertius. The translation in Bohn's edition will serve the purpose.

As for the greatest of the Greeks—a keen pleasure, intellectual and aesthetic, awaits the man who turns to Plato's *Republic* and his *Laws*. Jowett's great translation is in every public library. And we must read Aristotle's *Nichomachean Ethics* and his *Politics*. Here little attention is given to artistic form; but the preternatural acuteness of the man is overpowering. If we would understand some of the reasons which induced Plato and Aristotle to write of the state as they did, we can turn to chapter xiv of Grote's *Aristotle*.

With certain later classical moralists most of us are more or less familiar. Seneca, in his work *On Benefits*, gives a good picture of the moral emotions and judgments of an enlightened man of his time. He was a great favorite with Christian writers later. Cicero's work, *De Officiis—On Duties*—it is best known under the Latin title, is very clear and very clever. It is, in its last half, full of "cases of conscience." I venture to suggest to the teacher of undergraduates who find ethics a dry subject, that he give them a handful of Cicero's "cases" to quarrel over. Doing just this has brought about something resembling civil war in certain classes of my undergraduates. It has done them good, and it has vastly entertained me. But each teacher must follow his own methods. We can none of us dictate.

How many of us have drawn inspiration from the noble reflections contained in the *Thoughts* of Marcus Aurelius and in the *Discourses* of Epictetus, those great Stoics! The unadorned translations of George Long will serve to introduce us to these.

To get a good idea of how the moral world revealed itself to a Father of the Church in the fifth century, we have only to turn to that most fascinating of autobiographies, the *Confessions* of St. Augustine. His *City of God* is too long, though interesting. Augustine's thought influenced the world for centuries. Then we may take a long jump and come down to St. Thomas, the great Scholastic of the thirteenth century. To get acquainted with him, we may turn to the English versions by Rickaby, *Aquinas Ethicus*. Those of us who are smugly satisfied at belonging to the twentieth century must remind ourselves that there were great men in the thirteenth, and that many among our contemporaries are still listening to them. We Protestant teachers of philosophy are sometimes in danger of forgetting this. A strictly fresh century and a strictly fresh egg cannot claim to be precisely on a par.

I do not think that I shall add the modern moralists to this list. There are a great many of them, and many of them are very good. But they are discussed at length in Part VII, which deals with the schools of the moralists. Citations and references are there given. I think, however, that I ought to add here that I should regard an ethical collection incomplete that did not include at least one of the comprehensive works on morals lately offered us by certain sociologists. Westermarck's wonderful book—a mine of information—on *The Origin and Development of the Moral Ideas*, or the admirable book by Hobhouse, *Morals in Evolution*, will serve to fill the gap.

Information regarding editions of all the books I have mentioned can be had in most public libraries, or from any good publisher and book-seller.

As for the reading to accompany these Chapters, I-III, I suggest looking over the chapters by Westermarck and Hobhouse, indicated in foot-notes. He who would realize how men have differed in their moral outlook on life might read the lives of Aristippus, Epicurus and Zeno, in Diogenes Laertius; or follow the account, in Sidgwick's *History of Ethics*, of Aristotle's teaching, as compared with the ethics of the Church.

2. Chapters IV to VII.—These chapters on ethics as science and on ethical method do not appear to me to call for extensive notes. Several foot-notes are given which might be followed up. I think it would be a very good thing for the student to read chapters i and vi in Sidgwick's admirable work, The *Methods of Ethics*.

3. Chapters VIII to X.—To undertake to give any adequate list of references on the chapters which treat of man's nature and of his material and social environment would take us quite too far afield. I merely suggest looking up the articles on "Anthropology" and "Sociology" in the *Encyclopedia Britannica*. References are given there. And one should not overlook Darwin's great book on *The Descent of Man*. It will never be rendered superfluous, although the men of our day criticize it in detail. A recent work of value is "Heredity and Environment in the Development of Men," by Professor Edwin Grant Conklin, 1918.

4. Chapters XI to XVI.—Here my notes must be somewhat more detailed, for we are on quite debatable ground. At any rate, there is much dispute, between men of unquestionable ability, on the one side and on the other. I may be pardoned for thinking that the general argument of these chapters is reasonable and sound.

In commenting upon Chapter XI, I suggest that the reader look up what Hobhouse has to say on impulse, desire and will, in his volume, *Morals in Evolution*; also that he consult the same topics in James' *Psychology*. McDougall's *Social Psychology* might be read with much profit.

Some admirable writers have a repugnance to using the word "volition" in speaking of the brutes. I cannot help thinking that this is a dispute touching the proper use of a word, rather than that any important distinction in *kind* is marked. Some human volitions stand out very clearly as such. There are free ideas present, there is the tension of desires, there is deliberation, and there is clearly conscious choice, or the final release of tension. But how many of the decisions—I see no objection to the word,—

which we make during the course of a day, are of this character! It would be difficult to set a lower limit to volition.

Muirhead, who writes, in his *Elements of Ethics*, clearly and well of desires, emphasizing the presence of "tensions," follows the Neo- Hegelian tradition in speaking of will. He describes it as the act by which the attention is concentrated upon one object of desire, and he calls the act of choice the *identifying of oneself* with one object or line of action.

Naturally, it is not easy to think of the bee or the ant or the spider, perhaps not even of the cat or dog, as "identifying itself" with some object of desire. I suggest that the reader, after a perusal of Muirhead, reflect upon what Hobhouse has to say of the lower animals; or that he look up Miss Washburn's book on *The Animal Mind*, (second edition, 1918), where a really serious study of the brute is undertaken.

On Chapter XII, I find no comment necessary. As to Chapter XIII, I recommend to the reader a reading or re-reading of the fascinating pages in which James treats of instinct in his *Psychology*. And let him look up the same subject in McDougall's *Social Psychology*. At the same time, I enter a note of warning against reading even such good writers uncritically. There is no little dispute in this field. Dr. H. R. Marshall's volume *Mind and Conduct* gives an unusually thoughtful account of instinct (N. Y., 1919).

Comment on Chapter XIV is not imperatively necessary. But I must speak with detail of Chapter XV, for the best of men quarrel when they come upon this ground:

Sec 49. The psychologist takes into his mouth no word more ambiguous than "feeling." It may be used to indicate any mental content whatever— John Stuart Mill could speak of consciousness as composed of a string of feelings. Herbert Spencer divided conscious processes into "feelings" and "relations between feelings." James obliterates the distinction, and finds it possible to speak of "a feeling of *and*, a feeling of *if*, a feeling of *but*," etc. (*Psychology* I, p. 154, ff.).

Some writers do not distinguish between emotions and feelings. Thus, Darwin, in his *Descent of Man*, calls pleasure and pain "emotions." Marshall (*op. cit.*, chapter ii) makes emotions, and even intuitions, "instinct-feelings." Dewey, in his *Ethics* (p. 251), appears to treat emotions as synonymous with feelings. Gardiner, in his interesting and careful study, *Affective Psychology in Ancient Writers after Aristotle* (*Psychological Review*. May, 1919), treats of "what are popularly called the feelings, including emotions."

223

On the other hand, in ethical writings the word, "feelings," very often means no more than pleasure and pain. Thus, *Seth* (*A Study of Ethical Principles*, p. 63), makes feelings synonymous with pleasure and pain. Muirhead (*Elements of Ethics*, p. 46), says, "by feeling is meant simply pleasure and pain"; and to have "interest" in, he defines as to have pleasure in (p. 46).

This narrowing of the meaning of the word on the part of ethical writers is, perhaps, natural. The hedonistic moralists made pleasure and pain the only ultimate reasonable stimulants to action. Many moralists opposed them (see, later, Chapters XXIV and XXV). So pleasure and pain became "the feelings," *par excellence*. Both Dewey and Alexander sometimes speak as if, by the word "feeling," we meant no more than pleasure and pain. So does Kant.

The modern psychologist sometimes distinguishes pleasure and pain from "agreeableness" and "disagreeableness." Marshall, a high authority on pleasure and pain, refuses to draw the distinction (*op. cit.*, Part III. chapter vi). But he also refuses to call pleasure and pain sensations, regarding them as "qualifications of our sensations," like intensity, duration, and the like.

Are pleasures, as pleasures, alike? and are pains, as pains, alike? Jeremy Bentham refused to distinguish between kinds of pleasures. On the other hand, John Stuart Mill did so (see Chapter XXV in this volume); and S. Alexander, in his work entitled *Moral Order and Progress*, maintains that pleasures differ in kind, and cannot be compared merely in their intensity (see page 202).

The whole matter is complicated enough, and there is occupation for the most disputatious. But I do not think that these disputes very directly affect the argument of my chapter.

Sec 50. That there is a relation between feeling and action, but that the two are by no means nicely adjusted to each other, has been recognized in many quarters.

Darwin, discussing the mental and moral qualities of man, points out that the satisfaction of some fundamental instincts gives little pleasure, although uneasiness is suffered if they are not satisfied. Seth (*op. cit.*, p. 64) says that feelings "guide" action; and he claims that the energy of a moving idea lies in the feeling which it arouses (p. 70). On the quantity of emotion, and its relation to action, see Stephen, The Science of Ethics, ii, iii, 25.

Sec 51. It appears to be repugnant to Green to admit that feeling—pleasure—can be the direct object of action; and he denies roundly that a sum of pleasures can be made an object of desire and will at all (*Prolegomena to Ethics*, Sec 221; see Sec 113 of this book). Moreover, he maintains, and in this Dewey follows him, that the making of pleasure an object is evidence of the existence of unhealthy desires. I cannot but think this, taken generally, an exaggeration. Of course, what is called "a man of pleasure" is a pretty poor sort of a thing.

Sec 52. In this section I do not touch at all upon the immemorial dispute concerning what has been called "the 'freedom' of the will."

Indeed, I leave it out of this book altogether. The moralist must, I think, assume that man has natural impulses and is a rational creature. Those who are interested in the problem above mentioned, may turn to my *Introduction to Philosophy*, chapter xi, Sec 46, where the matter is discussed, and references (in the corresponding note) are given.

Chapter XVI. — The matter of this chapter appears, clear enough, but it may be well to give a few references touching the two conceptions of the functions of Reason.

Men of quite varying views have inclined to the doctrine which appeals to me. I think it is to be gotten out of Hegel. Green, who is much influenced by him, takes, as the rational end of conduct, a "satisfaction on the whole," which implies a harmonization and unification of the desires (see, in this book, Chapter XXVI, Sec 122). Spencer, in his *Study of Sociology*, defines the rational as the consistent. Stephen, in his *Science of Ethics*, chapter ii, Sec 3, says: "Reason, in short, whatever its nature, is the faculty which enables us to act with a view to the distant and the future." He claims that rationality tends to bring about a certain unity or harmony. Hobhouse, *Morals in Evolution*, (pp. 572-581), says that reason harmonizes the impulses.

The champions of the opposite view are the intuitionists proper—such men as Kant, Reid, Price, even Sidgwick. To judge of their doctrine—they were great men, be it remembered, and worthy of all respect—I suggest that the reader wait until he has read the chapter on *Intuitionism* in this volume, Chapter XXIII.

5. CHAPTERS XVII TO XIX.—What is said in Chapter XVII seems too obviously true to need comment. Indeed, it may be questioned whether the chapter is not full of platitudes. But even platitudes are overlooked by some; and there is some merit in arranging them systematically. Besides, they may serve as a spring-board.

As to Chapter XVIII, I suggest reading chapter vii, of Westermarck's book on *The Origin and Development of the Moral Ideas*. It is entitled *Customs and Laws as Expressions of Moral Ideas.*

For Chapter XIX, one may read Hobhouse, *Morals in Evolution*, Part I, chapter vi, where he shows how the mere "group morality" gradually gives place to a wider morality in which the concept of humanity plays a part. In the same work, Part II, chapters i and ii, the author treats of religious or sub-religious ideas as affecting conduct. Compare Westermarck, *op. cit.*, chapter xl. See, also, *The Ancient City*, by Fustel de Coulanges.

6. CHAPTERS XX TO XXII.—What is said in Chapter XX may be well reinforced by turning to Hobhouse (*op. cit.*), Part I, chapter iii, where he traces the gradual evolution of rational morality in the field of justice. See, also, Westermarck, (*op. cit.*) chapters ix and x, i. e., "The Will as the Subject of Moral Judgment and the Influence of External Events," and "Agents under Intellectual Disability." In the last chapter referred to, animals, drunkards, idiots, the insane, etc., come on the stage. The chapter is full of curious information.

In Chapter XXI (Sec 86), I have spoken of the hesitating utterances of moralists touching any duties we may owe to the brutes. I suggest that before anyone dogmatize in detail on this subject he read with some care such a comprehensive work as Miss Washburn's *The Animal Mind*. The book is admirable. Chapters x and xliv of Westermarck's work are instructive and entertaining on this subject. Hegel disposes of the animals rather summarily. See his *Philosophy of Right*, Sec 47. Sidgwick, *The Methods of Ethics*, Book III, chapter iv, 2, is well worth consulting. See in my own volume, Chapter XXX, Sec 141.

For Chapter XXII, I give no references. I appeal only to the common sense of my reader.

7. Chapters XXIII to XXIX.—For the chapters on the Schools of the Moralists, XXIII to XXIX, I shall give briefer notes than I should have given, were the chapters not already so well provided with foot-notes.

So far as the first four of these chapters are concerned, I shall assume that enough has been said, drawing attention only to two points which concern Chapter XXIII.

It is very interesting to note that one of our best critics of intuitionism, Hemy Sidgwick, was himself an intuitionist. His *Methods of Ethics* deserves very close attention. Again Intuitions are often spoken of as if they had been shot out of a pistol, and had neither father nor mother. To understand them better it is only necessary to read chapter viii of Dr. H. R. Marshall's little book, *Mind and Conduct*, which shows how difficult it is to mark intuitions off sharply, and to treat them as if they had nothing in common with reason.

Those interested in the ethics of evolution, treated in Chapter XXVII, should not miss reading the fourth chapter of Darwin's *Descent of Man*. Huxley's essay, *Evolution and Ethics*, might be read. The "Prolegomena" to the essay is, however, much more valuable than the essay itself. Spencer's general theory of conduct is best gathered from his *Data of Ethics*, which was reprinted as Part I of his *Principles of Ethics*. The volume by C. M. Williams, entitled, *A Review of Evolutionary Ethics*, gives a convenient account of a dozen or more writers who have treated of ethics from the evolutionary standpoint. It is well not to overlook what Sidgwick has to say of evolution and ethics; see *The Methods of Ethics*, Book I, chapter ii, Sec. 2.

As for Chapter XXVIII, on "Pessimism," it is enough, I think, to refer the reader to Book IV, in Schopenhauer's work on *The World as Will and Idea*. The Book is entitled *The Assertion and Denial of the Will to Live, where Self-consciousness has been Attained*. See also his supplementary chapters, xlvi, on "The Vanity and Suffering of Life," and xlviii, "On the Doctrine of the Denial of the Will to Live." For the doctrine of von Hartmann, see chapters xiii to xv, in the part of his work entitled, *The Metaphysic of the Unconscious*.

For the chapter on Kant, Hegel and Nietzsche, I shall give but a few references, though the literature on these writers is enormous. The English reader will find T. K. Abbott's translation of Kant's ethical writings a very convenient volume (third edition, London, 1883). The translation of Hegel's *Philosophy of Right*, by S. W. Dyde (1896), I have found good, where I have compared it with the original. The word "Right" in the title is unavoidably ambiguous, for the German word means both "right" and "law." Hegel is dealing, in a sense, with both. I have indicated, in a footnote, that Nietzsche ought to be read in the original. He is a marvellous artist.

Perhaps I should add that Nietzsche will be read with most pleasure by those who do not attempt to find in his works a system of ethics. I recommend to the reader, especially, his three volumes: *The Genealogy of Morals*; *Beyond Good and Evil*; and *Thus Spake Zarathustra*; (New York, 1911).

8. CHAPTERS XXX TO XXXVI.—I shall not comment on Chapter XXX. It is sufficiently interpreted by what has been said earlier in this book. Nor do I think that Chapter XXXI needs to be discussed here. I need only say that

many moralists have commented upon the negative aspect of the moral law. It will be remembered that the "demon" of Socrates—a dreadful translation—was a negative sign. I do not think that those who have dwelt upon the negative aspect of morality have reflected sufficiently upon the moral organization of society. We are put to school unavoidably as soon as we are born.

I shall not dwell upon Chapters XXXII and XXXIII. Here I appeal merely to the good sense of the reader.

But Chapter XXXIV demands more attention. He who is ignorant of history, and has come into no close contact with the organization and functioning of any state other than his own, is as unfit to pass judgment upon states generally, as is the man who has never been away from his native village to pass judgment upon towns generally—towns inhabited by various peoples and situated in different quarters of the globe. His lot may, it is true, happen to be cast in a good village; but how he is to tell that it is good, I cannot conceive. He has no standard of comparison.

Fortunately, his ignorance is not as harmful as it might be. The Rational Social Will, which is penetrated through and through with traditions wiser than the whims of the individual, carries him along upon its broad bosom, and makes decisions for him.

The sociologist and the political philosopher should be consulted, as well as the historian, by one who would make a satisfactory list of books touching the subject of this chapter. But the moralist may be allowed to suggest a few titles, some of them very old ones. Plato's *Republic* is fascinating, and Aristotle's *Politics* is the shrewdest of books. But compare the state as conceived by these men with our notions of a modern democracy! More's *Utopia* is a delight. To get back to earth and see what *history* means to a state, and to its constitution and laws, read Sir Henry Maine's *Ancient Law*. States are not made in a day, although, under abnormal conditions, governments may be upset, and new ones set up, within twenty-four hours. After such unhistorical proceedings, one can scarcely expect "fast colors." One or two washings will suffice to show what was there before.

He who has a weakness for the operatic can peruse Rousseau's *Social Contract* and the *Declaration of the Rights of Man* published in the great French Revolution. As an antidote, I suggest Bentham's essay on *Anarchical Fallacies*.

But reading will do little good—even historical reading—unless one also thinks. It is wonderful how much knowledge a man may escape, if he is born under the proper star. I once knew an undergraduate in an American university, who attended compulsory chapel for more than three years, and who still thought that the Old Testament was a history of the Ancient Romans.

There is quite too much to say about Chapters XXXV and XXXVI. The only thing to do is to say nothing. I shall touch upon just one point in each chapter. I venture to beg the teacher, when he treats of International Ethics, to read in class, with his students, those pages in which Sir Thomas More describes the principles upon which the Utopians conducted their wars. Remember that Sir Thomas was not merely a statesman, but, by common consent, a learned, a great, and a good man. Mark the reaction of the undergraduate mind.

The one matter upon which I shall comment in Chapter XXXVI, is the question of belief as an object of approval or of censure. Westermarck states (*The Origin and Development of the Moral Ideas*, Volume I, chapter viii, p. 216), that neither the Catholic nor the Protestant Church regarded *belief, as such*, as an object of censure. Yet each was willing to punish heresy. The point is most interesting, and I hazard an explanation. The churches were organizations with a definite object. They made use of reward and punishment. This was reasonable enough, abstractly considered. However, doctrine was the affair of the theologian. Now the theologian, like the philosopher, is a man who assumes that he is concerned with *proofs*, and with proofs only. If a thing is *proved*, how can a man *help* believing it? Only if he *will* not, which is sheer obstinacy or perversity. Let him, then, be punished on account of his defective character (see Westermarck, I, chapter xi, p. 283).

I think the apparent quibbling here can be gotten rid of by recognizing the truth emphasized in Sec Sec 167-168, namely, that logical proofs play but a subordinate part in the adoption or rejection of beliefs touching a vast number of matters both secular and religious. If we can influence men's emotions, we can influence their beliefs. Both State and Church have this power. It is a power that can be abused. But it is, on the whole, a good thing that men's beliefs can thus be influenced. There would be no stability in human society could they not. Every ignorant man—and many men are ignorant—would be at the mercy of every clever talker; and he would change his beliefs every day. As men act on beliefs, this means that he would zig-zag through life to the detriment of all orderly development. I beg the reader, learned or unlearned, to put aside prepossessions, and to look at things as they are in this field.